DEFINING MOMENTS
THE SCOPES
"MONKEY TRIAL"

DEFINING MOMENTS
THE SCOPES
"MONKEY TRIAL"

Anne Janette Johnson

615 Griswold, Detroit MI 48226

Omnigraphics, Inc.

Kevin Hillstrom, *Series Editor*
Cherie D. Abbey, *Managing Editor*

Peter E. Ruffner, *Publisher*
Frederick G. Ruffner, Jr., *Chairman*
Matthew P. Barbour, *Senior Vice President*

Kay Gill, Vice President – *Directories*
Elizabeth Collins, *Research and Permissions
    Coordinator*
David P. Bianco, *Marketing Director*
Kevin Hayes, *Operations Manager*

Barry Puckett, *Librarian*
Allison A. Beckett, Linda Strand, Mary Butler,
    Research Staff
Cherry Stockdale, *Permissions Assistant*
Shirley Amore, Martha Johns, Kirk Kauffman,
    Administrative Staff

Copyright © 2007 Omnigraphics, Inc.
ISBN 0-7808-0955-6

Library of Congress Cataloging-in-Publication Data

Johnson, Anne.
  The Scopes "Monkey Trial" / Anne Janette Johnson.
    p. cm. -- (Defining moments)
  Summary: "Examines the famous Scopes "Monkey Trial" and the continuing debate over evolution
and religion in American society. Features include narrative overview, biographical profiles, primary
source documents, detailed chronology, and annotated sources for further study"--Provided by pub-
lisher.
  Includes bibliographical references and index.
  ISBN 0-7808-0955-6 (hardcover : alk. paper) 1. Scopes, John
Thomas--Trials, litigation, etc. 2. Evolution--Study and teaching--Law and legislation--Tennessee. I. Title.
  KF224.S3J64 2006   345.73'0288--dc22
                                                                                              2006026439

The information in this publication was compiled from the sources cited and from other sources considered reliable.
Additional copyright information can be found on the photograph credits page of this book. While every possible effort
has been made to ensure reliability, the publisher will not assume liability for damages caused by inaccuracies in the data,
and makes no warranty, express or implied, on the accuracy of the information contained herein.

This book is printed on acid-free paper meeting the ANSI Z39.48 Standard. The infinity symbol that appears above indi-
cates that the paper in this book meets that standard.

Printed in the United States

TABLE OF CONTENTS

PRIMARY SOURCES

PREFACE

Throughout the course of America's existence, its people, culture, and institutions have been periodically challenged by—and in many cases transformed by—profound historical events. Some of these momentous events, such as women's suffrage, the civil rights movement, and U.S. involvement in World War II, invigorated the nation and strengthened American confidence and capabilities. Others, such as the McCarthy era, the Vietnam War, and Watergate, have prompted troubled assessments and heated debates about the country's core beliefs and character.

Some of these defining moments in American history were years or even decades in the making. The Harlem Renaissance and the New Deal, for example, unfurled over the span of several years, while the American labor movement and the Cold War evolved over the course of decades. Other defining moments, such as the Cuban missile crisis and the terrorist attacks of September 11, 2001, transpired over a matter of days or weeks.

But although significant differences exist among these events in terms of their duration and their place in the timeline of American history, all share the same basic characteristic: they transformed the United States' political, cultural, and social landscape for future generations of Americans.

Taking heed of this fundamental reality, American citizens, schools, and other institutions are increasingly emphasizing the importance of understanding our nation's history. Omnigraphics' *Defining Moments* series was created for the express purpose of meeting this growing appetite for authoritative, useful historical resources. This series, which focuses on the most pivotal events in U.S. history from the 20th century forward, will be of enduring value to anyone interested in learning more about America's past—and in understanding how those historical events continue to reverberate in the 21st century.

Each individual volume of *Defining Moments* provides a valuable resource for readers interested in learning about the most profound events in our nation's history. Each volume is organized into three distinct sections—Narrative Overview, Biographies, and Primary Sources.

- The **Narrative Overview** provides readers with a detailed, factual account of the origins and progression of the "defining moment" being examined. It also explores the event's lasting impact on America's political and cultural landscape.

- The **Biographies** section provides valuable biographical background on leading figures associated with the event in question. Each biography concludes with a list of sources for further information on the profiled individual.

- The **Primary Sources** section collects a wide variety of pertinent primary source materials from the era under discussion, including official documents, papers and resolutions, letters, oral histories, memoirs, editorials, and other important works.

Individually, each of these sections is a rich resource for users. Together, they comprise an authoritative, balanced, and absorbing examination of some of the most significant events in U.S. history.

Other notable features contained within each volume in the series include a glossary of important individuals, places, and terms; a detailed chronology featuring page references to relevant sections of the narrative; an annotated bibliography of sources for further study; an extensive general bibliography that reflects the wide range of historical sources consulted by the author; and a subject index.

Acknowledgements

This series was developed in consultation with a distinguished Advisory Board comprised of public librarians, school librarians, and educators. They evaluated the series as it developed, and their comments and suggestions were invaluable throughout the production process. Any errors in this and other volumes in the series are ours alone. Following is a list of board members who contributed to the *Defining Moments* series:

Gail Beaver, M.A., M.A.L.S.
Adjunct Lecturer, University of Michigan
Ann Arbor, MI

Melissa C. Bergin, L.M.S., NBCT
Library Media Specialist
Niskayuna High School
Niskayuna, NY

Rose Davenport, M.S.L.S., Ed.Specialist
Library Media Specialist
Pershing High School Library
Detroit, MI

Karen Imarisio, A.M.L.S.
Assistant Head of Adult Services
Bloomfield Twp. Public Library
Bloomfield Hills, MI

Nancy Larsen, M.L.S., M.S. Ed.
Library Media Specialist
Clarkston High School
Clarkston, MI

Marilyn Mast, M.I.L.S.
Kingswood Campus Librarian
Cranbrook Kingswood Upper School
Bloomfield Hills, MI

Rosemary Orlando, M.L.I.S.
Library Director
St. Clair Shores Public Library
St. Clair Shores, MI

Comments and Suggestionsa

We welcome your comments on *Defining Moments: The Scopes "Monkey Trial"* and suggestions for other events in U.S. history that warrant treatment in the *Defining Moments* series. Correspondence should be addressed to:

Editor, *Defining Moments*
Omnigraphics, Inc.
615 Griswold
Detroit, MI 48226
E-mail: editorial@omnigraphics.com

HOW TO USE THIS BOOK

*D*efining Moments: The Scopes "Monkey Trial" provides users with a detailed and authoritative overview of this event, as well as the principal figures involved in this pivotal episode in U.S. history. The preparation and arrangement of this volume—and all other books in the *Defining Moments* series—reflect an emphasis on providing a thorough and objective account of events that shaped our nation, presented in an easy-to-use reference work.

Defining Moments: The Scopes "Monkey Trial" is divided into three primary sections. The first of these sections, the **Narrative Overview**, provides a detailed, factual account of the 1925 Scopes trial in Dayton, Tennessee. It explores the perspectives of both the supporters and opponents of the teaching of evolution, explains how the trial was set in motion by town leaders eager to reap a tourism bonanza, follows each day of testimony and courtroom maneuvering, and discusses how the battle between supporters of evolution and "intelligent design" proponents is being waged in twenty-first century America.

The second section, **Biographies**, provides valuable biographical background on leading figures involved in the trial, including famed attorneys Clarence Darrow and William Jennings Bryan, high school teacher John T. Scopes, and journalist H.L. Mencken. Each biography concludes with a list of sources for further information on the profiled individual.

The third section, **Primary Sources**, collects essential and enlightening documents from the Scopes "Monkey Trial," including excerpts from Clarence Darrow's historic cross-examination of William Jennings Bryan at the trial; excerpts from Charles Darwin's *Descent of Man*; controversial dispatches from trial watcher H.L. Mencken; and documents from the 2005 *Kitzmiller v. Dover School Board* "intelligent design" court proceedings. Other primary sources featured in *Defining Moments: The Scopes "Monkey Trial"* include excerpts from official documents, papers, memoirs, and other important works.

Other valuable features in *Defining Moments: The Scopes "Monkey Trial"* include the following:

- Attribution and referencing of primary sources and other quoted material to help guide users to other valuable historical research resources.

- Glossary of Important People, Places, and Terms.

- Detailed Chronology of events with a *see reference* feature. Under this arrangement, events listed in the chronology include a reference to page numbers within the Narrative Overview wherein users can find additional information on the event in question.

- Photographs of the leading figures and major events associated with the trial.

- Sources for Further Study, an annotated list of noteworthy trial-related works.

- Extensive bibliography of works consulted in the creation of this book, including books, periodicals, Internet sites, and videotape materials.

- A Subject Index.

NARRATIVE OVERVIEW

PROLOGUE

Curiosity is fundamental to the human condition. For thousands and thousands of years, human beings have studied the natural world around them and the skies above, pondering the essential question: Was all this *made,* or did it *just happen?*

Every culture has grappled with how we came to be here, inhabitants of a richly diverse planet. Creation stories describe the roles of otherworldly agents, while scientists seek clues in the complex structure of DNA and the fossil record. One prominent account of the creation of humankind, for example, can be found in the Book of Genesis in the Bible. The Book of Genesis declares that humans were *made* by God. Meanwhile, the leading scientific theory on the origins of life on earth—and the ultimate development of *Homo sapiens,* the "thinking man"—was first set forth by Charles Darwin in his 1859 book *The Origin of Species.* According to Darwin and many other scientists who have followed him, humans *just happened* through a process called *evolution.*

Over the years, Darwin's evolutionary theory and the creation story contained in the Book of Genesis have often been seen as being in conflict with one another. Believers in the Biblical story of creation, in particular, came to see evolutionary theory as a challenge to basic Christian beliefs and a threat to humankind's relationship with God.

This simmering confrontation finally exploded in Tennessee in 1925. It was here that the state legislature passed a law called the Butler Act that made it illegal "to teach any theory that denies the story of the divine creation of man as taught in the Bible, and to teach instead that man has descended from a lower order of animals." A few months later, a young Tennessee high school teacher named John Thomas Scopes was ordered to stand trial after admitting that he had taught evolution to his biology class.

Scopes's deed was a simple infraction, a misdemeanor carrying a modest fine. But Americans of every political and religious persuasion recognized that the stakes involved in the celebrated Scopes "Monkey Trial" in Dayton, Tennessee, were very high. Indeed, the stakes were so high that the trial attracted some of the most famous orators and legal minds of a generation to the sleepy town of Dayton.

For the prosecution: William Jennings Bryan, a three-time nominee for president, famous worldwide as a champion of the common folk. Bryan had been crusading against evolution for four years by the time he arrived in Dayton. He drew support from a group of Christians called "fundamentalists" for their belief in the literal truth of the Bible. While no longer the vigorous young reformer he was in the 1890s, Bryan still wielded considerable power in national politics. His fight against teaching evolution in classrooms had begun to influence educational policy in a number of Southern states. Bryan saw the "Monkey Trial" as part of a vital mission to defend American children from unproven ideas that would erode their faith in God.

For the defense: Clarence Darrow, admitted agnostic and "attorney for the damned," a canny lawyer who believed that if American schools only taught scientific theories that met with the approval of religious fundamentalists, the nation's social and economic progress would be at risk. "Civilization is at stake," Darrow proclaimed when he joined John Scopes's defense team.

For the record: H. L. Mencken, the cynical Baltimore journalist who had made a name for himself by challenging many of the values and beliefs held dear by middle-class Americans of his time. Mencken had a field day at the

"Monkey Trial," where his critical remarks about the "yokels" and their persecution of the "infidel Scopes" presented an unflattering vision of a nation under mob rule.

At the "center of the storm": A quiet young man in horn-rimmed glasses who had been hired to teach math and coach the football team. John Scopes could not have imagined that his decision to challenge the Butler Act would provoke such a sensational trial. Plucked from obscurity into the limelight, Scopes became renowned as a person who let conscience be his guide against a law he felt to be unjust.

A whole nation listened via live radio broadcast as these assorted individuals came together in the carnival atmosphere of a tiny Tennessee town to debate and determine a fundamental question: Were we *made,* or did we *just happen?*

Chapter One

EVENTS LEADING UP TO THE SCOPES TRIAL

<figure decorative />

> Probably all organic beings which have ever lived on this earth have descended from some one primordial form, into which life was first breathed. There is grandeur in this view of life that, whilst this planet has gone cycling on according to the fixed law of gravity, from so simple a beginning endless forms most beautiful and most wonderful have been, and are being evolved.
>
> —Charles Darwin, *The Origin of Species*

Scientists and theologians have long disputed the geologic age of the earth and various aspects of human history. This debate over the age of the earth and the descent of human beings has been waged in many corners of the world, but it has been particularly contentious in the United States. Certainly it raged as a national issue in 1925, when John T. Scopes became the defendant in the celebrated "Monkey Trial."

In the 1920s many of America's strictest Christians still believed in a creation timeline set forth by Bishop James Ussher, a prominent seventeenth-century theologian in the Church of Ireland. Ussher placed the beginning of God's creation at October 23, 4004 BC—approximately 6,000 years ago. Ussher arrived at this date by using known dates from Middle Eastern history, including the reigns of ancient Babylonian kings, and then counting backwards by the ages of Israelite forefathers as recorded in the Bible. By the 1920s Ussher's timeline had become firmly established in American religious thought. Some versions of the King James Bible, including the one on the judge's desk at the Scopes trial, included Ussher's calculations in an appendix.

Bishop James Ussher (1581-1656) fixed the date of Creation precisely at 4004 B.C.E.

During the nineteenth century, however, scientists uncovered evidence that the earth was far older than Ussher and others claimed. French anatomist Georges Cuvier is widely considered the founder of paleontology, the study of fossils. Cuvier used the growing collection of fossils at the French Museum of Natural History to set forth a lengthy timeline of earth's history that included extinction events. Still, Cuvier agreed with other scientists and scholars of his era who believed that species did not change over time. According to their view of planetary history, the extinction of larger animals such as dinosaurs simply allowed other creatures already in existence (from kangaroos to elephants) to increase in numbers and maintain their existence into the modern era.

Another nineteenth-century French scientist, Jean-Baptiste Lamarck, challenged this viewpoint. Lamarck felt that species could undergo genetic changes if their environments changed around them. He also believed that animals were capable of passing beneficial traits along to their offspring. Lamarck used giraffes as an example. He noted that giraffes with longer necks would be able to reach higher into tree canopies for leaves in times of food scarcity, giving them a survival advantage over other giraffes. These giraffes would also be more likely to pass along the genetic trait of a long neck to offspring.

Many scientists of the early nineteenth century disagreed with Lamarck, though. They pointed out that if it was true that giraffes developed longer necks with each generation, people ought to see changes at work in the animals around them. In fact, however, the genetic differences between each generation of animals seemed minimal.

Charles Darwin Proposes "Survival of the Fittest"

This scientific impasse was solved by a naturalist named Charles Darwin, who proposed that species actually changed very gradually over long periods of time (see Darwin biography, p. 123). As a passenger on the HMS *Beagle* from 1831 to 1836, Darwin collected thousands of specimens of animals and plants from South America and the Pacific islands, including the remote Galapagos Islands. Working with specialists on comparative anatomy, Darwin learned that the birds he collected in the Galapagos were not from different families as he originally thought. They were actually all finches, even though they looked completely different from island to island. Darwin and his colleagues also determined that some of the fossil bones he found on his voyage were extinct larger relatives of animal species that could still be found in South America.

Darwin thus conceived the theory of evolution by natural selection. The centerpiece of this theory was "survival of the fittest," which held that animals would change gradually over long periods of time because the "fittest" in any given environment—those with genetic traits that gave them a survival edge over their contemporaries—would produce more offspring. Some of these offspring would inherit those beneficial traits, and they too would have more offspring. Meanwhile, other members of the species without these important genetic traits would be at a competitive disadvantage and would gradually die out.

Many nineteenth-century Christians felt that the theory of evolution by natural selection challenged the whole notion that animals and people had been created by a benevolent God. They viewed Darwin's evolutionary theory as one that framed the world as a cruel place in which individuals competed to be the "fittest" without intervention or guidance from a deity. They also strongly objected to some specific claims made by Darwin, such as his theory that human beings had descended from some ancestral ape, probably in Africa.

Darwin published two major works on the subject of evolution: *The Origin of Species by Natural Selection; Or, The Preservation of Favoured Races in the Struggle for Life* (1859), and *The Descent of Man, and Selection in Relation to Sex* (1871). He knew his books would provoke controversy, and they certainly did. Many scientists (especially paleontologists) embraced Darwin's theory of evolution enthusiastically. Most Christian leaders condemned his books initially, but as the nineteenth century drew to a close, some liberal theologians had reconciled the idea of evolution with the workings of God. The

Charles Darwin (1809-1882) explained his theory of evolution in two ground-breaking books, *The Origin of Species* (1859) and *The Descent of Man* (1871).

world, they said, was not created in a day, but rather in periods. God set evolution into motion in order to produce the ultimate species, the human being.

A great many deeply religious people disagreed with this effort to reconcile Biblical teachings with the fossil record, though. They interpreted the theory that humankind had descended from apes as a direct insult to God, and they charged that only an atheist could hold such a view. These people came to be called "fundamentalists" for their literal reading of Biblical scriptures.

Searching for Missing Links

Darwin's suggestion that humans had descended from apes led certain adventurers to seek out the "missing links" in the development of the human species. Two years before Darwin published *The Origin of Species,* workers in Germany's Neander Valley unearthed a portion of a skull that looked slightly different from that of a modern human. A nearby natural history teacher hurried to the site and found limb bones associated with the skull. "Neanderthal Man" became the first fossilized human discovery. For thirty years scientists argued over classification of the specimen. Some felt it was a different species altogether, while others thought it a very robust example of early *Homo sapiens,* or man.

Debate also raged over the location of humankind's evolution from ape. Darwin felt it must be Africa because of the similarities between people and chimpanzees. Other scientists, however, believed that Asia formed the cradle of civilization, pointing to Asian primates like orangutans and gibbons and *their* similarities to humans. A Dutch doctor named Eugène Dubois felt strongly that Asia must be the site of ancestral pre-humans. He set out to find the "missing link" on the East Indian island of Java. Dubois sacrificed his social standing, his fortune, and his health in seeking out proof of this theory. Surprisingly, he was successful. In 1891 he discovered some limb bones and a tooth that bore resemblance to *Homo sapiens* but looked more primitive. He called his find *Pithecanthropus erectus*, or "upright ape." For the remainder of his life he defended his discovery, sometimes against bitter opposition. Today Dubois is recognized as the discoverer of *Homo erectus*, a human that is now well-documented in the fossil record.

Possibly the best known "missing link" at the time of the Scopes trial, however, was "Piltdown Man," *Eoanthropus dawsoni*. In 1908 an amateur fossil collector, Charles Dawson, announced that he had discovered ancient skull fragments in a gravel pit in England. Some four years later, other workers at the same site found a complete jawbone that was distinctly primitive and ape-like. Combining the large skull bones with the simian jaw, such distinguished anatomists as Britain's Arthur Smith Woodward proclaimed "Piltdown Man" to be the missing link promised by Darwin. The unveiling of "Piltdown Man" on December 28, 1912, merited front page coverage in the *New York Times*.

The discovery of "Piltdown Man" continued to be regarded as a major scientific event for the next four decades. Certainly, the believers in evolution who assembled in Dayton, Tennessee, for the Scopes "Monkey Trial" accepted "Piltdown Man" as a legitimate scientific milestone. In 1953, however, a research team led by Dr. William Le Gros Clark declared that "Piltdown Man" actually was an elaborate hoax. Clark's studies, which included the use of more accurate chemical dating methods and analysis of other fossil evidence from Africa and Asia, clearly indicated that "Piltdown Man's" skull was that of a modern-age human and the jawbone was that of an orangutan (complete with teeth that had been cleverly filed to resemble that of a human). Even today no one is certain how many people were involved in carrying out the hoax, but researchers agree that Dawson played a major role.

Another noteworthy event that set the stage for the Scopes trial was a paper written by a South African doctor named Raymond Dart. His paper, which was published just a few months before the trial, discussed the discovery of a fossil ape skull in an African cave. This tiny but complete skull belonged to a child, but it was distinctly different from *Homo sapiens*. The "Taung Baby" had a small brain case and more modern teeth. Dart named his find *Australopithecus africanus*, or "dawn ape." This find was not a hoax. Today the fossil is recognized as an example of an upright hominid, or prehuman ape, with close ties to the human family tree. In his autobiography,

Center of the Storm, John T. Scopes wrote that he recalled reading about Dart's discovery in the spring of 1925, mere weeks before his celebrated trial began.

Social Darwinism and the Reform Movement

Farmers and pet owners had been selectively breeding animals for millennia when Darwin wrote about the "survival of the fittest." In fact, Darwin used examples from pigeon breeders in *The Origin of Species*. Some of Darwin's ideas in this regard, however, were seized on in ways that the scientist never imagined. Many scientists and educated men saw a new use for Darwin's key idea: selective breeding of people in order to "weed out" undesirables and speed the evolution of the human race. This controversial idea was called eugenics. By the late nineteenth century, some of the nation's most respected scholars were openly advocating the sterilization of disabled people, alcoholics, and the mentally retarded in order to improve the human genetic stock. The idea of creating a "master race"—a concept later and forever stained by the genocidal actions of the Nazis during World War II—was widely accepted as a legitimate goal at the turn of the twentieth century.

> *Social Darwinism allowed the wealthy few to rationalize their accumulation of vast fortunes, even as they paid their workers subsistence wages and used violence and intimidation to keep union organizers out of their factories.*

In the meantime, many wealthy American and European businessmen used the notion of "survival of the fittest" to explain their own success. According to this convenient theory of "Social Darwinism," the rich had succeeded simply because they were more "fit" or advanced than the poor workers who toiled in their factories, mines, and other industries, not because of the significant advantages that many of them enjoyed in education, financial resources, and business connections. Social Darwinism allowed the wealthy few to rationalize their accumulation of vast fortunes, even as they paid their workers subsistence wages and used violence and intimidation to keep union organizers out of their factories.

Rarely has the gulf been wider between factory owners and their workers than it was between 1890 and 1914. A series of bitter strikes erupted in America during that era. Reform movements arose to oppose the exploitation of workers. Some reformers worked in the private sphere, founding settlement houses and offering aid to women and children who toiled long hours in factories. Other reformers used the political arena to sway public opinion.

Bryan and Darrow

One of the leaders of this reform movement was William Jennings Bryan, one of the giants of American politics (see Bryan biography, p. 111). A staunch Democrat, Bryan reached out to ordinary folk with a message of women's suffrage, the right of workers to organize in unions, the end to business monopolies, and debt relief for poor farmers. From the outset of his long and distinguished career, Bryan was a vocal opponent of eugenics and Social Darwinism. He considered them shameful attacks upon society's most vulnerable citizens.

William Jennings Bryan emerged as a populist firebrand in the American heartland during the late nineteenth century.

Gifted with a magnificent speaking voice and the dramatic presence of an actor, Bryan received the Democratic nomination for president by his thirty-sixth birthday. He would eventually be nominated a total of three times for the presidency (in 1896, 1900, and 1908) by the party he helped to build. Nicknamed "The Great Commoner" in recognition of his ability to bond with ordinary Americans, Bryan was beloved by his millions of followers as a man of the people.

Another notable personality in the turbulent years bridging the end of the nineteenth century and the beginning of the twentieth century was Clarence Darrow (see Darrow biography, p. 118). A self-educated lawyer from a small town in northern Ohio, Darrow defended union leaders in a variety of high-profile cases, including that of Eugene Debs and the Pullman rail workers in 1894, the Woodworkers' Union in 1898, and the murder trial of a radical Socialist union leader named William "Big Bill" Haywood in 1908. Since these court cases received widespread coverage in the press, Darrow became famous as a legal champion of organized labor.

Clarence Darrow was known as one of the most formidable—and controversial—attorneys in America during the 1910s and 1920s.

William Jennings Bryan and Clarence Darrow achieved worldwide fame in the same decades and for many of the same reasons. Both of them fought for the underdogs: Bryan through politics, Darrow through the courts. Their paths diverged, though, on one crucial subject—religion. Bryan was a devout Christian who couched most of his speeches in religious terms. Darrow, on the other hand, was an agnostic whose well-known opposition to the death penalty was grounded in his belief that there was no life after death.

As they aged, both men became more devoted to their views. Bryan was a national leader in the drive to pass the Eighteenth Amendment, a provision in the U.S. Constitution that outlawed possession or use of alcoholic beverages beginning in 1920. This amendment, which ushered in the Prohibition era in American history, was widely seen as a momentous victory for Christian social activism (though Prohibition only lasted thirteen years before it was repealed). Darrow, meanwhile, was outraged by the passage of the Eighteenth Amendment. He saw it as part of a worrisome trend in American society away from intellectual and cultural freedom and toward a society based on strict Biblical teachings.

The "Roaring Twenties" Bring National Divisions

Prohibition arrived at the beginning of a decade that brought other enormous and sometimes disorienting changes to the lives of all Americans. At the beginning of the decade, only affluent Americans owned motorcars. Henry Ford changed that with his mass-produced, affordable Model T. Americans took to the roads, making the Sunday drive a habit and the family vacation a national pastime. Social changes were not confined to transportation, either. Large companies such as General Electric began massive advertising campaigns for labor-saving devices such as electric washing machines, stoves, and refrigerators.

This movement of industrialization out of the factories and into the homes and garages of American families was widely embraced. The last years of the 1910s had been marked by the ravages of World War I and the deadly influenza epidemic of 1919, and Americans were more than ready to enter a new era of increased comfort and "normalcy," as President Warren G. Harding put it.

"Normalcy" proved hard to define, though. Having gained the right to vote with the Nineteenth Amendment in 1920, many women became more politically and socially active. Especially in the big cities, women dressed in shorter skirts, began smoking cigarettes, visited "speakeasies" that sold illegal alcohol, and became more visible in unionizing activities. At the same time, many American veterans from the First World War voiced cynicism about the carnage they had seen and their involvement in the war in the first place. This defiant and cynical attitude was not confined to veterans. Many young people began to challenge the societal values their parents and grandparents held dear. Writer Gertrude Stein called these fast-living, disillusioned young people the "Lost Generation."

Some writers of the era, such as Baltimore journalist H. L. Mencken, appealed to this growing segment of educated but skeptical Americans (see Mencken biography, p. 134). His columns and essays repeatedly criticized the religious, middle-class "ignoramuses" and "boobs" populating small-town America. He also challenged religious, social, and democratic institutions and ideas that had long been important parts of the fabric of American society. In addition, Mencken helped to popularize a new style of realistic literature that cast America in a dark light—works such as Theodore Dreiser's *Sister Carrie* and F. Scott Fitzgerald's *The Great Gatsby*.

While Mencken and the realist novelists appealed to the "smart set" in the cities, William Jennings Bryan worked his magic in rural areas. As a candidate for president, Bryan had crossed the country by rail, speaking at each town along the way. In the 1920s he continued this practice, attracting huge audiences of fundamentalist Christians. These supporters were unnerved by the great changes taking place in American culture, business, and science, and they viewed the new generation of sophisticated city-dwellers with great alarm. America, they felt, was moving away from its Christian principles into lawlessness, hedonism, and disdain for the Bible. To these men and women, standing with William Jennings Bryan represented a possible way to stem the agnostic tide that threatened to sweep across their nation.

Journalist H. L. Mencken was one of the most famous literary voices of the "Jazz Age" of the 1920s.

The Crusade Against Evolution

In 1921 Bryan's efforts to reverse America's perceived slide into cultural and moral decay began to focus on one specific issue: the teaching of evolution in public schools. As Bryan himself declared on many occasions, how could children embrace God and His teachings if they were taught in schools that they descended from monkeys?

Two of Bryan's most popular lectures of the early 1920s—"The Menace of Darwinism" and "The Bible and Its Enemies"—attacked Darwin's theory on a number of fronts. Bryan particularly stressed the negative impact of eugenics and Social Darwinism. He also felt that Darwin's theory had not been proven by the facts. He scoffed at the teeth and skull fragments found by the likes of Dawson and Dubois, and he challenged scientists to explain how an organ as sophisticated and unique as the eye might have evolved through "survival of the fittest."

Bryan's primary concern about evolution, however, was the impact it could have on schoolchildren. Bryan believed that if students could not be taught religion in public schools, then they also should not be taught scientific theories that, in his view, ran *counter* to religion. Bryan thought that the teaching of evolutionary theory was entirely capable of turning religious chil-

16

dren into atheists. He recognized that he could not advocate putting the Bible into the classroom since that was unconstitutional. But Bryan determined that he *could* try to remove the teaching of evolution from the classroom because it cast doubt on the Bible.

Aided by fundamentalist pastors in states such as Florida, North Carolina, Texas, Tennessee, and Kentucky, Bryan began to campaign for state laws banning the teaching of evolution in public schools. He couched his arguments in simple terms. Bryan painted the scientific community touting evolutionary theory as a small minority. Ordinary taxpayers funded the public schools, observed Bryan, and if a majority of those taxpayers objected to the teaching of evolution, it should not be taught. To Bryan, this was a simple and democratic solution to a serious societal problem.

Bryan's new crusade drew opposition from numerous fronts. "Modernist" pastors from large mainstream denominations argued that it was perfectly possible to reconcile Darwinian evolution with Christian doctrine. University professors were horrified by the idea that American students might not receive essential instruction in their biology classes. Many ordinary Americans, represented by "free-thinkers" like Clarence Darrow and H. L. Mencken, condemned the idea of allowing any group of citizens to influence school curricula according to their own religious beliefs.

In 1922 and 1923 Bryan delivered speeches to the state legislatures of West Virginia and Kentucky, urging them to pass some sort of anti-evolution statute. Kentucky lawmakers considered passage of a law, but stiff resistance developed. In his memoir, John Scopes recalled that two of his favorite professors at the University of Kentucky traveled to the state capital to lobby against the bill. Some of the state's newspapers, and many of the region's best known mainstream clergymen, opposed it as well. Some lawmakers even poked fun at the legislation, proposing a corollary law to make it illegal for water to run downhill. The Kentucky anti-evolution statute failed.

The Butler Act of 1925

In Tennessee, however, anti-evolution forces scored a major victory. On January 20, 1925, a Tennessee state senator named John A. Shelton introduced a bill to make it a felony, or criminal act, to teach evolution in the state's public schools. A similar bill was introduced the next day by John

Washington Butler of the state's House of Representatives. Although citizens of Memphis, Nashville, Knoxville, and Chattanooga peppered the newspapers with letters opposing the bill, organized opposition never developed. Instead, a host of popular national preachers descended into the state, urging quick passage of the bill.

> *Nationally-known radio evangelist Billy Sunday undertook an 18-day crusade in Memphis in support of Butler's anti-evolution bill. Night after night, Sunday's audiences grew until more than 200,000 people had heard him preach about the evils of evolution.*

One nationally-known radio evangelist, Billy Sunday, undertook an 18-day crusade in Memphis in support of the bill. Night after night, Sunday's audiences grew until more than 200,000 people had heard him preach about the evils of evolution. If state lawmakers had been reluctant to pass an anti-evolution bill, the crowds clamoring for Sunday and other big-name evangelists changed their minds. Many politicians became convinced that a vote in favor of preserving the teaching of Darwinism in public schools would bring their political careers to an end.

The only other organized opposition to the anti-evolution statute might have come from the professors at the University of Tennessee. But they relied on state funds to operate their school, and the governor, Austin Peay, had not finalized their budget for the year. When several professors who were critical of the Butler Act had their contracts terminated, other faculty members quieted down. With clear citizen majority support for the statute, the state legislature conducted only brief debates on the issue behind closed doors.

John Butler's version of the act was passed into law on March 13, 1925, by a wide margin in both houses. The State Senate voted 24-6 in its favor, the House, 71-5. Governor Austin Peay, a devout Baptist, signed it enthusiastically.

The text of the Butler Act was short and to the point. It required teachers to avoid any instruction that denied the Biblical account of creation. Anyone who violated the statute could be arrested, tried in court, and fined. The maximum fine, $500, represented about three months' salary for a public school teacher in 1925.

A Quick Challenge to the Butler Act

Ironically, this ambitious anti-evolution bill exceeded William Jennings Bryan's desires. He never intended the teaching of evolution to be a *crime*, with fines levied against guilty teachers. Bryan recognized that in their zeal to pass legislation to please a fundamentalist majority, the Tennessee state lawmakers had opened the possibility of extended courtroom battles. A teacher might appeal his or her conviction to the state Supreme Court, and possibly all the way to the U.S. Supreme Court.

Just as Bryan suspected, the ink had hardly dried on the Butler Act before its first challenger emerged. He was a shy young bachelor in a small mountain town, better known as a football coach than as a biology teacher. He wore horn-rimmed glasses and smoked cigarettes. He could not even remember whether or not he had covered evolution in the science classes he was asked to teach.

Nevertheless, John Thomas Scopes (see Scopes biography, p. 142) allowed himself to be arrested for violating the Butler Act. From the moment he was drawn into the trial that would bear his name, Scopes felt he was acting on behalf of every teacher in the state. In his view, he was defying an unjust law that could severely diminish the quality of education that all Tennessee students deserved. Still, the lanky football coach did not foresee that his name would be forever linked with the teaching of evolution in public schools—or that his trial would become one of the most dramatic events in twentieth-century courtroom history.

Chapter Two

TWO SIDES
PREPARE FOR TRIAL

⧯⧖⧖⧯

Geology teaches that millions of years ago, life upon the earth was very simple, and that gradually more and more complex forms of life appeared, as the rocks formed latest in time show the most highly developed forms of animal life. The great English scientist, Charles Darwin, from this and other evidence, explained the theory of evolution. This is the belief that simple forms of life on the earth slowly and gradually gave rise to those more complex and that thus ultimately the most complex forms came into existence.

—George William Hunter, *A Civic Biology,* 1914

The American Civil Liberties Union (ACLU) was founded in 1917 as the National Civil Liberties Bureau. It was officially chartered as the ACLU on January 19, 1920. Then as now, the ACLU existed to protect the free speech of citizens with minority viewpoints, no matter how unpopular their messages might be. Composed primarily of wealthy New York-based attorneys, the ACLU set out to defend American Communists and Socialists who had been jailed for expressing dissatisfaction with capitalism. From its earliest years, the ACLU also paid close attention to issues relating to academic freedom, especially the right of teachers in all ranks to decide what and how they should teach.

When the Butler Act became law in the spring of 1925, the ACLU issued a press release and sent it to the newspapers in Tennessee's largest cities. The press release appeared in the *Chattanooga Times* on May 4, 1925. It flatly stated that the ACLU was prepared to provide defense attorneys free of charge to any schoolteacher in Tennessee who would step forward to challenge the Butler Act.

The ACLU concentrated on the big cities in Tennessee because the attorneys thought it more likely that urban dwellers would support their point of view. They were quite surprised when only one lone teacher accepted their offer. That teacher, John Scopes, lived in rural Rhea County in the southeastern part of the state, almost 40 miles from Chattanooga.

A Young Teacher in Dayton

John Scopes earned a bachelor's degree in law from the University of Kentucky in 1924. A short time later, he accepted a position at Central High School in Dayton, Tennessee, the county seat of Rhea County. When Scopes arrived Dayton's population stood at about 1,800 people. That number had declined from the 1890s, when miners had worked regional deposits of coal and iron ore that supported a local blast furnace operation. A town built for 3,000 people in the late nineteenth century now stood half empty, better known for its strawberry farms and illicit corn liquor than for any industry it had been able to attract.

When Scopes began working there in the autumn of 1924, he taught math, chemistry, and physics and served as the coach of the school's football team. He felt much more comfortable in the classroom than he did roaming the sidelines of the football field—he had never played football in his life.

Many young bachelors would have found Dayton dull, but Scopes wrote in his autobiography that "I enjoyed the people [of Dayton] and my job from the beginning." Born in Kentucky, Scopes spent his high school years in the small town of Salem, Illinois—William Jennings Bryan's birthplace. He thus felt comfortable in the sleepy mountain town. He attended a local church, since almost all of Dayton's social events revolved around its churches, and went dancing on weekends at a resort in Morgan Springs, higher in the hills. His friendships were drawn from the seniors at his school and the few single women who worked in town. After a few months in Dayton, Scopes recognized everyone, and he was by all accounts a popular and well-liked teacher.

Scopes and *A Civic Biology*

In the spring of 1925, the principal at Central High School—who also was the school's biology instructor—became ill and had to take a leave of absence. He asked Scopes to serve as the school's biology teacher during his absence. Scopes reviewed the biology curriculum with his new students, using a 1914 textbook approved by the state of Tennessee: *A Civic Biology*, by George William Hunter.

This biology textbook, however, contained material that had escaped the notice of the state legislators who had passed the Butler Act earlier that year. Specifically, *A Civic Biology* covered evolution and included humans as mammals in a diagram of the increasing complexity of organisms. The author of the textbook also praised Darwin as "great" and contended that the fossil record supported Darwin's theory.

After his trial ended, Scopes admitted that he could not remember if he had actually taught evolution during his brief tenure as a substitute biology teacher. But that was irrelevant to Scopes. The point, as he saw it, was that it was impossible for *any* biology instructor to teach life sciences *without* teaching evolution—especially when the state-approved textbook for the class described the evolutionary process.

A Scheme to Revitalize Dayton

When the American Civil Liberties Union put out its call for a Tennessee school teacher willing to challenge the Butler Act, the organization's offer immediately caught the attention of George W. Rappleyea, a native New Yorker who served as caretaker of the iron mines in the hills surrounding Dayton. A firm believer in Darwin's theory of evolution, Rappleyea was convinced that the ACLU's stand could be used to bring a splash of publicity—and economic activity—to sleepy Dayton.

Rappleyea tucked the May 4, 1925, edition of the *Chattanooga Times* under his arm and strolled over to Frank E. "Doc" Robinson's drugstore. Robinson wore many hats in Dayton. An energetic community booster, he owned the drugstore, served on the board of education, and even sold school textbooks along with soft drinks and pain relievers. Robinson was intrigued by Rappleyea's news, and before long the two men agreed to see if they could build enough community support to persuade a local schoolteacher to challenge the Butler Act.

Many Dayton residents were strong supporters of the Butler Act. Still, Rappleyea and Robinson had little trouble finding others who either supported Darwin's theory of evolution or agreed that the publicity of a trial might attract visitors and businesses to Dayton. School Superintendent Walter White supported the scheme, and the two city attorneys, brothers Herbert E. and Sue K. Hicks

George Rappleyea (right) believed that the sleepy town of Dayton, Tennessee, would receive a much-needed economic boost if it hosted a legal challenge to the Butler Act.

(the latter a man named after his mother), savored the idea of testing the constitutionality of the law. Wallace Haggard, another young Dayton lawyer, also foresaw a challenging case. Haggard and the Hicks brothers agreed to prosecute any local teacher who would agree to be "arrested" for violating the Butler Act.

These community leaders immediately settled on John Scopes as an ideal candidate. Whereas Central High School's regular biology teacher was a married man with children and deep ties to the community, Scopes was a footloose bachelor who had no intention of spending his life in Dayton. In addition, he had already become known as an independent-minded young man.

Robinson and Rappleyea knew that they needed to approach Scopes quickly, however. The school year had just ended, and the young teacher might soon be gone for the summer (as it turned out, Scopes had planned to visit his father in Illinois as soon as the school year ended, but he remained in Dayton an extra week in order to attend a church picnic with a young woman he had just met).

Scopes was playing tennis with some of his students on May 5 when he was summoned to Robinson's drug store by a delivery boy. Figuring that Robinson must have some school issue to discuss, Scopes hastened to the store. "I was wearing a shirt and trousers and the shirt was stained with sweat," Scopes recalled in his autobiography. "It was about three-quarters of a mile downtown to the drugstore, and I walked there dressed as I was."

A small committee of Dayton residents awaited Scopes at the drugstore, including Sue Hicks, Rappleyea, and Robinson. They treated the sweating teacher to a soft drink. Then Rappleyea said, "John, we've been arguing, and I said that nobody could teach biology without teaching evolution." Scopes agreed. He pulled a copy of *A Civic Biology* off the drugstore shelf and turned to the pages that covered evolution. He reminded the assembled men that the textbook was approved by the state.

Rappleyea asked Scopes if he had taught from that text. Scopes said yes. Robinson asked Scopes if he would agree to be the "accused teacher" for the ACLU's test case against the law. At this point the meeting turned awkward. Scopes and Sue Hicks were good friends, and the teacher feared that his participation in such a legal challenge might drive a wedge into the friendship. After all, Hicks would likely be one of the attorneys prosecuting Scopes for his actions. But Hicks assured Scopes that a trial would not threaten their friendship, and he emphasized the potential stakes involved. At that point, Scopes agreed to serve as a test case for the legality of the Butler Act.

Rappleyea rushed out to find a justice of the peace and swore out a complaint against Scopes. Robinson strode to the telephone and called the Chattanooga newspapers. Scopes returned to his tennis game, blissfully unaware of the stormy weather ahead. "I had been tapped and trapped by the rush of events," he wrote in his memoir. "That was all right with me."

"Doc" Robinson's position on the Dayton school board did not deter him from lending his enthusiastic support to Rappleyea's scheme to "put Dayton on the map."

A Trial Date is Set

On May 9, 1925, Rhea County's three judges formally acknowledged the complaint filed against Scopes. The judges scheduled an August hearing before a grand jury, at which time Scopes would either be indicted or have the charge against him dismissed. Scopes was released without having to post bail. He never spent a second behind bars.

The Tennessee newspapers picked up the story, and soon newspapers and radios all across the country were reporting on the events taking place in Dayton. An eccentric Knoxville attorney named John Randolph Neal drove to Dayton and pledged to help Scopes as a counsel. Neal had a scruffy appearance and a controversial past; he was a former politician who in 1923 had

The first lawyer to rush to the defense of Dayton teacher John Scopes (right) was pro-evolution attorney John Randolph Neal (left).

been ousted from a teaching position at the University of Tennessee because of his vocal support for evolution. The ACLU representatives counseling Scopes were leery of him. Scopes liked Neal, though, and was eager to accept the lawyer's help. This proved a wise decision. Neal had a firm grasp of Tennessee law, and he recognized that any attempt to strike down the Butler Act hinged on getting the case past a local trial and into the appeal process, where it might eventually wind its way to the U.S. Supreme Court.

Neal's early involvement in the case proved to be important. John T. Raulston, the circuit court judge for the Eighteenth District, decided to change his whole schedule to bring the Scopes issue to a speedy trial (see Raulston biography, p. 139). Raulston convened a special grand jury on May 25.

The proceedings did not last long. Raulston read the grand jurors the first chapter of Genesis, and then the passage on evolution from the textbook Scopes had used. District Attorney Tom Stewart then called on three students who testified that Scopes had taught them evolutionary theory (see Stewart biography, p. 147). A few hours later, the jury returned an indictment against Scopes. Raulston scheduled the trial for July 10.

Neal advocated moving the location of the trial to Knoxville or Chattanooga, arguing that such cities would provide a more neutral venue. The citizens of Dayton vocally opposed such a move, and Neal's request was denied. Excitement about the upcoming trial gripped the town and surrounding communities. Civic boosters began to plan for an influx of 30,000 or more people who would sit in their restaurants, sleep in their boardinghouses and hotels, purchase souvenirs and other goods—and then go home and tell all their friends about the charming Tennessee town set amid lovely mountains. Ignoring suggestions in the big city newspapers that the trial would expose Rhea County as a hotbed of ignorance, Daytonians prepared for the "big event" that would make their town famous.

The "Great Commoner" Volunteers to Prosecute

At the same time Rappleyea and his companions were initiating the Scopes trial in Robinson's drugstore, William Jennings Bryan was addressing delegates to the World's Christian Fundamentals Association (WCFA) in Memphis. During the conference, word reached Bryan that a Tennessee teacher had been arrested for violating the Butler Act. Bryan worked this information into his speeches. Officials in the WCFA urged "The Great Commoner" to join Scopes's prosecution team. Even though he had not practiced courtroom law for 30 years, Bryan agreed. He initiated correspondence with the local Dayton prosecutors to join their team. "I shall of course serve without compensation," he added in an early note.

> *"The real issue is not what can be taught in the public schools, but who shall control the educational system," Bryan declared.*

The addition of "The Great Commoner" to the prosecution team changed the whole tenor of the trial. The ACLU had hoped to focus strictly on the constitutionality of the Butler Act—whether a state could make a school teacher a criminal for teaching a theory that did not support the Christian Bible. But now that Bryan was part of the mix, the defense attorneys braced themselves for a massive clash on much larger issues: majority rule and taxpayers' rights. Bryan even predicted that the prosecution could claim victory in the upcoming trial without even mentioning evolution. "The real issue is not *what* can be taught in the public schools, but *who* shall control the educational system," he declared.

Bryan's entrance into the legal fray also overjoyed the citizens of Dayton, including residents that disagreed with him. One of the most famous orators in America, a three-time presidential nominee, would grace their town with his presence! Buoyed by this prospect, Dayton residents forecast even higher attendance figures for the upcoming trial.

Dayton Catches Darrow's Eye

Clarence Darrow learned of Scopes's decision to defy the Butler Act while lecturing in Richmond, Virginia. Journalist H. L. Mencken was in attendance at the lecture, and afterwards he and Darrow discussed the attorney's possible participation in the trial. Mencken was excited at the prospect. He thought Darrow was the perfect lawyer to argue against the undue influence of Christian fundamentalist religion in law and education.

Initially, however, Darrow declined to pursue the matter. He was reluctant to get involved in the Dayton case in part because he had become one of the most controversial lawyers in America over the previous year. In 1924 Darrow served as the defense attorney for two wealthy young men, Nathan Leopold and Richard Loeb, who had kidnapped and murdered a 13-year-old boy for the sheer challenge of committing the "perfect crime." The evidence against Leopold and Loeb was overwhelming. When arrested they confessed to the deed, although they blamed each other for the actual murder. The killers' parents hired Darrow not to seek an acquittal, but to save the young men from death sentences.

Most Americans thought that the death penalty for Leopold and Loeb was a foregone conclusion. After all, everyone agreed that the crime was despicable, especially given the victim's young age and the many luxuries that the murderers had enjoyed from birth.

Everyone expected Leopold and Loeb to plead not guilty by reason of insanity. Darrow, however, convinced them to plead guilty so they could avoid a jury trial that would almost assure them a death conviction. By pleading guilty, Leopold and Loeb's case moved straight to the penalty phase—life in prison, or death, to be decided by a judge.

Arguing the penalty phase before a judge (and a courtroom full of reporters), Darrow spoke eloquently for twelve hours, mustering every argument he could against a death sentence for the two young men. Notoriously, he used Darwinian evolution as a centerpiece of his argument against the death penalty, suggesting that the two defendants were victims of poor genetics. He also blamed their behavior on their upbringing by nannies and their infatuation with the German philosopher Friedrich Nietzsche. But the crux of Darrow's argument rested on his lifelong opposition to the death penalty. He spent hours attempting to persuade the judge that a lifetime spent in

In 1924 Clarence Darrow (left) saved notorious child-killers Nathan Leopold (right) and Richard Loeb (second from right) from the death penalty.

prison could suffice as punishment. Indeed, he insisted that a life sentence might be worse than death for two twenty-year-olds.

Darrow convinced the judge to spare the lives of Leopold and Loeb. Many Americans reacted with outrage to this news, and his success in saving the two murderers from execution struck many religious people as a terrible sin in itself. Bryan, meanwhile, seized on Darrow's use of Darwin in his Leopold-Loeb defense as yet another reason to outlaw teaching of evolution theory.

Scopes Chooses Darrow over ACLU Objections

When Darrow learned that William Jennings Bryan had joined the Scopes prosecution, the proud agnostic experienced a rapid change of heart. "At once I wanted to go [to Dayton]," Darrow recalled in his autobiography, *The Story of*

My Life. "To me it was perfectly clear that the proceedings bore little semblance to a court case, but I realized that there was no limit to the mischief that might be accomplished unless the country was aroused to the evil at hand."

Darrow teamed with an international divorce lawyer named Dudley Field Malone, and the two of them wired Neal that they would like to join in the defense of John Scopes. Malone had ties to the ACLU but was better known for his occasional work on behalf of union organizers and other poor defendants who might not otherwise be able to get proper legal representation (see Malone biography, p. 131). Both men offered their services free of charge—Darrow for the first and last time in his life.

> *"To me it was perfectly clear that the proceedings bore little semblance to a court case, but I realized that there was no limit to the mischief that might be accomplished unless the country was aroused to the evil at hand."*
>
> *—Clarence Darrow*

Anyone could volunteer to defend John Scopes, but ultimately the choice of counsel was his. In early June Scopes and Neal traveled to New York City to confer with the ACLU and Malone. The ACLU had chosen its own team of top lawyers and hoped to convince Scopes to allow those lawyers to represent him. The ACLU leadership also reminded Scopes that Darrow was an admitted agnostic, that he would turn the trial into a showdown between religion and science, and that he would bring the Leopold-Loeb baggage with him to Dayton.

Scopes decided, however, that he wanted an attorney with a reputation equal to that of Bryan. In addition, he recognized that despite his controversial name, Darrow was an excellent defense attorney. He chose Darrow and Malone. "Ballyhoo was already drowning out the original issues that ACLU wanted to emphasize," Scopes later wrote in his memoir. "We should expect a gouging, roughhouse battle, for which Darrow and Malone were best suited."

As a courtesy to the ACLU, Scopes also agreed to the presence of Arthur Garfield Hays on his defense team (see Hays biography, p. 128). Hays served as general counsel for the ACLU. He was instructed to keep the constitutional issues surrounding the Butler bill in the forefront during the trial.

In the Spotlight

During his trip to New York, John Scopes came to realize that his days of anonymity were over. He was mobbed by the press wherever he went and photographed with university professors, museum curators, and fossil collectors. On the way back to Dayton he stopped in Washington, D.C., and visited the Library of Congress, where he was photographed with the original copy of the Constitution. Reporters asked him if he believed in God. Stories circulated that he had been offered enormous sums to appear in movies. Everything he did and said found its way into print.

Meanwhile, back in Dayton, advocates for both sides of the approaching clash began to gather. The town's business owners, meanwhile, seized on the upcoming trial's central underlying issue—humankind's alleged evolutionary links to primates. The citizens got down to "monkey business," decorating shop and automobiles with pictures of apes and chimpanzees. Live monkeys seemed to materialize out of nowhere, including trained chimpanzees rented or purchased by publicity-hungry business owners. Like John Scopes, the town of Dayton would forever be changed by the famous "Monkey Trial."

Chapter Three
THE SCOPES TRIAL BEGINS

—◦◦◦◦◦—

I came all the way from New York to find that the defendant was a man, the prosecutor was a man, the judge a man, the jury all men, the attorneys on both sides men.... One would think there weren't any women in this world, or that they didn't do any thinking.

—Suffragette Doris Stevens, wife of Dudley Field Malone,
July 16, 1925

John Tate Raulston was the elected judge for Tennessee's eighteenth district, where the Scopes trial would take place. As a circuit court judge, he traveled from county to county in his district. Upon his arrival in a county seat, he would hear all the cases that had accumulated since his last visit. Rhea County, where Dayton was located, was one of a half dozen counties within his jurisdiction.

Before Scopes declared that he had taught evolution in defiance of the Butler Act, Raulston had not been scheduled to visit Rhea County until sometime in the autumn of 1925. Raulston quickly rearranged his schedule, however. He was as eager as the boosters in Dayton to arrange a speedy trial in the Scopes matter. Mindful that he faced a re-election campaign the following year, Raulston did everything in his power to court publicity and get his picture in the national newspapers. He also willingly sat for interviews in which he consistently cast himself as a God-fearing man. "It has always been and is now one of the great passions of my life to ascertain the truth about all matters, especially relative to God," he told the *Nashville Banner* for its May 25 edition. "But I am not so much exercised over the question as to whence man cometh as I am to wither he goes."

Scopes's alleged crime was only a misdemeanor. It was no more significant then a charge of producing illegal liquor or shoplifting merchandise from a store. Raulston heard scores of such petty cases in his travels. But the judge knew that the Scopes trial was different, for it was going to stray into controversial philosophical areas. He also knew that the presence of icons such as William Jennings Bryan would heighten the tension surrounding the case. "Big issues are involved," the judge told the *Nashville Banner.*

A Carnival Atmosphere Envelops Dayton

Once Raulston announced a trial date of July 10 for the Scopes case, the citizens of Dayton—and many early-arriving visitors—prepared for an onslaught of curious tourists and newspaper reporters. Many Daytonians recognized that the impending trial had the potential to be a moneymaking event for the town.

Doc Robinson, for example, hung a banner outside his store reading "Where It Started" and began selling "simian sodas." He also brought in Joe Mendi, a trained chimpanzee, to attract business. The little chimp was a big hit, eventually becoming one of the most famous attractions in all of Dayton. Meanwhile, anti-evolution forces staked out positions throughout town. One religious group erected an enormous banner within sight of the courthouse. Its simple message: "Read Your Bible." Members of the Anti-Evolution League set up a sidewalk stand where they sold copies of Bryan's books and a bestseller by an author named T. T. Martin called *Hell and the High Schools.* Evangelist preachers planted themselves under the shade of swaying trees, delivering impassioned sermons.

Then came the thrilling news that the trial would be broadcast live by Chicago radio station WGN, and that the station would make its broadcast feed available to other stations all over America. Technicians arrived to wire Dayton's courthouse with microphones. Newsreel companies sent cameramen to record film footage for distribution to movie houses. In addition, the Scopes story brought more than 200 print journalists into Dayton, some from as far away as London. The *New York Times* announced its intention to print the entire court transcript while still using a corps of reporters to cover the trial highlights.

Celebrity chimpanzee Joe Mendi poses with "Doc" Robinson (center) at Robinson's Drug Store in Dayton.

H. L. Mencken was the most famous journalist who covered the Scopes trial. In addition to his regular columns for the *Baltimore Evening Sun,* he edited an influential magazine, *The American Mercury.* It was in the pages of the latter that he coined the name "Monkey Trial" for the Scopes proceedings. Even before arriving in Dayton he began painting the Scopes event as a classic battle between the powers of enlightenment (the defense) and the unruly, uneducated lower classes (represented by Bryan, the "Great Commoner"). For the duration of the trial, Mencken never wavered in his support for Darrow and the defense—or in his hostility toward Bryan and his fundamentalist backers. He repeatedly branded Bryan as ignorant, and dismissed the religious folk of Dayton as "half-wits" and "yokels."

The legal teams involved in the Scopes case were joined in Dayton by anti-evolution organizations such as the Anti-Evolution League, which did a brisk sidewalk business selling anti-Darwinist books by William Jennings Bryan and T. T. Martin.

Bryan Arrives in Dayton

William Jennings Bryan and his wife, Mary, arrived in Dayton by train on July 7, just three days before the commencement of the trial. A hero's welcome awaited him at the train station. A large crowd gathered to greet him with cheers and waving handkerchiefs. The temperature hovered in the 90s, as it would throughout the trial, and Bryan wore an African safari-type pith helmet to protect his head from the sunshine. "Just say that I am here," he told his supporters. "I am going right to work, and I am ready for anything that is to be done." The town's Progressive Club invited Bryan to a banquet in his honor that night. He accepted.

William Jennings Bryan (center, in bow tie) received a hero's welcome when he arrived in Dayton, Tennessee, to lead the prosecution team.

At the banquet, Bryan delivered a lengthy speech to enthusiastic applause. He openly described the upcoming trial as a clash of national interests. "The contest between evolution and Christianity is a duel to the death," he said. "The atheists, agnostics and all other opponents of Christianity understand the character of the struggle, hence their interest in this case. From this time forth Christians will understand the character of the struggle also."

Bryan joined a swelling prosecution team that included Bryan's son, William Jr.; Sue and Herbert Hicks; Wallace Haggard; Gordon McKenzie, a Dayton resident who vehemently opposed evolution on religious grounds; McKenzie's father, Ben, a retired attorney general for the eighteenth circuit; and Tom Stewart, the current attorney general for the eighteenth district. With the exception of Bryan and his son, all of the prosecuting attorneys lived in Tennessee.

Stewart stood out among this team of attorneys. Young, handsome, and businesslike, he wanted to prosecute the Scopes case as if it were any other minor misdemeanor. He did not want any expert witnesses to debate issues of majority rule, moral decay among the young, or scientific evidence for evolution. To Stewart, the case rested on very simple ground: Scopes had broken a Tennessee law. Stewart could produce witnesses to prove it, and that should be that.

The Defense Gathers

The Scopes defense team presented an altogether different profile. Arthur Garfield Hays was a Jewish New Yorker who financed his free work on behalf of the American Civil Liberties Union (ACLU) by serving wealthy corporations. Dudley Field Malone was a lapsed Catholic divorce lawyer, married to a suffragette named Doris Stevens (her continued use of her maiden name was a scandalous breach of propriety in that era). Clarence Darrow hailed from Chicago and made no effort to hide his doubts about the existence of God, heaven, or hell. John Neal, the scruffy professor who still fumed about his dismissal from the University of Tennessee, was the sole Tennessean on the team.

As the opening of the trial drew near, the Hicks brothers gave newspaper interviews in which they bluntly described their opponents as socialists and atheists, big-city outsiders who had no business bringing their minority viewpoints to Dayton. On behalf of his colleagues, Malone parried with his own interviews. In one, he said: "No more serious invasion of the sacred principle of liberty than the recent act against the teaching of evolution in Tennessee has ever been attempted."

As he departed New York for Dayton, meanwhile, Darrow famously announced that "Scopes is not on trial. Civilization is on trial. Nothing will satisfy us but broad victory, a knockout which will have an everlasting precedent to prove that America is founded on liberty and not on narrow, mean, intolerable and brainless prejudice of soulless religio-maniacs."

Darrow, Hays, and Malone all arrived for the trial on July 9. Hays and Malone reached Dayton in the morning, while Darrow arrived on the late train after dark. A small but courteous crowd greeted Darrow at the station, and the Progressive Club invited him to a banquet in *his* honor. Darrow accepted.

John Scopes (left) shakes hands with Clarence Darrow upon the latter's arrival in Dayton, Tennessee, for the "Monkey Trial."

The night before the trial, Judge Raulston attended an open air prayer service on the courthouse lawn. He offered the benediction for the evening, stating: "I am much interested that the unerring hand of Him who is Author of all truth and justice should direct every official act of mine." Such an ardent statement of Christian faith on the sitting judge's part did not fill Scopes and his defense team with confidence that the teacher would receive a fair trial.

In reality, though, Scopes and his lawyers did not necessarily *want* a fair trial. They wanted Scopes to be found guilty so that they could appeal the case to higher courts, where the constitutional issues of academic freedom and separation of church and state would become paramount. "Civilization" might not be on trial in the minds of the ACLU attorneys and Neal, but the constitutionality of the Butler Act certainly was.

To Bryan and Darrow and their legal allies, then, the stakes for the approaching courtroom showdown could not have been higher. Put simply, both sides were trying to set the future course of the United States in vital social, educational, and spiritual matters.

Trial Begins in a Packed Courthouse

On Friday, July 10, 1925, the Scopes "Monkey Trial" commenced at nine o'clock in the morning in the Rhea County courthouse. Spectators who hoped to gain a seat in the second-floor courtroom started arriving at dawn. The courthouse was large and modern, spruced up inside with a new coat of paint. But it was not built for the volume of movie cameramen, radio technicians, telegraph operators, newspaper reporters, and curious onlookers who descended on the courthouse. By nine o'clock the courtroom was packed and the overflow of spectators settled for places on the lawn, where they could listen to the proceedings through a loudspeaker.

The throngs of tourists never arrived, however. Dayton's boosters had estimated that as many as 30,000 people might seek overnight shelter in the town. Instead, only some 500 visitors took accommodations in and around Dayton, and many of these individuals were associated with the trial in some way. Those who could not find rooms in the few hotels received hospitality from homeowners. The defense team and its witnesses, for example, roomed together in a large unoccupied mansion in Dayton.

Still, the trial produced a lively mix of individuals. Rural residents of the mountains surrounding Dayton arrived in horse-drawn wagons, the traveling evangelists held court, some interested spectators motored in from Chattanooga, and all regular business in Dayton ceased.

Battling the Heat

A heat wave had settled over Dayton by the time the trial began. Despite the addition of new electric fans, the courtroom quickly became stifling—a "blast furnace," in Mencken's words. Judge Raulston announced that gentlemen need not wear their coats and ties, and that no smoking would be allowed in the courtroom. This last pronouncement brought groans from the press corps and the spectators. The edict also became a source of frustration for almost every attorney except Bryan, who was a nonsmoker.

The arrival of the prosecution and defense teams on the morning of July 10 underscored the publicity surrounding the trial. Flashbulbs popped as each team entered the courtroom, and again as Bryan and Darrow greeted each other cordially. Although they had both been giving dramatic speeches about the case in the weeks leading up to the trial, Bryan and Darrow had

Defense attorneys Dudley Malone (left), John Randolph Neal (center), and Clarence Darrow (right) led a talented legal team dedicated to defending evolution from fundamentalist attacks.

long been on good terms. Neither one objected to posing for photos. They even smiled at one another with genuine affection. Judge Raulston agreed to pose for the cameras as well, and he even advised the press about possible picture-taking opportunities in the coming days.

The trial participants quickly accepted Raulston's dress code, divesting themselves of suit coats and ties. Bryan unbuttoned and removed the collar from his shirt and rolled up his sleeves. Even so, the oppressive heat began to bother him almost immediately. Throughout most of the trial he fanned himself constantly with a hand-held palm leaf fan. Only one attorney retained his

41

America's First Major Media Event

The modest size of the "live" audience that descended on Dayton, Tennessee, for the Scopes "Monkey Trial" did not accurately reflect the level of national interest in the proceedings. Throughout its duration, the Scopes Trial dominated the front pages of every major metropolitan daily newspaper. These stories were usually accompanied by photographs and often featured complete transcripts of even the most tedious legal details. Countless Americans, meanwhile, followed the trial via live radio broadcasts that transmitted every legal twist and turn from the Dayton courthouse.

In addition, the entire event was filmed on newsreel cameras. This footage—the first film of a trial in U.S. history—was whisked away every day by plane to New York, Cleveland, Chicago, Detroit, and other northern cities, where it was shown in a multitude of movie halls. "America was in the middle of the roaring twenties [and] ... into media sensation, and this was the greatest media sensation of a media sensation-loving decade," said trial historian Edward J. Larson in an interview with C-SPAN's *Booknotes*.

coat and tie. Dudley Field Malone came dressed impeccably in a custom tailored suit. Even as the temperature in the courtroom rose toward 100 degrees, Malone never removed a single article of clothing. The reporters began to joke that he did not sweat.

When the greetings and the posing for photographs concluded, Raulston placed his personal Bible and a Tennessee statute book on the judge's bench and took his seat. He called for order. The trial began.

Prayer in the Courtroom

By Tennessee law, any court case could begin with a prayer. Judge Raulston invited a local fundamentalist pastor to do the honors. The pastor prayed that the Holy Spirit "may be with the jury and with the accused and with all the attorneys," so that all of them would remain "loyal to God." The lengthy prayer drew a chorus of "amens" from spectators—and stony stares from the defense table. These daily prayers would become a major source of contention between Darrow and the judge as the trial progressed.

Because Judge Raulston had called the original Scopes grand jury so quickly, the term of the grand jury had expired. He thus found it necessary to reconvene the grand jury and re-issue the indictment against Scopes. The same men who had issued the first indictment took their seats in the jury box. Again, as on May 25, Raulston read them the Butler Act and the first chapter of the Book of Genesis.

Attorney General Stewart then called some of Scopes's students to the witness stand. Each student took the stand and testified that Scopes had taught them Darwin's theory of evolution. They were not asked to explain the theory or comment upon it. Years later, Scopes wrote that he actually played an important role in securing the testimony of one of the students: "As the new proceedings were about to get under way, a friend reported that one of the boys didn't want to go on the stand. He was afraid he would hurt me. To prevent his loyalty from delaying the trial I went to see the youngster and told him to go ahead and testify to what he had been told to say because he would be doing me a favor."

After hearing the testimony from Scopes's students, the grand jury again indicted Scopes for violating the Butler Act. Raulston then announced a lunchtime recess, after which the assembled attorneys would choose the jury for Case Number 5232: *The State of Tennessee v. John Thomas Scopes.*

> *"Scopes is not on trial," said Darrow. "Civilization is on trial. Nothing will satisfy us but broad victory, a knockout which will have an everlasting precedent to prove that America is founded on liberty and not on narrow, mean, intolerable and brainless prejudice of soulless religio-maniacs."*

Twelve Jurors Take Their Seats

Dayton's populace included women and African Americans, of course, but only white males served on juries during this era in Tennessee history. One hundred potential jurors had been summoned, and to a man they keenly desired a prize front seat for the trial.

According to custom, the local sheriff determined the order in which potential jurors would be presented for questioning by the defense and prosecution. Darrow, however, asked that potential jurors be drawn from a hat instead (Darrow surmised that since the sheriff knew most of the potential jurors, he might choose them in a prejudiced manner.)

Darrow was renowned for grilling potential jurors, so most observers expected a lengthy jury selection process. After all, in a community like Dayton, it might prove impossible to find twelve men who did not attend church services or profess a deep belief in the Bible.

In this case, however, Darrow fully expected—indeed, wanted—jurors who would deliver a guilty verdict. "Because it was a trial geared for the national media, he wanted to expose to the public that these jurors didn't know anything about evolution," explained trial historian Edward J. Larson in an interview for C-SPAN's *Booknotes*. "The idea was to show the specter of having a trial where the merits of a scientific theory [are judged] by people who didn't know the scientific theory."

Darrow, though, also hoped to find jurors who might be open-minded enough to at least consider and weigh defense arguments. With this in mind, he posed three questions to every potential candidate, using slightly different wording each time. Basically his queries ran thus:

- Do you know anything about evolution?
- Do you have any opinion on whether the Bible is against evolution?
- Would you be willing to form an opinion based on the evidence presented here in court?

Darrow accepted one juror who admitted that he could not read because he was "uneducated." The man's honesty appealed to Darrow. It also helped boost the defense's chances of introducing expert witnesses on the science of evolution and the opinions of more liberal clergymen.

Another potential juror, a traveling pastor, at first claimed to have no opinion on evolution. Because he was a pastor, though, Darrow grilled him more intensely. Under the scrutiny of the wily attorney, the pastor finally admitted that he had preached against evolution in his churches. His statement drew applause from the spectators—and a warning by Judge Raulston that further outbursts would lead to expulsion from the courtroom. The warning was not heeded and was never enforced.

Darrow refused several jurors who could not conceal their fundamentalist views. Throughout the afternoon, he was able to find only one man who did not attend church. That man was admitted to the jury. All of the others were church-goers, and all met the approval of Stewart, who led the questioning for the prosecution. In his memoir, Scopes said he knew each and every one of the twelve jurors.

The jury selected for the Scopes trial poses for the camera. Standing at far right is John T. Raulston, who presided over the famous trial.

Jousting Over "Expert" Witnesses

One procedural matter remained to be discussed. Darrow wanted a ruling on the admissibility of the expert witness testimony he planned to use in Scopes's defense. Usually this step occurred only after the prosecution had concluded its case. Judge Raulston patiently reminded Darrow of this fact. Darrow countered by pointing out that his witnesses would have to travel great distances to get to Dayton; he wanted to spare them the trip if they would not be allowed to testify. District Attorney Stewart urged Raulston not to permit such testimony. Eager to restrict the trial to its simple legal limits, Stewart insisted that "It isn't competent to bring into this case scientists who testify as to what the theory of evolution is or interpret the Bible or anything of that sort."

Raulston refused to rule on the admissibility of expert witnesses at that point in the trial. He adjourned for the weekend, and the crowd spilled out

45

into the streets of Dayton. The reporters submitted their stories. The defense attorneys retired to their mansion to plot their strategy. William Jennings Bryan and his wife returned to a private home where he and his family had been invited to stay.

Bryan had Sunday sermons to write. He had been invited to preach at every church in Dayton. Given the number of people eager to hear his words, he decided to deliver his oration at the Methodist church, the largest church in Dayton. Later Sunday afternoon, he preached again for an outdoor audience estimated at 3,000 people. Judge Raulston attended the Methodist church service and sat in the front pew.

Bryan used his weekend remarks to undermine the defense attempts to introduce expert testimony on evolution. Darrow, meanwhile, told newspaper reporters that the wording of the Butler Act made it essential for him to be able to present evidence refuting the contention that Darwin's theory absolutely contradicted the Bible. In this way Darrow could introduce theologians who felt that evolutionary theory and the Book of Genesis could be reconciled.

For his part, Bryan believed that attempts to reconcile Christian belief with evolutionary theory at best produced only a "half truth" that would be "worse than a lie." Nonetheless, to protect themselves in case Raulston decided the issue in favor of Scopes, the prosecution contacted several nationally-known professors of theology who believed that it was impossible to reconcile Darwinism with the Bible. These individuals included fundamentalist leader John Roach Straton, who denounced Piltdown Man as a forgery (correctly, as it turned out); William Bell Riley, president of the World's Christian Fundamentals Association; and J. Frank Norris, a popular preacher from Dallas who had been campaigning for anti-evolution legislation in Texas. All three men were personal friends of Bryan. Armed with this insurance, the prosecution prepared for the trial to begin in earnest.

Chapter Four

FIREWORKS IN THE COURTROOM

─━━⊷╎⊶━━─

Every step in human progress, from the first feeble stirrings in the abyss of time, has been opposed by the great majority of men. Every valuable thing that has been added to the store of man's possessions has been derided by them when it was new, and destroyed by them when they had the power. They have fought every new truth ever heard of, and they have killed every truth-seeker who got into their hands.

—H. L. Mencken, "Homo Neanderthalensis,"
Baltimore Evening Sun, June 29, 1925

The Scopes "Monkey Trial" re-convened on Monday morning, July 13, 1925. Once again the temperature and humidity combined to create stifling conditions in the courtroom. Judge Raulston opened the proceedings by inviting a local pastor to offer a prayer. This time the defense really fumed. Darrow stood and politely asked that the court dispense with the prayers, since the case held religious issues and the prayers might influence the jury. The judge waved off Darrow's concerns and called the pastor forward.

The pastor, Reverend Moffett, prayed: "Oh God, our Father, Thou who are the creator of the heaven and the earth and the sea and all that is in them. Thou who are the preserver and controller of all things, Thou who wilt bring out all things to Thy glory in the end, we thank Thee this morning that Thou does not only fill the heavens, but Thou doest also fill the earth." Whether the pastor had planned his remarks before Darrow's objection or changed them at that moment, they expressed clear support for the prosecution team.

Once the prayer concluded, the first order of business was to seek relief from the heat. Coats and ties were removed and slung over chairs. Even Raulston, who had a personal electric fan at his disposal, removed his suit coat. Only Malone remained in his impeccably tailored clothing. By now his self-discipline had been noted by everyone.

Defense Moves to Quash the Indictment

"If a dramatist with a keen ear for dialogue and a rapid imagination had tried to write a script, he couldn't have outdone the Dayton trial," Scopes wrote in his memoir. "As soon as it opened that morning, it created friction. Every sentence was pointed and loaded with conflict."

> *"If a dramatist with a keen ear for dialogue and a rapid imagination had tried to write a script, he couldn't have outdone the Dayton trial," Scopes said. "As soon as it opened that morning, it created friction. Every sentence was pointed and loaded with conflict."*

Scopes's defense team went right to work. The attorneys immediately sought to quash Scopes's indictment, asserting that the law he was accused of breaking was itself in violation of the Constitution of the State of Tennessee. This move ensured that if Scopes was found guilty, the defense would have the option of filing an appeal with Tennessee's Supreme Court.

Raulston promptly ordered the jurors to leave the room and to be sequestered where they could not hear procedural arguments. The jurors had been sworn in simply for the misdemeanor case, not for complicated debates on the constitutionality of the Butler Act.

Defense attorney John Neal, his unkempt appearance in stark contrast to Malone, asked the judge to set protocol for the discussion on constitutionality. Neal wanted the defense to offer opening remarks. Then the prosecution could rebut, after which the defense would have the right to deliver final arguments. Neal was the defense attorney who knew the most about Tennessee law. He believed this defense motion might be the only chance Scopes's side had to present its views, especially since Raulston still had not indicated whether he would allow testimony from the defense's expert witnesses.

Raulston agreed to Neal's request. The flamboyant Neal then launched into a lengthy and rambling speech detailing how the Butler Act violated the

Tennessee Constitution's separation of church and state clause. He reminded the judge that the Constitution existed to protect the minority—in this case, those who supported evolution in science classes—from decisions by the majority. He ended his remarks by declaring that the Butler Act established the teaching of religion in public schools, a clear violation of Tennessee's Bill of Rights.

At the conclusion of Neal's speech, ACLU attorney Arthur Garfield Hays rose to address the judge. Hays insisted that passage of the Butler Act was akin to passing a law ordering teachers to tell students that the sun revolved around the earth. (Hays used this analogy in part because Kentucky legislators had recently used this argument to defeat a proposed anti-evolution statute in their state.) "The Copernican theory [that the Earth and other planets in our solar system revolve around the sun] is a matter of common knowledge," Hays reminded the court. "Evolution is as much a scientific fact as the Copernican theory. The State may determine what subjects shall be taught, but if biology is to be taught, it cannot be demanded that it be taught falsely."

McKenzie Takes the Floor

The prosecution began its rebuttal with a speech by former Rhea County attorney general Ben McKenzie. A retired Tennessee lawyer with a "country gentleman" Southern drawl, McKenzie knew that he could count on support from the audience. He courted this local approval by couching his remarks in humor. He nonetheless managed to stick barbs into the defense attorneys at several points.

First McKenzie ridiculed Hays's linkage of the Copernican theory and Darwin's evolutionary theory as scientific theories that were equally deserving of a place in Tennessee's public school curriculum. "It is not half so much kin to this case as he says we are to the monkeys," McKenzie quipped.

McKenzie then threw out his own challenge. "The questions [based on the Butler Act and Scopes's indictment] have all been settled in Tennessee," he said, "and are favorable to our contention. If these gentlemen have any laws in the great metropolitan city of New York that conflict with it, or in the great white city of the Northwest [Darrow's Chicago] that will throw any light on it, we will be glad to hear about it. They have many great lawyers and courts up there." In his own folky, Southern way, McKenzie was implying that

Prosecuting attorney Ben McKenzie (at left with arm around Clarence Darrow) established a recurring prosecution theme when he implied that Scopes's defense attorneys, most of whom hailed from large northern cities, had no business litigating a case in a rural court in Tennessee.

city lawyers like Hays, Malone, and Darrow had no business litigating a case in a rural court in Tennessee. McKenzie's remarks met with loud applause and cheers from the assembled spectators.

Malone objected vigorously. "We are here, rightfully, as American citizens," he said.

Judge Raulston responded that McKenzie was renowned for his sense of humor.

"Why, you all ain't acquainted with me," McKenzie added. "I love you."

Malone again demanded that McKenzie stick to the issues under discussion.

Undaunted, McKenzie replied: "I love you."

"Sure you do," Darrow snarled in response.

More heated debate followed after the lunch break. Making his first appearance for the prosecution, young Tom Stewart proved a worthy foe for the seasoned lawyers across the aisle. Stewart vigorously denied that the Butler Act ran counter to the provisions for separation of church and state in the Tennessee Constitution. He noted that John Scopes had every right to lecture on the theory of evolution anywhere but in a public classroom. He reminded the judge that taxpayers funded the public schools, and asserted that taxpayers should have ultimate authority—through their elected state representatives—over what could be taught in the schools. Finally, he pointed out that the Butler Act did not require that students attend one particular church, or any church at all.

Darrow interrupted at that point. He reminded Stewart that the Tennessee Constitution protected citizens from the "preference" of one religion over any others. But he charged that the Butler Act gave preference to the Bible. "Why not the Koran?" he asked.

"If your Honor please, the Saint James version of the Bible is the recognized one in this section of the country," responded Stewart. "The laws of the land recognize the Bible; the laws of the land recognize the law of God and Christianity as a part of the common-law."

Malone responded that this view would be prejudiced against any Jewish Tennesseans. Stewart replied that people of that faith were permitted to worship as they pleased, and that this matter had nothing to do with his main point: that taxpayers had a right to influence curriculum in taxpayer-funded schools.

Darrow Challenges the Butler Act

On the afternoon of July 13, Clarence Darrow gave his first lengthy statement of the trial. Darrow had visualized the entire Scopes trial in advance as a grand master might contemplate a chess game. He desperately wanted to avoid allowing Bryan to make any closing remarks. He knew Bryan had been working on a summation speech for weeks. The defense had the power to conclude the case without any summation. It could simply ask the jury to find Scopes guilty. Darrow was prepared to take this step, but he wanted to make as many points about evolution and theology as he could before doing so.

Standing before the judge with his thumbs hooked in his old-fashioned bright suspenders and his shoulders hunched, Darrow hardly seemed to epit-

Lead defense attorney Clarence Darrow condemned the Butler Act as unconstitutional and a product of "ignorance and bigotry" during the opening day of the trial.

omize the urbane intellectual from Chicago. In fact he looked and talked like the man he was—a blunt, self-educated native of small-town America. But Darrow was also a master at delivering well-crafted, emotionally charged courtroom speeches. This talent was on full display that afternoon.

Darrow began his remarks with a cutting response to McKenzie's suggestion that big-city outsiders had no business participating in the trial. Darrow reminded the judge that William Jennings Bryan, Jr., a "very pleasant gentleman," hailed from California. Then, in his first acidic remark of the afternoon, Darrow added: "Another who is prosecuting this case, and who is responsible for this foolish, mischievous and wicked act ... comes from Florida." This was a clear reference to Bryan, an Illinois native who spent much of his life in Nebraska before he and his wife moved to Florida for her health.

Darrow then moved on to describe the Butler Act not only as "foolish" and a product of "ignorance and bigotry," but also a dangerous setter of legal precedent because it allowed one particular religious sect—Christian fundamental-ists—to limit the constitutional right of everyone else, even other Christians.

Darrow also returned to the points his fellow defense attorneys had made earlier in the day. He reminded the judge that the indictment against Scopes stated that the teacher had taught *evolution*. But the attorney then pointed out that the Butler Act made no explicit mention of evolution; it simply said that it was illegal to teach any theory of human origins that contradicted the book of Genesis in the Bible.

Building on this point, Darrow argued that in order to comply with the Butler Act, every science teacher in Tennessee would have to study the Bible in depth so as to ensure that they never contradicted any scripture at any time. If they were forced to take such steps, said Darrow, science teachers would be required to teach that the earth was flat and that the sun revolved around it. They could not teach chemistry or offer instruction on how to build a locomotive or an engine, since this information could not be found in the Bible. "Just imagine making it a criminal code that is so uncertain and impossible that every man must be sure that he has read everything in the Bible and not only read it, but understand it, or he might violate the criminal code."

Darrow stated that he personally would applaud and defend anyone who took solace from the Bible, which he described as "a book primarily of religion and morals." But he noted that many other people worshipped in other ways, and he asserted that those religions held their own validity too. "Here is the State of Tennessee, living peacefully, surrounded by its beautiful mountains, each one of which contains evidence that the earth is millions of years old—people quiet, not all agreeing upon any one subject and not necessary," said Darrow. "If I could not live in peace with people I did not agree with, why—what—I could not live! Here is the State of Tennessee going along in its own business, teaching evolution for years, state boards handing out books on evolution, professors in colleges, teachers in schools, lawyers at the bar, physicians, ministers, a great percentage of the intelligent citizens of the State of Tennessee, evolutionists, have not even thought it was necessary to leave their Church. They believed that they could appreciate and understand and make their own simple and human doctrine of the Nazarene [Jesus Christ], to love their neighbor, be kindly with them, not to place a fine on and not to try to send to jail some man who did not believe as they believed, and got along all right with it too."

Throughout Darrow's remarks, the stifling courtroom was so quiet the crowd could hear the clicks of the telegraph operators as they sent the lawyer's words across the wires to the newspapers. He concluded by voicing his fears about the possible legacy of the Butler Act and similar legislation: "If today you can take a thing like evolution and make it a crime to teach it in the public school, tomorrow you can make it a crime to teach it in the private schools, and next year you can make it a crime to teach it ... in the church.

"At the next session you may ban books and newspapers. Soon you may set Catholic against Protestant, and Protestant against Protestant, and try to foist your own religion upon the minds of men. If you can do one, you can do the other. Ignorance and fanaticism are ever busy and need feeding. Always they are feeding and gloating for more. Today it is the public school teachers, tomorrow the private. The next day the preachers and the lecturers, the magazines, the books, the newspapers.

> *In his column for the Baltimore Evening Sun, Mencken wrote that the impact of Darrow's speech on the courtroom observers in Dayton "seem[ed] to be precisely the same as if he had bawled it up a rainspout in the interior of Afghanistan."*

"After awhile, your Honor, it is the setting of man against man and creed against creed, until with flying banners and beating drums we are marching backward to the glorious days of the sixteenth century when bigots fired [kindling] to burn the men who dared to bring any intelligence and enlightenment and culture to the human mind."

When Darrow finally sat down, Judge Raulston adjourned court for the day. As Darrow collected his papers—and a round of hearty handshakes from his colleagues—some audience members hissed. Few spectators seemed to have been moved by his words.

The following day, the Memphis, Tennessee *Commercial Appeal* ran an editorial cartoon depicting Darrow as the Anti-Christ, alone on a hill surrounded by skulls, demons, and Satan. In his column for the *Baltimore Evening Sun*, Mencken wrote that the impact of Darrow's speech on the courtroom observers in Dayton "seem[ed] to be precisely the same as if he had bawled it up a rainspout in the interior of Afghanistan."

More Debate about Courtroom Prayers

A thunderstorm hit Dayton the evening after Darrow's speech, knocking out the electrical power. By morning the power had been restored, but Judge

Clarence Darrow's lengthy remarks concerning the Butler Act's potential impact on the future of American law left most courtroom spectators unimpressed.

Raulston had not yet completed his opinion on the defense motion to quash Scopes's indictment. Raulston announced that he would need a few more hours to work privately. Nevertheless, he called forward a pastor to open the court day with a prayer.

This time Darrow rose to formally object to the daily prayer and its potential impact on the jurors. "I object to prayer and I object to the jury being present when the court rules on the objection," he said. Darrow claimed that Raulston was turning the courtroom "into a meetinghouse." Darrow also pointed out that in Raulston's regular duties as circuit court judge, the court did not always open with a prayer.

A heated debate then erupted between Ben McKenzie and Stewart for the prosecution and Malone and Hays for the defense. Stewart accused Scopes's

Arthur Garfield Hays and other defense attorneys strongly objected to Judge Raulston's decision to allow each day of the trial to open with a prayer.

defense team of being "agnostics" who needed to remember that Tennessee was a "God-fearing country." Malone denied being an agnostic (while declaring that he supported Darrow's right to be considered one) and assured Stewart that New York City was just as God-fearing as Tennessee. Stewart countered by insisting that the Scopes case was not about religion in any case; it was about determining whether the defendant had broken a legal statute.

Raulston overruled the defense's objection and invited yet another fundamentalist pastor to deliver a prayer. This one, Dr. Stribling, ended his address: "May there be in every heart and in every mind a reverence to the Great Creator of the world." On that note, the court adjourned until after lunchtime.

As the court reconvened for an afternoon session, Hays handed Raulston a petition from Dayton's small number of "modernist" pastors. The petition asked that they be given an opportunity to offer morning prayers, just as their fundamentalist colleagues had been doing over the first few days of the trial. Raulston said he would ask the local pastors' association to choose the persons who would pray for the rest of the trial. This decision drew laughter and applause from the assembled crowd, because most of Dayton's pastors were decidedly anti-evolution. Nevertheless, for the duration of the trial, modernist clergymen alternated with fundamentalist clergymen in delivering the opening prayers.

A Newspaper Scoop

After receiving the pastors' petition, Raulston disappeared from the packed courtroom for a lengthy period of time. The rainstorm had done nothing to quell the heat, and everyone suffered as they waited for the judge's return.

When Raulston did return from his chambers, he was furious. He had learned that some afternoon newspapers were already reporting his ruling on

Songs Devoted to the "Monkey Trial" Controversy

The uproar surrounding the Scopes "Monkey Trial" inspired numerous songwriters and poets to pen new works on the subject. Nearly all of these works expressed support for William Jennings Bryan and the anti-evolution perspective. But the tone of these works varied enormously. Some songs, such as "Fiddlin' John" Carson's "There Ain't No Bugs on Me" adopted a lighthearted, amused viewpoint on the whole issue. But many others took a much more serious tone, and Bryan's death shortly after the trial's end triggered a wave of respectful eulogies such as "The Death of William Jennings Bryan" by Charles O. Oaks.

The following song, "The John Scopes Trial" by Carlos B. McAfee, is representative of the solemn tone that most "Monkey Trial"-inspired songs and poems took:

All the folks in Tennessee
Are as faithful as can be
And they know the Bible teaches what is right
They believe in God above and his great undying love
And they know they are protected by His might

CHORUS

You may find a new belief—it will only bring you grief
For a house that's built on sand will surely fall
And where-ever you may turn—there's a lesson you will learn
That the old religion's better after all
Then to Dayton came a man
With his new ideas so grand
And he said we came from monkeys long ago
But in teaching his belief
Mister Scopes found only grief
For they would not let their old religion go
Then the folks throughout the land
Saw his house was built on sand
And they said we will not listen any more
So they told him he was wrong and it wasn't very long
Till he found that he was barred from ev'ry door
Oh you must not doubt the word
That is written by the Lord
For if you do your house will surely fall
And Mister Scopes will learn where-ever he may turn
That the old religion's better after all

Robison, Carson J. (Carlos B. McAfee, pseud.) "The John T. Scopes Trial," 1925. Special Collections, Leonard H. Axe Library, Pittsburg State Iniversity.

the constitutionality of Scopes's indictment, even though he had not yet read his decision in court. "If I find that [reporters] have corruptly secured such information I shall deal with them as the law directs," Raulston railed. He promptly adjourned the court without issuing his ruling and ordered five well-known journalists (not including H. L. Mencken) to determine how the press had learned of his decision in advance.

In his memoir *Heathen Days*, Mencken described how the "scoop" occurred. During the lunch break, William K. Hutchinson of the Hearst newspaper chain slyly asked Raulston if, after he gave his decision, court would adjourn until the next day. Raulston replied that it would.

Raulston had made a foolish mistake. If he had decided to uphold the defense's charge that the indictment was unconstitutional, *the trial would have ended at that point and there would be no "next day" of the trial.* By stating that the case would go on, the judge unwittingly revealed to Hutchinson his intention to deny the defense's motion to dismiss the indictment.

The following morning, Day Four of the Scopes trial, began with a more conciliatory prayer. Judge Raulston then asked the committee of journalists for their findings on the "scoop." By Mencken's account, the five journalists spent the better part of the previous night playing poker. After a few hours' rest, they dressed in their best attire, reported to the courtroom, and allowed their committee chairman, Richard Beamish, to defend Hutchinson. Beamish played to Raulston's vanities, acknowledged that professional ethics had been breached, and then beseeched the judge's pardon on behalf of his colleague.

Raulston had probably figured out what had happened by that time. He pardoned Hutchinson, but warned the assembled press corps against future challenges of the court's authority. Proceeding with the business of the trial itself, Raulston then issued his widely anticipated ruling against the defense's motion to quash the indictment. The two sides would now commence making their arguments.

Opening Statements

The jury, which had missed most of the excitement of the trial's first three days, was called into the courtroom. They filed in and took their seats in the jury box. The prosecution then opened its case against John Scopes.

Stewart began the prosecution of *Tennessee v. Scopes* with a two-sentence declaration. John Scopes had broken the law by teaching that "mankind is

In his opening statement, Dudley Malone (standing at far right with paper in hand) claimed that Scopes had not violated the Butler Act because it was possible to reconcile evolutionary theory with the Biblical story of creation.

descended from a lower order of animals." This teaching, Stewart said, directly violated the Butler Act of 1925. Stewart estimated that the prosecution would need one hour to prove its case.

Malone opened the case for the defense with a longer speech. Setting aside the question of whether the Butler Act was constitutional for the moment, Malone claimed that Scopes had actually never broken the law. The defense would make its case by producing experts from the realms of science and theology who believed in both evolution *and* the workings of God in humankind. "We believe there is no conflict between evolution and Christianity," Malone stated.

Local prosecutor Tom Stewart maintained throughout the trial that the paramount issue was not the validity of evolutionary theory, but whether John Scopes had broken a legal statute.

Dudley Field Malone had known William Jennings Bryan for many years and had even worked for Bryan as an undersecretary of state. Now Malone turned his former colleague's words against him by quoting from an article Bryan had written twenty years earlier that took a much broader view of religious belief and condemned any measure that might favor one particular belief over another. "We of the defense appeal from [Bryan's] fundamentalist views of today to his philosophical views of yesterday, when he was a modernist, to our point of view," Malone said.

When Malone continued to single Bryan out as the person behind the fundamentalist legislation, Stewart finally objected. Bryan then rose to his own defense. "I ask no protection from the court," he states, "and when the proper time comes I shall be able to show the gentlemen that I stand today just as I did, but that this has nothing to do with the case at bar."

This opening blast from "The Great Commoner" drew such lengthy and enthusiastic applause from the spectators that Judge Raulston worried out loud that the courthouse floor might collapse.

Simple Questions

Stewart called four witnesses. The first was Rhea County School Superintendent Walter White, one of the instigators of the charges. Under Stewart's questioning, White told the jury that Scopes admitted teaching evolutionary theory from the pages of Hunter's *A Civic Biology*.

During cross-examination, Darrow read the passages from Hunter's textbook that mentioned Darwin and the relationship between man and mammals. He asked White if those were the passages in question, and White said yes. Darrow then asked White if the textbook had been approved by the state for use in Tennessee high schools. White said yes.

Stewart then called two of Scopes's students, a freshman named Howard Morgan and a senior named Harry Shelton. Both stated that Scopes had taught about evolution. During cross-examination by Darrow, both boys were clearly nervous and uncomfortable with all the attention. Both youths, though, declared that they had not been harmed by the instruction. Shelton, in fact, testified that he still attended church regularly and believed in God.

The prosecution's last witness was Frank "Doc" Robinson, the drugstore owner who had helped convince Scopes to challenge the law. During his testimony Robinson recalled how Scopes had taken the copy of Hunter's *A Civic Biology* from the drugstore shelf and stated that no Tennessee teacher could teach biology without teaching evolution. Darrow enjoyed cross-examining Robinson, who was a member of the Rhea County school board. When the druggist admitted that he sold Hunter's textbook in his store, Darrow even insinuated that the board member might be a Butler Act violator himself for keeping the textbook on sale.

When Robinson stepped down from the stand, Stewart rested the state's case. The hour had come to defend John T. Scopes.

Chapter Five

BRYAN AND MALONE CROSS SWORDS

—⟨⟨⟨⟨⟨⟨⟩⟩⟩⟩⟩⟩—

Tell me that the parents of this day have not any right to
declare that children are not to be taught this doctrine? ...
Shall be detached from the throne of God and be compelled
to link their ancestors with the jungle? Tell that to these children! Why, my friend, if they believe it, they go back to scoff
at the religion of their parents!

—William Jennings Bryan, July 16, 1925

The Scopes defense team began presenting its case on the fourth day of
the trial. By law, if John Scopes was to take the stand, he would be the
first witness for the defense. His attorneys, however, did not call him to
testify. Clarence Darrow and his colleagues—and Scopes himself—feared that,
during cross-examination, he might have to admit that he was not initially
hired as a biology teacher and that he could not remember whether he actually
taught evolution during his stint as a substitute. Scopes also worried that he
did not know enough about biology to answer sophisticated questions on evolutionary theory. As a result, he never took the stand in his own defense.

Instead, Darrow stated that even though Scopes had taught evolution, he
had not defied the Butler Act. The defense's case, Darrow argued, would rest
on the contention that evolutionary theory did not necessarily contradict the
Biblical version of creation as presented in Genesis. In other words, the
defense contended that it was perfectly reasonable to believe that God used
evolution as his *means* of creation.

To that end, the defense called its first witness, Dr. Maynard Metcalf of
Johns Hopkins University. Metcalf seemed the ideal defense witness. He had

By the fourth day of the Scopes trial, it was clear that the legal teams headed by both Clarence Darrow (left) and William Jennings Bryan (right) were convinced of the righteousness of their respective positions.

attended Oberlin College and earned his doctorate degree in zoology at Johns Hopkins. He was also a devoted Christian who taught Sunday school at a modernist church in Baltimore.

Darrow asked Metcalf to state his credentials and his work experience. Then Darrow asked the professor: "Will you state what evolution is, in regard to the origin of man?"

Stewart leaped up immediately. He declared that the prosecution objected to any discussion of the theory of evolution and any attempt to prove that evolution and Biblical creation could be compatible.

The moment had come in which Judge Raulston would need to rule on the admissibility of expert testimony from the defense. Judge Raulston excused the twelve jurors and had them sequestered. Once the jury had left the room, the prosecution reminded Judge Raulston that the statute made it a crime to teach evolution, even if the instruction did not explicitly contradict the Bible. The defense team responded that the law applied *only* to the teaching of evolution *that directly contradicted the book of Genesis.* The defense asserted that it could use expert testimony to prove that some interpretations of evolutionary theory could be reconciled with Genesis.

Judge Raulston decided to allow Metcalf to testify—but not in front of the jury. This ruling was an acknowledgement of the defense's desire to secure Metcalf's testimony in the event of a later appeal. In addition, Raulston was understandably curious about what Metcalf might say.

Metcalf spent the afternoon lecturing the court on the difference between the provable *fact* of evolution and the ongoing debate about the *theory* of evolution in its many particulars. He testified that all university-level biologists accepted evolution as a fact, and that evolution was continuing to the present day. He also offered a highly technical description of natural selection, using certain living and extinct species as examples. By the time Raulston adjourned the court for the day, Metcalf still had not addressed how the facts of evolution could be seen as compatible with the creation story of Genesis. Everyone assumed he would take the stand again the next morning to address that subject.

Fifth Day Provokes Heated Debate

The blazing heat continued on Day Five of the Scopes trial. Once again the second-floor courtroom became so packed with journalists and spectators that Raulston cautioned that the cumulative weight of people might cause the floor to buckle. After hearing the day's opening prayer, the prosecutors repeated their objection to any defense attempt to place a scientist on the stand to talk about evolution.

William Jennings Bryan Jr. took the lead in this regard. He stood and delivered the nation's rules for admitting expert evidence in criminal court cases. He patiently enumerated case after case in which such evidence was ruled inadmissible. Soft-spoken and clearly affected by the heat, Bryan Jr. delivered his statement in a dull, dry manner totally unlike that of his colorful father.

William Jennings Bryan Jr., son of the famed "Great Commoner," took the lead in explaining the prosecution's opposition to defense efforts to call expert witnesses to the stand.

When Bryan Jr. concluded his remarks, arguments raged back and forth between the prosecution and defense. Almost every attorney on both sides of the aisle made some contribution. The prosecution steadfastly maintained that the court should limit itself to issues directly pertaining to whether Scopes had broken a standing law. "This is a court of law, it is not a court of instruction for the mass of humanity at large," stated Herbert Hicks. The defense countered that without expert witnesses, it could not make its case that Scopes had never technically violated the law. "Jurors cannot pass upon debatable scientific questions without hearing the facts from men who know," Hays declared. "Is there anything in Anglo-Saxon law that insists that the determination of either court or jury must be made in ignorance?"

Ben McKenzie jumped in to the fray as well, claiming that the defense lawyers "are seeking to reconcile [evolution] ... and come right along and prove by the mouth of their scientist that when he said God created man in his own image, ... created him out of the dust of the ground and blew into him the breath of life, and he became as a living creature, they want to put words into God's mouth, and have him to say that he issued some sort of protoplasm, or soft dish rag, and put it in the ocean and said, 'Old boy, if you wait around about 6,000 years, I will make something of you.'" The spectators roared with laughter and applauded.

When Hays objected to McKenzie's humorous characterization of the defense position, McKenzie asked the defense attorney point blank if he believed in Genesis. "That is none of your business," Hays retorted.

At this point William Jennings Bryan Sr. noted that he would like to make some remarks on the subject at hand. Raulston promptly adjourned court for lunch so that "The Great Commoner" could speak without interruption in the afternoon.

Bryan in the Spotlight

News spread quickly that Bryan would address the court after lunch. Those who could not find seats in the courtroom sought space under the trees outside, where they could hear the loudspeakers. Even the roving evangelists and monkey-toting photographers quieted for the big event.

The only Rhea County residents to miss Bryan's speech, it seemed, were the twelve jurors. Even as Judge Raulston continued to hear arguments regarding the admissibility of expert witnesses for the defense, the jurors remained sequestered, waiting for the trial proper to resume. By this point several jurors undoubtedly realized that the front-row seats that had looked so enticing during jury selection had actually deprived them of the chance to witness much of the legal action.

William Jennings Bryan Sr. found the overheated courthouse very hard to bear. Throughout the first four days he had said little but had fanned himself constantly with his palm-leaf fan. His wife, wheelchair-bound due to arthritis, sat behind him, her face creased with anxiety. As he rose to deliver his first major address, however, Bryan seemed to transcend the heat. "He was suddenly the fighting evangelist," Scopes recalled in his memoir.

"This is not the place to try to prove that the law ought never to have been passed," Bryan said. "The place to prove that, or teach that, was to the legislature." Like his colleagues before him, Bryan maintained that lawyers from big cities like New York and Chicago had no business rolling into Tennessee and disparaging the state's laws as "ignorant" and the work of "bigots." What might work in New York, Bryan said pointedly, should not be touted in Tennessee.

"The people of this state passed this law," Bryan declared. "The people of this state knew what they were doing when they passed the law and they knew the dangers of the doctrine so that they did not want it taught to their children... It isn't proper to bring experts in here to try to defeat the purpose of the people of this state by trying to show that this thing that they denounce and outlaw is a beautiful thing that everybody ought to believe in."

Bryan became so animated by his subject that he forgot he was in a courtroom. He turned his back on Judge Raulston and addressed the crowd. He reminded the judge and the spectators that a vast majority of Tennesseans worshipped God and believed in the Bible. He also noted that the Bible could not be taught in Tennessee's public schools due to the Tennessee Constitu-

On Day Five of the Scopes trial, William Jennings Bryan (standing) delivered a long speech denouncing evolution as a dire threat to American morality and religious belief.

tion's Bill of Rights for religious freedom. No one was asking for Biblical teaching in the public classroom, he insisted. "The question is can a minority in this state come in and compel a teacher to teach that the Bible is not true and make the parents of these children pay the expenses of the teacher to tell their children that what these people believe is false and dangerous?" he said. "Has it come to a time when the minority can take charge of a state like Tennessee and compel the majority to pay their teachers while they take religion out of the heart of the children of the parents who pay the teachers?"

The telegraph operators clicked Bryan's words to the nation. The live radio feed broadcast his message to the very big cities he condemned. "The

A Controversial Textbook

During the Scopes "Monkey Trial," William Jennings Bryan denounced many passages in *A Civic Biology*, the 1914 textbook that Scopes had allegedly used to teach evolutionary theory. The following passage from the textbook, which was written by George William Hunter, was just one of many that angered Bryan and fundamentalist Christians for its linkage of mankind with other species:

> If we attempt to classify man, we see at once he must be placed with the vertebrate animals because of his possession of a vertebral column. Evidently, too, he is a mammal, because the young are nourished by milk secreted by the mother and because his body has at least a partial covering of hair. Anatomically we find that we must place man with the apelike mammals, because of these numerous points of structural likeness.

Great Commoner" was acutely aware that he had never addressed a larger audience than the one he commanded now, not even at the many Democratic conventions he attended.

Bryan Describes the Dangers of Evolutionary Theory

Bryan then launched into the heart of his speech on the dangers of teaching evolution. He pulled many of his remarks from the anti-evolution speeches he'd been giving for years. The crowd hung on his every word, laughing and applauding as he made his points. Raulston warned against further outbreaks of laughter and applause, but to no avail.

Bryan made special use of a copy of Hunter's *A Civic Biology* textbook during this time. Flipping to several pages he had marked, Bryan ridiculed the textbook's animal classification system and its classification of man as "indistinguishable" from "3,499 other mammals." He then observed that Professor Metcalf, the only defense expert to testify thus far, had offered no explanation for the origins of life. Bryan charged that this was because no sci-

69

entist could do so. In fact, Bryan said, even Charles Darwin felt that "all life [is] a mystery that no one can explain."

Returning to the subject of expert witnesses, Bryan noted that everyone could understand the Bible, that it had been translated into hundreds of languages, and that even the illiterate could learn its truths by hearing it read.

He warned that for every scientist the defense produced, he could produce a Christian, learned or humble, who would reject evolution in its entirety. "Our witnesses will be just as good experts as theirs on a question of that kind," he said.

> *"Has it come to a time when the minority can take charge of a state like Tennessee and compel the majority to pay their teachers while they take religion out of the heart of the children of the parents who pay the teachers?"*
> — *William Jennings Bryan*

Bryan claimed that no court in the land, from the humble circuit court in Dayton to the mighty Supreme Court in Washington, could ever decide an issue like evolution that divided the nation "between believer and unbeliever." He defended the Bible as "the only expression of man's hope for salvation … the record of the Song of God, the Savior of the World, born of the Virgin Mary, crucified and risen again." This Bible, he declared, would never be driven from Tennessee by out-of-state experts.

"The facts are simple, the case is plain," Bryan concluded. "If those gentlemen want to enter upon a larger field of educational work on the subject of evolution, let us get through with this case and then convene a mock court, for it will deserve the title of mock court if its purpose is to banish from the hearts of the people the word of God as revealed!"

Exhausted, Bryan returned to his seat without acknowledging the thunderous applause that followed his remarks. The din in the courtroom masked the equally ecstatic response from the crowded lawn outside. Who would dare rebut this renowned orator, especially to an audience of fierce supporters?

Malone Takes the Stage

Dudley Field Malone, the dapper Paris-based attorney who had been born, raised, and educated in New York City, rose to answer Bryan's emotional appeal. Malone had never garnered the headlines that attended Darrow's court work. And up to this point in the trial, Malone had spoken only in brief bursts in response to various legal maneuvers by the prosecution. If he had become noted for anything during the proceedings to this point, it was for the fact that he never removed his suit coat or tie in court, despite the smothering heat.

Now, though, Malone stood, carefully removed his jacket, and draped it over his chair. The spectators fell completely silent. Speaking in a loud, clear voice, Malone opened his rebuttal to Bryan—his old boss in the U.S. State Department—by stating, "Whether Mr. Bryan knows it or not, he is a mammal, he is an animal and he is a man."

Having uttered that controversial statement, Malone then took care to note his respect for his former colleague, calling Bryan "my old chief and friend." But he also signaled his determination to highlight perceived flaws in the "Great Commoner's" reasoning. "This is not a conflict of personages," Malone said. "It is a conflict of ideas, and I think this case has developed by men of two frames of mind. Your

Dudley F. Malone's Day Five address was widely praised as the oratorical high point of the "Monkey Trial."

Honor, there is a difference between theological and scientific men." The theological mind could accept doctrine without corroborating evidence from geology or archeology. The scientific mind, Malone said, craves solid evidence and forward progress. Scientists are never satisfied to accept theories on faith alone.

Malone noted that the Archeological Museum in London had recently found evidence of an advanced civilization in Egypt that existed 14,000 years ago. He also alluded to the trials and tribulations of two famous Renaissance scholars, Galileo and Copernicus, who had been punished by authorities for their assertions that the earth revolved around the sun. "Are we to have our children know nothing about science except what the Church says they should know?" Malone asked. "I have never seen harm in learning and understanding, in humility and open-mindedness, and I have never seen clearer the need of that learning than when I see the attitude of the prosecution, who attack and refuse to accept the information and intelligence which expert witnesses will give them."

Malone also addressed Bryan's characterization of the defense lawyers as "foreigners." "If it be wrong for American citizens from other parts of the country to come to Tennessee to discuss issues which we believe, then Mr. Bryan has no right here either," he said. "We [the defense attorneys] feel at home in Tennessee; we have been received with hospitality personally... We have corrupted no morals so far as I know."

This observation brought Malone to his next theme: the alleged corruption of morals from the teaching of evolution. He reminded Judge Raulston that the young witnesses called by the prosecution said they had not been harmed by the theory. "I believe and we believe that men who are God-fearing, who are giving their lives to study and observation, to the teaching of the young—are the teachers and scientists of this country in a combination to destroy the morals of the children to whom they have dedicated their lives? Are preachers the only ones in America who care about our youth?"

Malone urged the assembled crowd to exhibit greater faith in their children. He then framed Bryan's anti-evolution stance as destructive to the youth of Tennessee. "We have no fears about the young people of America. They are a pretty smart generation. Any teacher who teaches the boys or the girls today an incredible theory—we need not worry about those children of this generation paying much attention to it... People, as a matter of fact I feel that the children of this generation are probably much wiser than many of their elders. The least that this generation can do, your Honor, is to give the next generation all the facts, all the available data, all the theories, all the information that learning, that study, that observation has produced—give it to the children in the hope of heaven that they will make a better world of this than we have been able to make it."

Malone reminded the court and the spectators that America still reeled from the twenty million dead of World War I. "Civilization is not so proud of the work of adults," he declared. "For God's sake let the children have their minds kept open—close no doors to their knowledge; shut no door from them. Make the distinction between theology and science. Let them have both. Let them both be taught. Let them both live!"

Dramatic Defiance, Surprising Response

With gathering force, Malone returned to his most important assertion. It was Bryan, he said, who had inserted religion into the Scopes trial. It was Bryan who had insisted that this particular case was a "duel between revealed religion and science." Was this duel to be one-sided, with a defendant who could not produce witnesses or evidence by order of the court? How could that be fair and just? "Is our weapon, the witnesses who shall testify to the accuracy of our theory— is our weapon to be taken from us?" Malone asked. "That isn't my idea of a duel. Moreover it isn't going to be a duel."

"There is never a duel with the truth," Malone concluded. "The truth always wins, and we are not afraid of it…. We feel we stand with science. We feel we stand with intelligence. We feel we stand with the fundamental freedom in America. We are not afraid. Where is the fear? We meet it! Where is the fear? We defy it!"

To the dismay of Bryan and the rest of the prosecution team, the entire courthouse erupted in cheers and sustained applause when Malone completed his remarks. A policeman charged with keeping order actually broke a desk by beating his nightstick against it in a show of approval. *Nation* reporter Joseph Wood Krutch observed that the response was "twice as great in volume and duration as that which had greeted Mr. Bryan."

"The truth always wins, and we are not afraid of it," Malone proclaimed. "We feel we stand with science. We feel we stand with intelligence. We feel we stand with the fundamental freedom in America. We are not afraid. Where is the fear? We meet it! Where is the fear? We defy it!"

By virtue of his dynamic performance and persuasive reasoning, Malone had bested Bryan in front of an audience packed with fundamentalist supporters of "The Great Commoner." As Krutch put it, "a dormant sense of fair play had turned even the fundamentalists for an instant against their leader." Even John Washington Butler, the author of the controversial law that Scopes was on trial for violating, told radio reporters he thought Malone's presentation was "the finest speech of this century."

End of Day Five

Day Five of the Scopes trial concluded with Tom Stewart's rebuttal to Malone's stirring speech. Stewart reminded the judge that no amount of expert testimony in praise of evolution could change the standing statute. "I submit, your Honor, that under a correct construction of this statute that this scientific evidence would be inadmissible," he said. "Let us not make a blunder in the annals of the tribunals in Tennessee, by permitting such as this. It would be a never-ending controversy."

Stewart, who had not previously issued any personal opinion on evolution, then threw his hands into the air. "They say it is a battle between religion and science," he declared. "If it is, I want to serve notice now, in the name of the great God, that I am on the side of religion... [The defense's] charge strikes at the very vitals of civilization and Christianity, and is not entitled to a chance."

Judge Raulston adjourned the court, telling those assembled that he would rule the next day on the admissibility of scientific evidence into the Scopes case. Eager to escape the heat, the crowd surged for the doorways. Within minutes the large courtroom was empty except for Scopes, Malone, and Bryan. Scopes remembered in his memoir that Bryan sat alone, staring into space, his palm fan moving mechanically in his hand.

Finally, Bryan said, "Dudley, that was the greatest speech I have ever heard."

"Thank you, Mr. Bryan," Malone answered. "I am sorry it was I who had to make it."

More than forty years later, when he wrote his memoir, Scopes said that he thought Malone's speech formed the turning point of the trial: "Malone's words, read today, seem dry and uninspiring; delivered in full heat of battle in that stuffed and hot Dayton courthouse ... they were as electric as the emotions that had precipitated the controversy in the first place. His reply to Bryan was the most dramatic event I have attended in my life. The intervening decades have produced nothing equal to it; nor do I expect to see anything like it in my remaining years."

Chapter Six

A HISTORIC DUEL, A VERDICT REACHED

⧯⧯⧬⧯⧯

Do you, good people, believe that Adam and Eve were created in the Garden of Eden and that they were forbidden to eat from the tree of knowledge? I do. The church has always been afraid of that tree. It still is afraid of knowledge. Some of you say religion makes people happy. So does laughing gas. So does whiskey. I believe in the brain of man. I'm not worried about my soul.

—Clarence Darrow, *Why I Am an Agnostic, and Other Essays*

The Scopes "Monkey Trial" re-convened for its sixth day on Friday morning, July 17, 1925. After another pastor offered a morning prayer, Judge Raulston announced that the court would not allow the defense's expert witnesses to testify. This ruling was a crushing blow to the defense team's legal strategy.

Predictably, Darrow and Hays challenged Raulston vigorously. Hays asked that statements from each of the twelve scientists brought to Dayton for the trial be admitted into evidence either as sworn oral affidavits—testimony delivered outside of court—or in written form. Hays expressed a preference that the defense witnesses be allowed to give oral affidavits. When Bryan heard this, he declared that the prosecution should be allowed to cross-examine any defense witnesses who were allowed to introduce oral affidavits into the court transcripts.

The judge agreed with Bryan. If the scientists were allowed to speak for the record (so that it could be incorporated into any subsequent appeal to the Tennessee Supreme Court), then prosecution cross-examination of the witnesses should also be entered into the record.

This ruling deeply angered Darrow. He felt that Raulston had favored the prosecution from the outset of the trial, and he viewed this latest decision as yet another brazen example of favoritism from the bench. Indeed, Raulston's ruling led Darrow and the rest of the Scopes defense team to abandon the oral affidavit strategy and instruct their experts to submit written briefs.

When Darrow asked for an adjournment until Monday morning so that his scholars could prepare written remarks, Raulston retorted that Darrow's witnesses should not need that much time. Furious, Darrow replied that the judge himself had taken half a day to rule on the constitutional issues in the case. "I do not understand why every request of the State and every suggestion of the prosecution should meet with an endless amount of time and a bare suggestion of anything that is perfectly competent on our part should be immediately overruled," he grumbled.

Raulston's temper flared. "I hope you do not mean to reflect on the Court?" he said.

Darrow thumbed his suspenders and turned his back on the judge. "Well," he replied, "Your Honor has the right to hope!" In his fury, Darrow had overreached. He had insulted Judge Raulston and questioned his impartiality.

Raulston understood the meaning of Darrow's remark. "I have a right to do something else, perhaps," the judge growled. In fact, Raulston had every right to cite Darrow for contempt of court, a charge that carried steep fines and even possible jail time. Throwing up his hands, Darrow said, "All right. All right."

Raulston let the matter pass for the moment. He agreed to allow the defense's witnesses to have the weekend to prepare their written statements. Then he adjourned the court.

A Weekend of Plotting and Campaigning

Many of the newspaper reporters following the trial thought this last blow to Scopes's defense meant the end of the trial. "All that remains of the great cause of the State of Tennessee against the infidel Scopes is the final business of bumping off the defendant," wrote H. L. Mencken in the *Baltimore Evening Sun*. "There may be some legal jousting on Monday and some gaudy oratory on Tuesday, but the main battle is over, with Genesis completely triumphant."

This belief was probably the leading factor in Mencken's decision to leave Dayton on Saturday, before the trial's conclusion. Some historians have speculated that town reaction to Mencken's relentless mocking of Dayton's anti-evolution residents as "local primates" and "yokels" might also have been a factor in his early departure. A. P. Haggard, Dayton's chief commissioner and one of the town's leading citizens, told the *New York Times*: "We don't like the things Mr. Mencken is writing and we want him to know it. I hope nobody lays hands on him. I stopped them once, but I may not be there to dissuade them if it occurs to them again." But Mencken himself dismissed the idea that he had been chased out of town as ridiculous.

Bryan, meanwhile, used the weekend to once again take his message to pulpits and outdoor arenas. Throughout the hot and humid weekend, Bryan assailed the idea that humans could be lumped with animals and that they had anything in common with monkeys. He promised to take the fight for legislation against evolution to at least seven state legislatures in the South and Midwest.

Bryan's eloquence inspired some wealthy fundamentalists, among them fellow Floridian George F. Washburn, to push for creation of a William Jennings Bryan University in Dayton. Bryan was thrilled and honored by Washburn's pledge of funds for the project. Like many other fundamentalists, Bryan was concerned about the liberalism evident in the Northern divinity schools. Dayton, he said, would be a perfect location for a university founded on literalist Christian teachings.

Bryan's counterpart, Clarence Darrow, kept a lower profile over the weekend. He issued written statements in which he claimed that Bryan had come to Dayton to defend the Bible but now was avoiding the battle. "Bryan is willing to express his opinions on science and religion where his statements will not be questioned," the wily lawyer stated, "but Bryan has not dared to test his views in open court under oath." He issued this rebuke knowing full well that it would soon reach Bryan's ears.

> *"All that remains of the great cause of the State of Tennessee against the infidel Scopes is the final business of bumping off the defendant,"* wrote H. L. Mencken. *"There may be some legal jousting on Monday and some gaudy oratory on Tuesday, but the main battle is over, with Genesis completely triumphant."*

Darrow in Contempt of Court

On Monday morning, July 20, 1925, an overflow crowd packed into the courtroom despite the intense heat for Day Seven of the Scopes "Monkey

Judge John T. Raulston (seated in foreground) slapped defense attorney Clarence Darrow with a contempt of court charge at the beginning of Day Seven of the Scopes trial.

Trial." Certain that the trial was entering its final stages, the crowd not only wanted to hear closing arguments, but also the announcement of the verdict.

The daily prayer was delivered by a fundamentalist pastor who bitterly criticized Scopes's defense team. Invoking God, the pastor said: "Thou has been constantly seeking to invite us to contemplate higher and better and richer creations of Thine, and sometimes we have been stupid enough to match our human minds with revelations of the infinite and eternal."

Judge Raulston opened the proceedings by citing Clarence Darrow for contempt of court for his insulting remarks to the bench the previous Friday. He demanded that Darrow appear in court the next day to receive a sentence.

The judge set Darrow's bail at $5,000, more than a year's salary for many working people of the time. Darrow was expecting this decision. He said nothing.

The jury was again excused so that Hays could present the court with the written affidavits from the defense's experts. The lawyer asked that some passages be read into the official record of the proceedings. Raulston agreed, and Hays spent the rest of the morning reading from the statements, focusing particularly on affidavits from the theologians. Judge Raulston then adjourned the court for lunch.

During the break, Darrow sought out District Attorney Tom Stewart and offered to apologize in court for the remark that had brought a contempt citation. He also asked Stewart to put in a good word with the judge on Darrow's behalf. Stewart agreed to approach the judge before the beginning of the afternoon session.

When Raulston called the court back to order after lunch, Darrow moved quickly to address the contempt citation. Rising in his shirtsleeves and hooking his thumbs into his gaudy suspenders, Darrow offered a grudging apology for his remark. He said that he did not think his statements deserved a contempt citation, but he agreed that they were extremely insulting to the judge. "I am sorry that I made it ever since I got time to read it, and I want to apologize to the Court for it," he said.

Raulston accepted the apology, noting that he was personally moved by the spirit of Jesus Christ to be forgiving. Then the judge made an unexpected decision. He announced that the court proceedings for the rest of the day would move outdoors, under the trees on the lawn, where they might get some relief from the stifling heat.

Gathering papers and briefcases, the lawyers, reporters, and defendants joined the spectators who filed out of the building and took seats on the lawn. It was slightly cooler in the open air, and hastily gathered chairs and tables enabled both sides in the legal drama to get organized. But Darrow lost no time finding fault with the new setting. A huge banner saying "Read Your Bible" hung within easy reading distance. Darrow asked that it be removed. The judge agreed, and helpful citizens pulled it down.

Showdown in the Shade

Once the crowd had settled, Scopes's defense team asked to introduce one last witness, an "expert on the Bible." Hays announced that the defense

The unexpected showdown between William Jennings Bryan (seated, in black bow tie) and Clarence Darrow (standing at right) spellbound the crowd of spectators outside the Dayton courthouse.

wished to call William Jennings Bryan Sr. to the stand. He explained that Scopes's defense team needed Bryan's testimony as an expert on the Bible to complete its case for appeal.

Every prosecuting attorney except Bryan leaped to object, and Raulston seemed poised to rule for the prosecution. But Bryan, who was well aware of Darrow's weekend charges that he was avoiding a real debate on science and religious faith, stood and hushed the commotion. Excited by this opportunity to defend the Bible and refute Darrow's accusation, Bryan declared that he would be glad to take the stand and answer any and all questions put to him by the defense. He listed only one condition: that he be allowed to question Darrow, Hays, and Malone on the witness stand after his own appearance as a witness concluded.

With the jury still sequestered, Bryan was sworn in as an expert witness for the defense. Stewart shook his head in disbelief. As Bryan took his seat in the witness stand, the assembled crowd murmured in anticipation.

Darrow began questioning Bryan in a friendly, down-home manner. "You have given considerable study to the Bible, haven't you, Mr. Bryan?" he asked. Bryan responded that he had studied the Bible for fifty years, more closely as an adult than he had as a child. He, too, seemed confident and at ease.

Darrow pointed out that Bryan had written a great deal on the Bible for books and newspapers. Bryan agreed that this was true. Darrow asked if the works Bryan had authored were *interpretations* of the Bible, or literal summations of certain passages. Bryan said that some Biblical scriptures were meant to be taken as illustrations: For example, he quoted, "Ye are the salt of the earth." Bryan said: "I would not insist that man was actually salt or that he had flesh of salt, but it is used in the sense of salt as saving God's people."

Darrow's tone changed. His questions came more rapidly, and each one was designed to challenge Bryan and his belief in the literal truth of Biblical scripture. First he turned to the Biblical story of Jonah and the whale. He asked Bryan how he interpreted the Biblical passage that said Jonah was swallowed by a whale and remained in the whale's stomach for three days. Bryan contended that the whale was a "big fish," and that a God that could make a man could also make a fish big enough to swallow a human being.

Darrow then asked if God "fixed up" a special fish just for that purpose. Bryan said that since the Bible did not make this explicit, he could not give an answer. "One miracle is just as easy to believe as another," Bryan added. "The Bible doesn't make as extreme statements as evolutionists do."

Darrow on the Attack

Darrow moved on to question Bryan about other Biblical passages. How could God make the sun stand still, as reported in the Book of Joshua? Was it the sun that stood still, or the earth? If the earth revolved around the sun, it must have been the earth that stood still. Flustered, Bryan responded that a true believer need not worry about such specifics. What happened just happened.

"Mr. Bryan, have you ever pondered what would have happened to the earth if it had stood still?" Darrow asked.

"No," Bryan replied. "The God I believe in could have taken care of that, Mr. Darrow."

Darrow retorted: "Don't you know it would have been converted into a molten mass of matter?"

William Jennings Bryan (left) and Clarence Darrow (right) dueled for more than two hours under the broiling Tennessee sun.

As he would many times that afternoon, Bryan said that he had never given the issue much thought. Bryan remained on the stand long enough to regret this remark. Darrow began to hone in on just what Bryan *didn't* know and *didn't* ever think about, including ancient civilizations in Egypt and China and world religions other than Christianity. For his part, Bryan repeated his assertion that the Bible was the only book he needed, and all others were not important.

Darrow asked about the story of Noah. How could it be that all the various animals of the world (except the fishes, as Bryan pointed out) fit onto one boat? How could they have multiplied and spread across the world in just 4,000 years? (Here Darrow used Bishop Ussher's dating system for the exact moment of Noah's flood.) How could all the world languages have evolved from one moment in the Tower of Babel? Again and again Bryan fell back upon his faith in the literal truth of these Biblical passages, sometimes with frustration and sometimes with humor. When Darrow asked where Cain had gotten his wife, Bryan responded: "I will leave you agnostics to look for her."

Bryan Disappoints the Fundamentalists

The afternoon wore on. Every time the other prosecutors tried to halt Darrow's barrage of questions, Bryan halted *them* and pressed on. Both Darrow and Bryan became hostile. As they tried to outwit each other, it became clear that the fundamentalist lion was struggling with Darrow's relentless questioning.

At one point Bryan became so flustered that he said: "I do not think about things I don't think about."

Darrow smiled. "Well, do you think about things that you *do* think about?"

"Well, sometimes," Bryan answered feebly.

The audience laughed, a discomforting development to Bryan and the other prosecutors. Again Stewart tried to halt the questions, but once again Bryan insisted on continuing.

Earlier in the day, Bryan had confirmed his belief in Bishop Ussher's date for Noah's flood. Now, pointedly, Darrow turned to the first chapter of the Book of Genesis. "Do you think the earth was made in six days?" Darrow asked Bryan.

"Not six days of twenty-four hours," Bryan answered.

Under further examination by Darrow, Bryan stated that the six days mentioned in Genesis might actually be *periods* of uncertain length. This admission stunned the fundamentalists in the audience. Ussher's dating method specifically referred to days of twenty-four hours. "It seemed incredible that William Jennings Bryan, the Fundamentalist knight on the white charger, had betrayed his cause by admitting to the agnostic Darrow that the world hadn't been made in six days!" wrote Scopes in his memoir. "It was the great shock that Darrow had been laboring for all afternoon."

Bryan's error was not lost on his fellow prosecutors. Again Stewart jumped to his feet. "I want to interpose another objection," he said. "What is the purpose of this examination?"

Clearly agitated, Bryan declared that "the purpose is to cast ridicule on everybody who believes in the Bible, and I am perfectly willing that the world shall know that these gentlemen have no other purpose than ridiculing every Christian who believes the Bible."

"We have the purpose of preventing bigots and ignoramuses from controlling the education of the United States, and you know it, and that is all," responded Darrow.

Bryan exploded. "I am simply trying to protect the word of God against the greatest atheist or agnostic in the United States! I want the papers to know I am not afraid to get on the stand in front of him and let him do his worst!"

The audience, which had swelled to about 3,000 viewers by this time, burst into applause. Darrow watched the crowd for a moment, then drawled, "I wish I could get a picture of these clappers."

Lawyers on both sides used this lull to petition the judge about whether Bryan's testimony could be filed as an affidavit. The prosecutors said it was not pertinent to the case. The defense claimed that it should be part of the appeal process—and that Bryan's testimony should continue. Judge Raulston emphatically ruled that Bryan's testimony would not be allowed into the jury portion of the trial. As the attorneys for both sides returned to their respective camps, the incredible drama between Darrow and Bryan resumed.

Darrow returned to the Book of Genesis. Was Eve created from Adam's rib? Bryan said yes. Darrow then asked Bryan how Cain got his wife, and whether other people populated the earth at the time of the Biblical creation. Bryan said he did not know, and that he was not bothered to think about it. Darrow made sure Bryan repeated himself on his indifference to this matter.

Then Darrow returned to the literal interpretation of the first six days as described in the Bible. Again Bryan commented that the days could have been longer than twenty-four hours. They could, in fact, have been millions of years each. The fundamentalist members of the audience gasped.

Judge Halts Bryan's Testimony

Clarence Darrow seemed perfectly willing to question William Jennings Bryan on the literal interpretation of the Bible for hours and hours. And Bryan, though suffering from the heat and from Darrow's barbs, was equally unwilling to yield under the withering questions of his opponent. Gradually, however, Bryan realized that he had given too much ground. Darrow had tricked him into acknowledging that he himself sometimes turned to *interpretation* of the Bible rather than *literal acceptance* of the Bible. Bryan not only admitted he had never pondered the specifics of some Biblical tales, but he had also offered a non-literal perspective on the six-day creation story in Genesis. All of these missteps bolstered Darrow's contention that evolutionary theory could actually be reconciled with a non-literal interpretation of the creation story in Genesis.

Darrow moved from the six-day creation story to the verses pertaining to Adam and Eve. Bryan asked Darrow to read the passage in question from the Bible. Obliging the request, Darrow chose a St. James version Bible and read the verses about the serpent tempting Eve to eat the apple of knowledge.

"I am simply trying to protect the word of God against the greatest atheist or agnostic in the United States!" declared Bryan. "I want the papers to know I am not afraid to get on the stand in front of him and let him do his worst!"

Darrow quoted the verse in which God cursed the serpent: "Upon thy belly shalt thou go, and dust shalt thou eat all the days of thy life." Darrow paused. Then he asked Bryan: "Do you think that is why the serpent is compelled to crawl upon its belly?"

"I believe that," Bryan said.

"Have you any idea how the snake went before that time?"

"No, sir," Bryan responded.

"Do you think he walked on his tail, or not?"

As the audience erupted with laughter, Bryan recognized that he had walked into another trap set by his seasoned adversary. "Your Honor," he snapped, "I think I can shorten this testimony. The only purpose Mr. Darrow has is to slur at the Bible. But I will answer his question. I will answer it all at once and I have no objection in the world. I want the world to know that this man, who does not believe in God, is trying to use a court in Tennessee…"

"I object to that!" Darrow exclaimed angrily.

"… To slur at it, and while it will require time I am willing to take it."

"I object to your statement!" Darrow barked. "I am examining you on your fool ideas that no intelligent Christian on earth believes."

The two men glared at one another, their hands balled into fists. The level of antagonism had reached its boiling point. Neither Darrow nor Bryan wanted to yield a single point. Bryan had done so. But Darrow had made mistakes as well. By belittling Bryan's "fool ideas," Darrow had lost the good will of his audience and undermined his own performance.

Judge Raulston banged his gavel and ended the ordeal. Darrow's defense team—and a number of supportive spectators—mobbed him, shaking his hand and pounding him on the back. Bryan, meanwhile, wearily accepted the acclaim of those who remained loyal to him. A famous moment in courtroom drama thus passed into history.

Announcement of the Scopes Verdict

Bryan had only agreed to take the stand in defense of the Bible under the condition that he would have his own chance to grill Darrow, Hays, and Malone. Even after his difficult time in the witness box, Bryan remained eager to fight, and especially keen to deliver his closing oration. Fellow prosecutor Tom Stewart, though, urged Bryan to end the debate and keep the trial narrowly focused on whether Scopes had violated the Butler Act.

When the trial re-commenced on a rainy Tuesday morning for Day Eight, Judge Raulston announced that Bryan's testimony of the previous afternoon would be expunged from the court record. Darrow shrugged. Every newspaper in the country had covered the dramatic exchange, and the clash had been broadcast to radio sets from California to New England. Some larger periodicals, including the *New York Times,* ran the whole transcript of the historic Bryan-Darrow clash. The damage had been done. Bryan could not undo it.

At this point Darrow asked the jury to be admitted to the courtroom. Twelve very frustrated individuals entered. Darrow smiled at the jurors and told them that since none of the defense evidence was admissible in circuit court, the defense would rest its case by admitting that Scopes had taught evolution. Darrow reminded the jurors of the boys who had testified to that fact. He said that the defense did not call John Scopes to the stand at the trial's outset because Scopes would have had to admit he had taught evolution. Sadly, Darrow said, the case would have to be sent along to the court of appeals, where the defense would be able to introduce expert testimony and other evidence that Raulston had ruled as inadmissable. He then asked the jury to render a verdict of guilty against his client.

Dayton schoolteacher John Scopes (second from right) stands for sentencing at the conclusion of the Scopes "Monkey Trial."

By asking for a guilty verdict, Darrow made it unnecessary for either side to deliver closing arguments. Bryan's carefully-crafted summation lay on the table, never to be uttered in court. The jury filed out. Nine minutes later they returned. The foreman announced that they found John T. Scopes guilty as charged.

Tennessee law required that the jury fix the amount of fine to be imposed on Scopes. However, Judge Raulston stepped in and declared that Scopes would pay the minimum fine of one hundred dollars. When Stewart reminded Raulston that the jury should decide this matter, Raulston said that in misdemeanor cases a judge could impose the fine. Both prosecution and defense agreed to this arrangement.

Attorney John Neal, Scopes's first lawyer in the case, then reminded the judge that the defendant could now speak if he so chose. Raulston invited John Scopes to make a statement. The courtroom hushed as Scopes rose. "Your Honor, I feel that I have been convicted of violating an unjust statute," he said. "I will continue in the future, as I have in the past, to oppose this law in any way I can. Any other action would be in violation of my ideals of academic freedom, that is to teach the truth as guaranteed in our Constitution, of personal and religious freedom." He added that he thought the fine was unjust.

Judge Raulston rapped his gavel, and the case of *Tennessee v. John T. Scopes* concluded. Journalist H. L. Mencken eventually paid Scopes's fine.

Chapter Seven
THE BATTLE CONTINUES

⸺◄⸺

The trial and that summer constituted only one chapter in my life, and I didn't want it to influence or to control every step I took from then on… I suddenly had a taste of what happens in America to a young man who skyrockets to spectacular fame or notoriety.

—John T. Scopes, *Center of the Storm*

In the wake of his trial, John Scopes received letters and telegrams from all over the world, including a four-page note written in Chinese. Offers poured in from promoters who wanted him to embark on a national lecture tour. Others approached him about a career in the movies. Women proposed marriage. Evangelists sent long missives trying to save his soul.

Every day the postman arrived at Scopes's doorstep with a washtub full of mail. Scopes began to store the mostly unopened letters in a field. Soon they amounted to a "small mountain," as he recalled in his autobiography. One afternoon, Scopes and two of his friends set the entire pile of correspondence on fire and watched it burn to cinders.

The one offer Scopes did accept was a scholarship to the University of Chicago. A group of university professors had banded together to raise the funds to pay for Scopes's further education. Scopes earned a master's degree in geology, but when he applied for a doctoral fellowship, the president of the university denied it to him, saying that Scopes was an atheist who did not deserve the award.

Scopes took a job in the petroleum industry and tried to live as anonymously as possible. He received mail related to the trial for the rest of his life, but he never answered any of it.

Lingering Anger and Bitterness

Both the prosecution and the defense declared victory in the aftermath of the Scopes "Monkey Trial." Of course the prosecution had won a clear initial victory on the legal front. With Scopes's conviction, William Jennings Bryan proudly declared that religion had triumphed over America's pro-evolution forces. He took special pleasure in besting Darrow, who he felt embodied "all that is cruel, heartless and destructive in evolution." On the other side of the aisle, the defense attorneys claimed they had gained a moral victory by exposing the narrow-mindedness of fundamentalist views and the dangers of limiting the education of young adults.

Public opinion split along geographical lines. The Northern newspapers were generally critical of Bryan and his anti-evolution allies. The *New York Times* was particularly harsh, describing Bryan's time on the witness stand as "an absurdly pathetic performance." Southern newspapers were more generous to Bryan, with several declaring that the "Great Commoner" had succeeded in maintaining his dignity and defending his faith.

In the meantime, the famous leaders of the two legal camps continued to trade verbal blows. Frustrated that he had been unable to question Darrow on the witness stand, Bryan posed a series of written questions to Darrow on religion and evolution. These questions, along with Darrow's responses, were published in the July 22, 1925, pages of the *New York Times*.

Death of a Legend

In the days following the end of the trial, Bryan traveled across Tennessee, delivering the summation speech he had intended to deliver at the trial to enthusiastic crowds. His fundamentalist supporters seemed willing to forgive the broad interpretation of the first chapter of Genesis that he had offered on the witness stand.

During this victory tour, "The Great Commoner" predicted—correctly—that other state legislatures would follow Tennessee and ban the teaching of evolution. Meanwhile, donations toward the university to be founded in his honor continued to pour in to Dayton.

On Sunday, July 26, 1925, just five days after the Scopes trial ended, Bryan returned to Dayton to offer several sermons and speeches and to confer

Pallbearers carry the casket of William Jennings Bryan, who died in Dayton a mere six days after the end of the Scopes trial.

with the town fathers about the university. He and his wife attended a church service the following morning and then ate a hearty meal. Bryan told his wife he wanted to rest that afternoon in anticipation of an address he planned to give that night. Hours later his wife found him lying motionless in bed. He had died in his sleep.

Bryan suffered from diabetes and other ailments, and without benefit of an autopsy his personal physician listed diabetes as the cause of death. Almost everyone else in the country attributed "The Great Commoner's" sudden demise to the stress of the Scopes "Monkey Trial." He had not looked well during the proceedings. The heat weighed on him visibly, and many people speculated that the tensions of the trial, including Bryan's long hours on the witness stand, had taken an additional toll.

Mourners pay their respects to William Jennings Bryan, who was buried at Arlington National Cemetery.

Writing in the *Baltimore Evening Sun*, H. L. Mencken gleefully celebrated Bryan's end. He sarcastically predicted that parts of his body would become religious relics for the faith healers in Dayton. Other newspaper reporters and obituary writers took greater care to look back on Bryan's life with respect. They reminded the nation that Bryan had fought valiantly for working people and contributed greatly to the development of the Democratic Party. Bryan's many fundamentalist followers in the nation's "Bible Belt" and elsewhere, meanwhile, publicly mourned the loss of one of their great champions.

William Jennings Bryan was buried in Arlington National Cemetery, the famous military cemetery located in Arlington, Virginia. He had become eligible for this honor by serving as an officer in the Nebraska National Guard during the Spanish American War.

Lawyers Appeal Scopes Verdict

Meanwhile, a team of attorneys from the American Civil Liberties Union (ACLU) pressed for an appeal of the guilty verdict in the Scopes "Monkey Trial" to the Tennessee Supreme Court. These attorneys, with the exception of Arthur Garfield Hays, did not want Darrow to participate in the appeal.

Bryan's death played no small part in their decision. Prevailing opinion held that Darrow had alienated many middle-of-the-road Americans with his assault on the "fool ideas" of Christianity during the first trial. Country songs, poems, and sermons celebrated Bryan as a martyr and cited Darrow as the devil who killed "The Great Commoner." The ACLU felt that Darrow would bring all this negative baggage to a case they desperately wanted to win. Darrow refused to remove himself entirely from the case. But he was conscious of having alienated many mainstream Christians during the original trial, so he kept a low profile.

"Innumerable members of our greatest Christian scientists, philosophers, educators and ministers firmly believe in the truth of the origin of man as taught by evolution. The State has no right … to stifle by legislation the influence of such men."
— Tennessee Academy of Sciences

The appeal process dragged on for 18 months and was finally heard in January 1927. Darrow attended, but he curtailed his participation in the case significantly, allowing other members of the defense team to take a greater role in the proceedings. Scopes did not attend. He was occupied with his college work.

Both defense and prosecution presented the Tennessee Supreme Court with 400-page position statements. These briefs—and the oral arguments that accompanied them—generally repeated the arguments each side had made in Dayton.

The prosecution, for example, demanded the right of the majority of taxpayers to dictate what could be taught in public schools. Edward Seay, the leading attorney for the prosecution in the appeal, also cautioned that "If you permit the teaching that law of life is the law of the jungle, you have laid the foundation by which man can be brought to accept the doctrine of Communism and to the point where he believes it right to advocate murder." Seay then noted that Darrow had defended both Communists *and* cold-blooded murderers during his career. In addition, Seay claimed that the Butler Act did not violate the Tennessee Constitution, which forbade religious instruction in public schools, because the act did not instruct biology teachers to offer the Genesis version of creation as a hypothesis for the descent of humankind.

The defense countered by insisting that evolutionary theory did not necessarily contradict the Bible, and that many Christian people believed in both. In fact, the Tennessee Academy of Sciences presented a "friend of the court" brief in which it wrote: "Innumerable members of our greatest Christian scientists, philosophers, educators and ministers firmly believe in the truth of the origin of man as taught by evolution. The State has no right ... to stifle by legislation the influence of such men."

Darrow made the closing remarks for the defense. "The future of America's public school system and the complete education of her children can be safeguarded only by wiping this law off the statute books," he said. "We are once more fighting the old question, which after all is nothing but a question of the intellectual freedom of man."

A Stunning Decision

Over a period of two days, the judges of the Tennessee Supreme Court heard the arguments put forward by the two sides. When the court rendered its decision, it delivered a severe blow to the ACLU's hopes of striking down the Butler Act.

The Court ruled that in the case of *Tennessee v. John T. Scopes,* the guilty verdict against John Scopes should be overturned. But the Court did not issue this judgment as part of a larger move against the Butler Act. Instead, the decision to overturn the verdict was based only on a minor technicality; namely, that by usurping the jury's rightful duty to set the level of the fine against Scopes, Judge Raulston had violated Tennessee jury trial law. This minor technicality made it possible for the Tennessee Supreme Court to avoid making any ruling on the constitutionality of the Butler Act.

All the months of planning and hard work by Darrow, the ACLU, and their legal allies had come to naught. John Scopes would receive a refund of his fine, but the Butler Act would remain Tennessee law. Moreover, it seemed unlikely that another similar legal challenge to the law would ever flare up; in a remarkable move, the Tennessee Supreme Court urged state officials to refrain from prosecuting any other alleged violators of the Butler Act.

In a divided ruling (3-1, with one abstention) the Tennessee Supreme Court in 1927 overturned the guilty verdict handed down to John Scopes two years earlier. The Court only did so on the basis of a technicality, however, so the Butler Act remained Tennessee law for the next four decades.

After this ruling, it became clear that the state of Tennessee had seen and heard enough of the "Monkey Trial." No other teacher came forward to challenge the Butler Act. The state also approved the use of a new science textbook that did not cover evolution. Meanwhile, other states, including Texas, Arkansas, and Mississippi, passed legislation that removed evolutionary theory from school instruction and biology texts.

After the Trial

In the years following the 1927 overturning of Scopes's conviction, the main players in the legal drama went their separate ways. Bryan remained a legendary figure in the minds of many Americans, and Bryan University, the college named in his honor, opened its doors in 1930. Initially housed in the old Dayton high school, the institution struggled to stay intact during the Great Depression. But it survived those grim years and quietly flourished thereafter.

Bryan's old courtroom nemesis, Clarence Darrow, argued his final case in 1932. He died in 1938 after a long period of inactivity due to heart disease.

H. L. Mencken fell from public favor during the Depression era. A champion of individual destiny, Mencken objected to the New Deal legislation introduced by Franklin Delano Roosevelt during the 1930s. Since many people benefited from Roosevelt's agenda during the Depression, his opposition severely eroded his popularity.

Mencken then changed his tone somewhat. He published three memoirs during the Second World War, and all were bestsellers. *Heathen Days,* the last in the series, devotes a chapter to the Scopes trial. But the author avoids the harshly negative portrayals of Dayton's citizens, Bryan, and the evangelical Christians that had characterized his columns during the actual trial. Mencken suffered a stroke in 1948 that deprived him of the ability to read or write. He died in 1956.

Dudley Field Malone spent the last years of his life in Hollywood as an attorney for 20th Century-Fox Films. He also starred in a 1943 film called *Mission to Moscow,* in which he played British Prime Minister Winston Churchill. Malone died in 1950.

John Scopes worked in the petroleum and natural gas industry, first in Venezuela and later in Texas and Louisiana. As the years passed by, he steadfastly refused to answer any correspondence about the "Monkey Trial."

In his later years, though, Scopes became more willing to talk about the trial. He agreed to participate in a premiere tour for the 1960 film, *Inherit the Wind.* In 1967 he published a memoir called *Center of the Storm,* written with James Presley. As other trials on the teaching of evolution made national news, he expressed his support for intellectual freedom in the classroom in several interviews. He died in 1970.

The town of Dayton, Tennessee, returned to its rural character within weeks of the end of the trial. Today it is somewhat larger in population, due to the expansion of Bryan University and the development of local industries. The old courthouse in which the trial took place still stands. Its basement contains a small museum dedicated to the "Monkey Trial." Every summer some of its citizens stage a re-enactment of the trial that usually lasts for an afternoon. The event receives only local newspaper coverage and rarely draws a sizable crowd.

The Scopes "Monkey Trial" has never faded from the collective American memory, however. Even today its echoes can be heard from the popular stage—and in court battles that continue to rage on in the twenty-first century.

Chapter Eight

LEGACY OF THE SCOPES "MONKEY TRIAL"

⚬

[Intelligent design] is an interesting theological argument,
but ... it is not science.

—Judge John E. Jones III

With the repeal of Prohibition in 1933, the Christian fundamentalist movement retreated from social activism. Its membership did not decrease, however. Particularly in the "Bible Belt," its numbers grew considerably. Toward the end of the twentieth century, evangelical Christians emerged again as a potent political force. During this time, much of their political activism became focused on opposition to abortion rights, homosexual marriage, and the teaching of evolution in public schools.

In the meantime, powerful forces in science and education have strongly defended Darwin's theory of evolution by natural selection. This emphasis on defending evolutionary theory—and scientific inquiry in general—was given a significant boost during the mid-twentieth century. During and immediately after World War II, Americans recognized that scientific and technological advantages had been a pivotal factor in the Allied victory over Nazi Germany and Japan. The value of scientific knowledge was further underscored during the Cold War of the 1950s and 1960s. At that time, prominent educators declared that the Soviet Union and China had the potential to surpass America in the realm of technology if the United States did not improve its science and math programs. The American populace gave greater weight to these warnings after the Soviets beat the United States into space, launching the first satellite into orbit in 1957.

Inherit the Wind and the Scopes Trial

The Cold War also increased the fear of Communism in the United States. Between 1900 and the beginning of the Second World War, American Communists worked to advance their cause, and at times their political goals coincided with those of labor unions dedicated to expanding worker rights and other leftist organizations. When the Soviet Union became a clear political and military threat to the United States after World War II, though, any hint of Communist activity in America brought reprisals from the U.S. government. These reprisals ranged from imprisonment and execution to "blacklisting" and loss of employment.

The anti-Communist "Red Scare" reached fever pitch in America in the 1950s. A major factor in this escalation of fear was a Wisconsin senator named Joseph McCarthy, who claimed that Communist agents had infiltrated the U.S. State Department and other important American institutions. McCarthy and other legislators took special aim at the entertainment industry, hauling actors, directors, writers, and producers before various investigating committees. During this time, the careers of many actors, broadcasters, directors, and writers were ruined by accusations that they were Communists or Communist sympathizers.

In response to the turmoil of the McCarthy era, a pair of writers named Jerome Lawrence and Robert E. Lee created a play called *Inherit the Wind*. It was based on the events of the Scopes "Monkey Trial," but it was influenced more by the McCarthy-era "witch hunts" unfolding before their eyes. *Inherit the Wind* offers a simplified, melodramatic rendition of the events in Dayton, and it features fictionalized versions of all of the major figures who were involved in the Dayton trial.

In the opening act of the play, angry leaders of a small Tennessee town haul a schoolteacher named Bertram Cates from his classroom and throw him in jail for teaching evolution. The townspeople are painted as an unquestioning mob that blindly follows Matthew Harrison Brady, a populist lawyer and former presidential candidate who is a nationally recognized foe of evolution. He is opposed by Henry Drummond, a crusading attorney who slips into town to defend Cates, and E. K. Hornbeck, an acerbic journalist for the fictional *Baltimore Herald*. As the play unfolds, Drummond is characterized as a freedom-loving intellectual with many admirable traits, while Brady and his supporters are painted as fearful and ignorant.

In this scene from the 1960 motion picture *Inherit the Wind,* actor Spencer Tracy (playing a character based on Clarence Darrow) cross-examines actor Fredric March (playing a character based on William Jennings Bryan).

Inherit the Wind premiered on Broadway on April 21, 1955, and ran for three years. A team of actors took the production on the road throughout America after that. The large cast and controversial subject matter appealed to high school teachers. They introduced it into school productions and English classes. By 1960, when the play was turned into a film starring the ever-popular Spencer Tracy as Drummond, almost every American believed that *Inherit the Wind* offered an accurate portrayal of the Scopes trial. Its closing scene, in which the character of Drummond confidently carries both the Bible and Charles Darwin's *The Origin of Species* from the courtroom, sends a clear message to audiences about where its authors' sympathies lie.

The primary goal of the authors was to use *Inherit the Wind* to cast light on the McCarthy "witch hunt" for Communists and the dangers of mob rule, anti-intellectualism, and blind allegiance to political leaders. To many people who view it today, its theme is one of the triumph of tolerance over mindless bigotry. Unfortunately, both the play and the film grossly oversimplify the actual events of the Scopes case. "While *Inherit the Wind* remains faithful to the broad outlines of the historical events it portrays, it flagrantly distorts the details," wrote historian Carol Iannone in *First Things*.

Repeal of Anti-Evolution Laws

Tennessee's Butler Act remained on the books until 1967, some 42 years after the Scopes trial. The state's leading scientists had assailed the legislation for years, and in 1967 a Tennessee school teacher named Gary L. Scott threatened to challenge the statute in court. The ACLU promptly promised to provide legal representation for Scott. Many in the Tennessee legislature feared that the publicity of a "Scopes II" trial would reflect badly on the state. (The success of *Inherit the Wind* probably influenced this view.) After heated debate, the Tennessee state government overturned the Butler Act.

Around this same time, another "John Scopes" emerged to challenge the anti-evolution statute in Arkansas. A 27-year-old schoolteacher named Susan Epperson teamed with H. H. Blanchard, the father of two high school students, to challenge the law. Epperson brought her case in 1965, after the state issued new textbooks that included a chapter on Darwinian evolution. She claimed that the presence of that information in her classroom made her liable for prosecution under the state's anti-evolution statute, even though that law had never been enforced. Blanchard joined the lawsuit because he wanted his children to learn evolution in class.

Epperson won her court trial in Arkansas, but the verdict was overturned by the Arkansas State Supreme Court. This reversal paved the way for the United States Supreme Court to hear the case in November 1968.

Supreme Court Justice Abe Fortas—a Jew who had actually attended high school in Tennessee during the time of the Scopes "Monkey Trial"—lobbied his fellow justices to hear the Epperson case. Fortas saw the case as an opportunity for the Court to express its firm support for the Establishment Clause in the First Amendment of the Constitution, the cornerstone of American law separating church and state.

The Supreme Court heard brief arguments on behalf of Epperson and in defense of the law by an Arkansas deputy attorney general named Don

Langston. Langston defended the law simply out of professional obligation because his state's Supreme Court had upheld it. During these oral presentations, Epperson's lawyer noted that the Arkansas statute had been passed in 1928 in direct response to the Scopes trial.

The Supreme Court struck down Arkansas' anti-evolution legislation in a near-unanimous decision. Fortas wrote for the majority, stating that the law violated the Constitution's guarantee of separation of church and state. In his written decision, he repeatedly returned to the Scopes case as ammunition against the Arkansas law. (Three concurring judges sided with Fortas simply because the wording of the law was "vague.") The only dissenter, Justice Hugo Black, thought that repeal of the bill would give school teachers too much leeway to exercise their freedom of speech in the classroom.

Epperson v. Arkansas ended anti-evolution statutes in the two states where they remained, Arkansas and Mississippi. Within ten years, however, Christian social activists devised a new strategy to return the Biblical story of creation to the public classroom.

Creation Science and Intelligent Design

During the mid-1970s, a fundamentalist-backed movement promoting "creation science" made significant inroads into science education in the United States. "Creation science" sought to debunk evolutionary theory by challenging its particulars. Creation science advocates highlighted hoaxes like "Piltdown Man" and claimed that other fossils were forgeries. Supporters claimed that natural selection was an unproven "theory," challenged science-based estimations of the age of the universe, and promoted the view that Noah's flood (or perhaps the violence of earth's creation), had formed a misleading geologic record in the earth's rocks.

America's scientific community rejected creation science. Scholars in many fields said the creation science movement offered no evidence in its favor that could be tested under the accepted rules of scientific experimentation. These opponents said that the whole concept of creation science depended upon a "creator" and upon casting doubts on Darwin, sometimes by misrepresenting or ignoring facts. According to critics, then, "creation science" did not remotely resemble true science.

Undaunted, the creation science movement lobbied to have its position represented in school books and lecture halls. When these efforts proved successful in some states, a legal showdown became inevitable. In the 1987 U.S. Supreme Court case *Edwards v. Aguillard,* the High Court struck down a Louisiana law requiring science teachers to cover both evolution and creation science in biology classes. The 7-2 decision declared that creation science was an unacceptable breach of the separation of church and state, since it argued—without scientific evidence—that the universe was created by the actions of a Judeo-Christian god.

This decision left open the possibility that competing theories on the origin of life could be presented in classrooms. But to be eligible for presentation, any competing theory would have to adhere to basic standards of scientific research and testing.

The creationists responded to this setback in two ways. Some evangelical Christians removed their children from public schools in favor of homeschooling or private schools that taught *only* creation science. Others sought to develop a new way to advance their message into public schools and other institutions. This new "intelligent design" movement promoted the view that some unknown creator—not specifically the Judeo-Christian God of Genesis—had set the universe in motion.

Intelligent design removes the Christian deity from its language. But its theory is still based on the belief that the universe did not *just happen*, but was instead created by a higher power. Led by organizations such as Seattle's Discovery Institute (which has produced its own pro-intelligent design textbook called *Of Pandas and People*) and fundamentalist universities such as Bryan College, the intelligent design movement has attempted to find evidence in physics, molecular biology, geology, and astronomy to support its scenario of an unknown creator at work.

As of 2006, no paper on intelligent design has been accepted by peer scientists in secular colleges or universities. In some parts of the country, though, local school boards and state departments of education have actively promoted the introduction of intelligent design to public school curricula as an alternative to Darwin's theory of natural selection. President George W. Bush said in 2005 that he welcomed such additional instruction in public schools as a way to spark debate on the origins of life.

Intelligent Design on Trial

In October 2004 the local board of education for Dover, Pennsylvania, released a directive to its science teachers. Before offering any instruction on evolution, the board said, teachers had to read a statement noting that intelligent design was a competing theory, and that students could obtain more information about intelligent design by consulting *Of Pandas and People* (which had been purchased by the school).

Within weeks of this announcement, a group of local parents led by Tammy Kitzmiller brought suit against the Dover Board of Education. They claimed that the mandated teacher statement issued by the board violated the U.S. Constitution's guarantee of separation of church and state. This clash bitterly divided the community of Dover—especially after a slate of anti-Intelligent Design candidates united to challenge the incumbent board members in upcoming elections.

In the autumn of 2005, the case reached Justice John E. Jones III of the U.S. District Court, Middle District of Pennsylvania. Jones heard arguments from scientists who opposed intelligent design and scholars who promoted it. These legal proceedings were a stark contrast to the dramatic Scopes trial of eighty

Dover, Pennsylvania, resident Tammy Kitzmiller led a group of local parents who mounted a legal challenge to the local school board's decision to mandate discussion of "intelligent design" in the district's science classrooms.

years earlier. Still, the trial contained echoes of that long-ago case. The plaintiffs received representation from the American Civil Liberties Union and Americans United for Separation of Church and State. The defense lawyers representing the Dover school board hailed from the Thomas More Law Center, a Christian advocacy group. (The Discovery Institute, concerned that some school board members had cited religious views prior to the case, refused to participate.) Jones allowed each side to produce "expert witnesses," with no objections from either prosecution or defense.

In November 2005 all eight members of the Dover school board that had advocated teaching intelligent design in biology class were swept from office in local elections. They were replaced by eight citizens who were firmly opposed to intelligent design discussion in science classes. One month after the elections, Jones issued a decision firmly denouncing intelligent design as part of any legiti-

Megan Kitzmiller, a Dover Area High School senior and daughter of Tammy Kitzmiller, holds up a sign urging voters to support a slate of school board nominees opposed to "intelligent design" discussion in Dover's public schools.

mate science instruction. Jones, a Republican-appointed church-goer, said that his decision did not seek to debate the existence or nonexistence of an intelligent designer; it only found that "intelligent design" itself was religion and not science. Jones worded his ruling in a way that would make appeals difficult.

The Discovery Institute denounced Jones's ruling as "legislation from the bench," intended to stifle free speech and debate in public schools. The institute plans to continue pressing for the inclusion of intelligent design in biology classes around the country. To this end, the Discovery Institute has made a concerted effort to provide information and "talking points" on intelligent design directly to students via the Internet and print materials.

An Ongoing Debate

A Gallup poll conducted in March 2006 revealed that Americans are evenly split on the issue of evolution. Those who believe in the validity of Dar-

Stephen Cashman, a Dover student and son of James Cashman (one of eight Dover board members who adopted a policy mandating discussion of "intelligent design" in Dover public schools), urges voters to support the pro-ID incumbents in a November 2005 election. All eight pro-ID board members were voted out of office in the election.

win's theory tend to have more education, vote Democratic, and have higher household incomes. Those who support an intelligent design or Biblical origin scenario tend to vote Republican, attend church regularly, and be at or near retirement age. Other polls conducted in recent years have found that a clear majority of Americans reject Darwin's theory of evolution by natural selection.

Nonetheless, the primary debate across America today is not *whether* to teach evolution. Darwin's theory is entrenched in science classrooms, in part because fields as varied as genetics, geology, zoology, paleontology, and even botany have added to the wealth of information about the origins and relations of species. The primary debate is whether it is legitimate and appropriate to *complement* this instruction in evolutionary theory in public schools with teachings about intelligent design. When one considers the positions that both sides have staked out on this issue—and the intellectual, religious, and philosophical foundations of those positions—it seems unlikely that this debate will subside any time soon.

BIOGRAPHIES

William Jennings Bryan (1860-1925)
Populist Politician and Chief Prosecutor at the Scopes "Monkey Trial"

Williamson William Jennings Bryan was born in Salem, Illinois, on March 19, 1860. His father, Silas Bryan, was an educated and deeply religious attorney who also served as a judge. Bryan was very fond of his mother, Mariah Jennings Bryan. She schooled the intelligent youngster herself and saw to it that he developed a strong faith in the Bible. Ironically, Bryan was born in the same small town in which John T. Scopes attended high school.

Bryan's father was a Baptist, and his mother a Methodist. The young Bryan felt more comfortable in the Baptist church until he faced the prospect of his own baptism. Frightened of water, he joined the Presbyterian Church to avoid the full-immersion baptism practices of the Baptist faith. He remained an active member of that denomination until his death.

Gifted with a melodic voice and a flair for the dramatic, Bryan began honing his abilities as an orator while an undergraduate at Illinois College. He earned a bachelor's degree in 1881 and a law degree from Union College of Chicago in 1883. He married Mary Baird, his college sweetheart, in 1884 and set up a small law practice in Jacksonville, Illinois. Mary Bryan studied law and passed the bar as well in order to assist her husband's practice. The two remained a formidable team throughout their long and happy marriage, which produced three children.

Early Political Career

In 1887 the Bryan family moved to Lincoln, Nebraska. Bryan wanted to go into politics, and he saw Nebraska as a developing state with many career possibilities in that area. Moved by the plight of poor farmers and the perils facing striking union workers, Bryan embraced the Democratic Party and also established ties to the even more left-wing Populist Party, although he never joined it. Handsome and personable, he became the first Democrat ever elected to represent Nebraska in the U.S. House of Representatives.

Bryan won re-election to Congress in 1892. Around this time he became a vocal champion of a variety of liberal political causes, including a graduated personal income tax system (one in which poor Americans paid a lower percentage of their income in taxes than rich Americans). He also supported campaign finance reform, government ownership of railroads, federally insured bank accounts, women's suffrage, unionization, and passage of a corporate income tax.

Bryan's most visible crusade, however, was on behalf of the "free silver movement," one of the most controversial issues of the era. Republicans and financiers backed a gold standard for American currency, while the working classes (and the silver mine owners in the Western states) favored the more debtor-friendly silver standard. Bryan was able to unite Democrats and Populists in his home state by speaking in favor of the silver standard.

After serving two terms in Congress, Bryan ran for a U.S. Senate seat in Nebraska. He lost because in those days senators were not chosen by popular vote, but by the state legislative bodies. (The Seventeenth Amendment, for which Bryan fought, provided for direct public election of senators. It was ratified in 1913.) Unbowed by his defeat, Bryan began to contribute articles to the *Omaha World Traveler* and burnished his reputation as one of the nation's leading public speakers. In fact, he spent much of the early 1890s traveling by train to town halls and churches around the country. At each stop, he delivered passionate speeches on the issues of the day to ordinary working Americans from all walks of life. Many of the people he encountered on these travels became lifelong supporters of Bryan and his political causes.

Bryan's "Cross of Gold"

In 1896 the 36-year-old Bryan was named a delegate to the Democratic National Convention. Most of the Democrats favored the silver standard, and a committee asked Bryan to deliver the closing speech on that issue at the convention. The young ex-congressman rose to the occasion. The large hall fell silent as Bryan, without benefit of a microphone, delivered an eloquent, powerful speech. His address was so moving that its famous ending is sometimes still quoted: "You shall not press down upon the brow of labor this crown of thorns. You shall not crucify mankind upon a cross of gold!" The audience erupted into cheers and extended applause.

Bryan's famous speech inspired the convention delegates to name the young firebrand as the party's presidential nominee on the convention's fifth ballot. To this day, Bryan remains the youngest man ever to earn a presidential nomination from a major American political party.

The 1896 presidential race pitted Bryan against Republican William McKinley, a seasoned politician who supported the gold standard. The two men took quite different approaches to the race. McKinley campaigned from the front porch of his home, talking to visiting journalists and voters. Bryan took to the rails, traveling across the country to spread his message. His exhausting trek encompassed 18,000 miles and more than 600 speeches. Even so, Bryan's candidacy fell short, a victim of McKinley's superior campaign chest. In the end, Bryan lost the election by 600,000 votes.

It was during this campaign that Bryan earned the nickname that would stay with him the remainder of his life: the Great Commoner. This nickname stemmed not only from his ability to connect with ordinary Americans, but also from his political philosophy. "There are two ideas of government," he declared in his standard campaign speech. "There are those who believe that, if you will only legislate to make the well-to-do prosperous, their prosperity will leak through on those below. The Democratic idea, however, has been that if you legislate to make the masses prosperous, their prosperity will find its way up through every class which rests upon them."

Bryan earned the Democratic nomination for president two more times, in 1900 and 1908. He never reached the White House, but he helped expand the Democratic Party from its base in the post-Civil War South to include unionized workers, working class voters, and Americans who wanted to see the government take a larger role in addressing social issues. Many of the ideas he espoused at the beginning of the twentieth century later came to fruition in President Franklin Roosevelt's New Deal programs of the 1930s.

Guided by Religious Beliefs

Bryan's deep religious ideals guided his actions throughout his long public career. In 1913, for example, he was named Secretary of State by President Woodrow Wilson. But he had major differences with Wilson and other administration officials over the subject of entry into World War I. Bryan consistently advocated neutrality out of Christian concern for blood spilled by "brother against brother." When a German submarine torpedoed the luxury cruise ship *Lusitania* on May 7, 1915, Bryan continued to plea for neutrality. But the unprovoked attack increased U.S. tensions with Germany. Bryan resigned his post on June 8, 1915, noting that he and Wilson "find ourselves differing irreconcilably" on the issue of intervention in the war. Once the United States finally entered World War I against Germany in 1917, though, Bryan supported the American effort.

Bryan was also a leading supporter of the Eighteenth Amendment to the U.S. Constitution, also known as the Prohibition Amendment. This law banned the sale of alcoholic beverages from 1920 until 1933, when it was repealed. It was widely supported by voters in the Bible Belt and other rural areas. But the law also deepened a widening cultural divide between rural Americans and their urban counterparts, many of whom defied the Prohibition laws.

In 1921 Bryan and his wife moved to Florida for health reasons. Bryan quickly earned a fortune speculating in Florida real estate. He could have retired from public life, but instead he joined the Chautauqua lecture circuit (Chautauqua lectures were popular sources of entertainment and education in the days before radio become commonplace in American households; Clarence Darrow also spoke on the Chautauqua circuit).

One of Bryan's favorite topics on the Chautauqua circuit was the danger of evolutionary theory. Bryan objected to the teaching of evolution in public schools for a number of reasons. His greatest fear was that the teaching of evolution could undermine children's faith in God. But Bryan also objected to evolutionary theory because he felt that it contributed to the acceptance of eugenics, or the so-called "natural selection" of the "fittest" humans.

Advocates of eugenics during the early twentieth century—including some respected scientists—suggested that the human race could advance more quickly if certain "inferior" elements, such as the poor and disabled, were not allowed to reproduce. Bryan believed that acts of great evil might take place if such notions ever became widely accepted. Two decades later—years after Bryan's death—his worst fears were realized when eugenics became a leading rationalization for the Holocaust, the execution of six million Jews by Adolf Hitler and Nazi Germany during World War II.

Bryan urged state governments to enact laws against teaching evolution in their schools. He declared that since ordinary citizens paid the taxes that paid for public school operations, they ought to be able to choose what their children could be taught. If a majority of citizens in a state opposed evolution, then it had no place in public school classrooms according to Bryan. This stand enjoyed wide support in many American communities, especially those in the South and the Midwest.

Bryan expressed great satisfaction when Tennessee legislators passed a sweeping anti-evolutionary law, the Butler Act of 1925. But a legal challenge to the law was not long in coming. The long-brewing battle over the teaching of evolution in public schools reached its peak in 1925 in the sleepy town of Dayton, Tennessee. It was in Dayton that a schoolteacher named John T. Scopes, supported by the American Civil Liberties Union, declared that he had willfully violated the new state law against teaching evolution. Bryan quickly offered his services to the prosecution team free of charge.

A Celebrity in Dayton

Bryan received a hero's welcome in Dayton. Throngs of people followed him wherever he went, and he obliged them by delivering speeches around town and in surrounding communities. The Great Commoner was clearly favored by the partisan crowds both inside the courtroom and outside the trial. Bryan's son, William Jr., joined him in Dayton as a member of the prosecution team. His wife did not support his participation in the trial. She worried about his health, and she also saw the potential of an unfavorable outcome. Nevertheless she traveled with him to Dayton and graciously kept her peace, venting her anxieties only in letters to her daughters, Ruth and Grace.

The intense summer heat in Tennessee visibly affected Bryan during the trial. He fanned himself constantly with a palm leaf and mopped his brow frequently. But the sweltering conditions did not dampen his zest for battle. Four days into the trial, when the court heard arguments about whether to permit the testimony of scientists and liberal theologians, Bryan stood to deliver his first extended remarks. His first oration for the court encompassed almost all the arguments he had made against evolution in his speeches of the previous few years. Holding Tennessee's high school biology text aloft, he condemned the linkage of humans with animals in evolutionary thought. He also warned that students would have their faith in God shaken if they were exposed to evolutionary teachings.

Bryan's statement met with warm applause from courtroom spectators. But Dudley Field Malone, a member of Scopes' defense team, then stood and delivered an equally impassioned plea for academic "freedom of the mind." Malone's statement was so convincing and heartfelt that the pro-Bryan crowd reportedly gave him even greater applause when he completed his remarks.

Bryan took this setback to heart. But in his eagerness to regain the upper hand in the debate, he made a historic tactical error. When the trial resumed, defense attorney Clarence Darrow surprised everyone by calling Bryan to the witness stand as an "expert on the Bible." What followed was one of the most remarkable courtroom exchanges of the twentieth century.

A Battle of Titans

The questioning began with civility but quickly turned tense as Darrow grilled Bryan on particulars of the Old Testament and ancient history. Bryan faltered under the relentless questioning. As the minutes ticked by, he revealed that even *he* did not accept a literal reading of the book of Genesis, which contains the Biblical story of the origins of man and woman. Prosecuting attorney Tom Stewart tried to halt the questioning, but Bryan refused to step down. By the time Judge John Raulston finally called a halt to Bryan's testimony, most observers believed that Darrow had easily won the duel between the two legends.

Bryan's willingness to stay seated in the witness stand for such a long period of time was due in part to his belief that he would be given an opportunity to question Darrow in the same manner. Bryan never got that opportunity, however. After concluding his questioning of Bryan, the sly Darrow urged the jury to find his client guilty and end the trial. The jury promptly did so, which enabled Scopes and his defense team to appeal the verdict.

The sudden guilty verdict also deprived Bryan of the opportunity to deliver his carefully-crafted summation speech. Still, the trial looked initially like a victory for Bryan and his supporters. He spent several days traveling in Tennessee, delivering his summation speech to enthusiastic crowds. Bryan then returned to Dayton with his wife to prepare for a major address. He died there during an afternoon nap, just six days after the Scopes "Monkey Trial" ended.

Changing Public Perceptions

In the late twentieth century, most Americans formed their opinions of Bryan from the the play and film *Inherit the Wind*. That work featured a character, Matthew Harrison Brady, who was clearly based on Bryan. But in both the play and film, Brady appears an intolerant and pompous buffoon. This fictional portrait unfairly painted Bryan's role in the trial and made no mention of his historical importance in other areas. In fact, his contributions to the Democratic Party in America were significant, his sense of social responsibility commendable, and his devotion to democratic ideals unwavering.

During the Scopes trial, a philanthropist suggested that Dayton, Tennessee, would be a fitting place to erect a Christian college honoring Bryan. After Bryan's untimely death, donations poured in. Bryan College opened its doors in 1930 and today boasts ten buildings on a 110-acre campus. Most of Bryan's speeches and papers reside at the Library of Congress. He and his wife are buried in Arlington National Cemetery in Washington, DC.

Sources

"Active, Political and Civic Career of W. J. Bryan, Thrice a Presidential Candidate." *New York Times*, July 27, 1925.

Ashby, Leroy. *William Jennings Bryan: Champion of Democracy*. Boston, MA: Twayne, 1987.

Kazin, Michael. *A Godly Hero: The Life of William Jennings Bryan*. New York: Knopf, 2006.

Larson, Edward J. *Summer for the Gods: The Scopes Trial and America's Continuing Debate over Science and Religion*. Cambridge, MA: Harvard University Press, 1997.

Clarence Darrow (1857-1938)
Chief Defense Attorney at the Scopes "Monkey Trial"

Clarence Seward Darrow was born April 18, 1857, in the rural Ohio town of Kinsman. His parents were Amirus and Emily Eddy Darrow. Darrow's father, a furniture-maker and undertaker, was both religious and independent-minded, with a cynical outlook on life. As a youngster, Clarence Darrow was influenced deeply by the Civil War's impact on his community. As dead soldiers from the area were shipped back for burial, Darrow became shaken by a growing sense of the finality of death. After a while, he actively avoided the part of his father's workshop where he stored coffins for his undertaking business.

Darrow's father collected books, and as a youth Darrow read a wide variety of literature. In 1873-74 he attended Allegheny College. He then spent three years teaching school in another small Ohio town. He then embarked on an independent study of law with an eye toward becoming a lawyer. His formal training in the subject was restricted to one year at the University of Michigan, in 1877. At that time, however, young men could "read the law" and apprentice in law offices as an alternative route into the legal profession. Darrow was admitted to the Ohio bar at the age of 21 by passing an oral examination—a triumph that he attributed both to his own study and to a clerkship in a Youngstown, Ohio, law firm.

Darrow married his first wife, Jessie Ohl, in 1880 (they divorced in 1897). The couple settled in Andover, another rural town in northeastern Ohio. Legal work was sparse in Andover, but it was during this period that Darrow discovered his talent for public speaking. He particularly enjoyed taking part in debates in which he could argue the less popular position.

After a short time in Andover, the Darrows moved to the larger town of Ashtabula, Ohio, with their young son Paul, Darrow's only child. Darrow became active in local politics shortly after his arrival in Ashtabula. Around this same period, he read two books that profoundly influenced the direction of his life: *Progress and Poverty,* by Henry George, and *Our Penal Machinery and Its Victims,* by Peter Altgeld. George's book advocated unionization as a way to address the unequal distribution of wealth in America. Altgeld's book was among the first to demonstrate that the American legal system often unfairly victimized the poor.

Acting on a whim, Darrow moved to Chicago in 1887 and immediately introduced himself to Altgeld, who was a powerful superior court judge in the city. A friendship developed between them, and Altgeld used political connections to secure several positions for Darrow in Chicago city government. In 1891 Altgeld secured for Darrow a lucrative job with the Chicago and Northwestern Railway. One year later, Darrow served as a counselor and campaign worker on Altgeld's successful campaign for the governorship of Illinois.

Legal Crusader for Labor

Darrow's life took a dramatic turn in 1894, when a bitter labor strike was called against the railroad for which he worked. The bloody Pullman Strike was organized and led by labor leader Eugene V. Debs. It culminated in a violent confrontation between strikers and National Guardsmen who had been brought in by the U.S. government, which was firmly in management's corner. Nearly a dozen demonstrators were killed when the Guardsmen opened fire on a crowd of strikers, and Debs was arrested and thrown into jail.

This series of events bothered Darrow so much that he quit his job with the railroad in order to defend Debs in the courts. Thus began a period of 17 years in which Darrow defended a succession of union leaders and striking workers threatened with imprisonment under various charges. During these years, Darrow repeatedly condemned the oppressive tactics of the U.S. government and Big Business against miners, factory workers, and other American laborers. Ironically, this stance made him a political ally of a young progressive Democrat named William Jennings Bryan.

Darrow's legal work took him all around the country during the late 1890s and early 1900s. Much of this work came from Samuel Gompers, president of the American Federation of Labor, the largest union in the country. Darrow returned to Chicago in 1903 and opened a firm that included future federal judge Francis Wilson and future fiction writer Edgar Lee Masters. He also married Ruby Hamerstrom, a wife who would remain faithful to him through hard economic times and occasional infidelities.

119

In 1907 Darrow undertook another sensational case, the murder trial of radical union leader "Big Bill" Haywood. Haywood had been implicated in the murder of a former governor of Idaho who had long been strongly anti-union. Darrow was able to win acquittal for Haywood and his alleged accomplices, in part by casting doubt on the testimony of a key witness for the prosecution. Although the trial was held in Boise, Idaho, it was covered by the national press and secured Darrow's reputation as a master courtroom orator.

Darrow then reluctantly agreed to defend two brothers accused of dynamiting the offices of the *Los Angeles Times* in 1910. Twenty-one people had been killed in the blast, and evidence against the men was overwhelming. Darrow persuaded them to plead guilty so he could argue against the death penalty. Reports then surfaced that prospective jurors in the case had been offered bribes by members of Darrow's defense team after the trial got underway in 1911. Darrow was arrested and charged with bribing jurors. Although he was acquitted in one trial and received a hung jury decision in a second related case, the negative publicity damaged his reputation. He returned to Chicago, where his law firm associates promptly disowned him. Darrow did not undertake another organized labor case for the rest of his career.

The Leopold and Loeb Case

World War I helped to restore Darrow's image. He was a staunch supporter of the war and made speeches praising U.S. intervention. He also rebuilt his law practice through criminal defense work in Chicago, most notably his efforts in the sensational Leopold-Loeb murder case of 1924.

Nathan Leopold and Richard Loeb were wealthy, high-achieving college students who kidnapped and murdered Bobby Franks, a 13-year-old boy. Leopold and Loeb had no apparent motive for their actions save the ambition to commit a "perfect crime." The cold-blooded nature of the attack and the young age of the victim drew national attention. Hired to defend the two young murderers, Darrow urged them to plead guilty in order to avoid a jury trial and go straight to a sentencing hearing before a single judge. Darrow fully expected his clients to receive the death penalty, but he argued passionately for the trial judge to spare their lives. He claimed that their upbringings played a factor in their immoral conduct, and that the carnage of the First World War had diminished their regard for human life. In addition, he asserted that they had been influenced by their exposure to the writings of philosophers like Friedrich Nietzsche, who challenged modern concepts of morality and the meaning of life. Finally, he declared that a life spent in prison might actually be a far tougher punishment than execution. To the amazement of Darrow and many Americans, the judge spared the lives of Leopold and Loeb.

Fresh off this victory of sorts, Darrow offered his services free of charge—for the first and only time—to John T. Scopes. For years Darrow had watched as William Jennings Bryan crusaded against teaching evolution in American classrooms. Bryan's words and actions alarmed the maverick lawyer. Darrow saw them as a threat to the Constitutional guarantee of church-state separation. He also saw Bryan and his anti-evolutionary allies as a dangerous threat to scientific research and inquiry. Darrow saw the Scopes trial as much more than a local matter. "Scopes is not on trial, civilization is on trial," he stated famously.

The American Civil Liberties Union (ACLU) had already agreed to provide attorneys for Scopes's defense, and the organization did not want the openly agnostic Darrow to participate in the case. But Scopes lobbied for Darrow, especially upon hearing that Bryan would be arguing for the prosecution. Bowing to Scopes's desires, the ACLU made room for Darrow.

Darrow in Dayton

Darrow arrived in Dayton prepared to challenge the whole notion of using Biblical principles to influence public education. Hooking his thumbs in his lavender suspenders, he delivered the defense's opening statement, setting the tone for the subsequent arguments. He then called upon experts from the fields of biology, geology, and liberal theology as witnesses for the defense. When his experts were not allowed to testify beyond the submission of written statements, Darrow took the unprecedented step of summoning Bryan himself to the stand as an "expert" on the Bible.

On a warm Monday morning in Dayton, one of the most memorable moments in twentieth century courtroom history unfolded under the shade trees outside the courthouse (where the court had been moved to seek relief from the heat). For more than two hours Darrow questioned Bryan about the literal truth of the Bible. Not surprisingly, the argument grew heated, as Bryan accused Darrow of atheism and Darrow insulted Bryan's "fool ideas." As time passed, though, Bryan faltered. Trapped by Darrow's skillful questioning, Bryan gradually revealed that even he did not support a literal interpretation

121

of the Book of Genesis. Bryan's struggles did not end until Judge John T. Raulston finally halted the cross-examination after two hours.

The jury brought back a guilty verdict, as expected. This enabled Darrow and his allies to appeal the Scopes verdict to a higher court. Certain that the Butler Act was unconstitutional, their aim was to appeal all the way to the U.S. Supreme Court if necessary. But the guilty verdict returned against Scopes was overturned on a technicality well before then.

At the end of the Scopes trial, the American Civil Liberties Union—and many American liberals—thought Darrow had done more harm than good for the cause of separation of church and state. By hurling insults at Bryan's "fool religion" and belittling the Bible, Darrow alienated all Fundamentalists and many religious people with moderate beliefs. Anti-evolution laws were passed in other states, and no defendant stepped forward to challenge them again for more than 40 years. Both sides in the Scopes trial claimed victory, but in the immediate aftermath it was Bryan, not Darrow, who prevailed in the eyes of a majority of Americans.

Darrow's Final Years

Darrow lived another 11 years after the Scopes trial. He spent much of this time in the courtroom, championing the underdog in highly publicized cases. During these years, Darrow also found time to write his autobiography, *The Story of My Life*, which was first published in 1932. He admitted in those pages that much of his intellectual activity over the years had been inspired by a desire to think about something besides his mortality. He truly was an atheist who did not believe in life after death.

In declining health as the 1930s advanced, Darrow retired and lived quietly in the Chicago apartment that had been his home for decades. He suffered from heart disease and spent his last months as an invalid, tended by his wife, Ruby. Darrow died of a heart attack a month shy of his eighty-first birthday in Chicago. He was survived by his wife and by his son.

Sources
Clarence Darrow Home Page. http://www.law.umkc.edu/faculty/projects/ftrials/Darrow.htm.
"Clarence Darrow Is Dead in Chicago." *New York Times,* March 14, 1938.
Darrow, Clarence. *The Story of My Life.* New York: Charles Scribner's Sons, 1932, 2nd ed. New York: Da Capo Press, 1996.
Darrow, Clarence. *Attorney for the Damned.* Edited by Arthur Weinberg. New York: Simon & Schuster, 1957. Reprint. Chicago, IL: University of Chicago Press, 1989.
Tierney, Kevin. *Darrow: A Biography.* New York: Crowell, 1979.

Charles Darwin (1809-1882)
Geologist, Naturalist and Writer Who Devised the Theory of Evolution by Natural Selection

Charles Robert Darwin was born on February 12, 1809, in Shrewsbury, Shropshire, England. His father, Robert Waring Darwin, was a physician who owned a large estate in the country. His mother, Susannah Wedgwood, was the daughter of the famous fine china maker Josiah Wedgwood. She died when Darwin was eight, and he was raised by his father and three older sisters.

During his youth, Darwin displayed a greater interest in exploring the woods and fields of his father's estate than in his studies at his Anglican (Church of England) school. His interest in natural science was further nurtured by family vacations in Northern Wales, where he went on many extended hiking trips. At 16 his father sent him to study medicine at Edinburgh University. Darwin paid little attention to medicine at Edinburgh but dove into lively campus debates about science and religion. He also learned how to conduct field work by assisting Robert Edmond Grant, a specialist on sponges who was conducting research into the relationship between various species of sea-living invertebrates.

In 1828 Darwin's father demanded that the young man cease his studies in naturalism and study for the clergy at Christ's College in Cambridge, England. Darwin agreed, in part because he did harbor religious beliefs and in part because many clergymen of that era engaged in nature study in their free time. He graduated in 1831, and by all measures he seemed destined to live the life of a well-to-do country minister.

Shortly after graduating, though, the 22-year-old Darwin was offered a berth on the HMS *Beagle,* a scientific research vessel captained by a 26-year-old adventurer named Robert Fitzroy. Fitzroy planned to circumnavigate the globe in order to survey frontier areas little known in England at the time. Darwin joined the crew as a collector of specimens.

Setting Sail on the *Beagle*

When the *Beagle* set sail in December 1831, Darwin began a travel diary that would eventually run to 770 pages. He also compiled 1,750 pages of notes and collected 5,436 specimen samples (mostly skins, bones, and carcasses). The ship sailed along the coast of South America, lingering in Uruguay, Patagonia, Argentina, and Chile. Everywhere Darwin went he collected specimens and observed the ecology and geology of his surroundings. During these explorations, Darwin collected extremely large animal bones that he could not link to any living species on the continent. He initially assumed that they belonged to extinct rhinoceros and mastodon species.

The entire *Beagle* voyage contributed to Darwin's appreciation of ancient eras of earth's past, and of the vanished species that once thrived in the regions he visited. In hindsight, historians have highlighted the ship's visit to the Galapagos Islands, but at the time these exotic volcanic outposts did not excite any specific attention from the young naturalist. Darwin dutifully collected bird specimens from each island but did not believe they were related species since they looked so different. It was only later, when the specimens were studied by zoologists in England, that their close genetic relationships were revealed.

The *Beagle* returned to England in October 1836, almost five years after its departure. Armed with an allowance from his father, Darwin did not need to seek employment upon his return. He instead prepared his voyage diaries for publication and worked on scientific classification of the numerous specimens he had collected over the previous five years. He was named a fellow of the Royal Geographic Society in 1837.

Darwin's efforts were greatly aided by a financial grant from the English treasury. This assistance enabled him to recruit the best zoologists of his time for his research efforts. These experts helped him document that the large bones he had collected during his years on the *Beagle* were giant ancestors of creatures still living in South America. They also discovered that all the little birds gathered on separate islands in the Galapagos Islands were finches— and that each species had adapted in unique ways to the environmental conditions of its particular island. By 1843 he had published not only his travel diary but a volume entitled *Zoology of the Voyage of the H.M.S. Beagle,* which detailed many of his research findings.

Darwin then retired to a quiet country estate in Downe, England. He enjoyed the lively debates of his scientific colleagues, but he also suffered from bouts of poor health. There he and his wife Emma Wedgwood (a cousin) had ten children while amassing a fortune from investments in real estate and railroads.

The Origin of Species

Like most men of his generation, Darwin believed in God. But he was never deeply religious, and the scientific research he conducted during and after his extraordinary voyage on the *Beagle* eroded those beliefs. He studied the question of the origin of man and other species throughout the 1840s and 1850s, but he did so quietly. Darwin's low-key behavior was partly due to the fact that he was still sorting out his own beliefs and research data. But it was probably also due to his recognition that any work that was interpreted as questioning the existence of God would be harshly condemned in many quarters.

Historians believe that Darwin may have written most of his theory of evolution by natural selection in the early 1840s. Yet he did not publish the book *The Origin of Species by Natural Selection; Or, The Preservation of Favoured Races in the Struggle for Life,* until 1859. He might have waited even longer, but he learned that another naturalist, Alfred Russel Wallace, had prepared a paper with similar conclusions about the origins of species for delivery to the prestigious Linnean Society. Darwin arranged to have his work presented at the same meeting, but he did not attend.

When Darwin's book was published, it generated tremendous controversy, as he had anticipated. Many scientists hailed the work as an inspired and convincing explanation for the fossil record. They also praised his views on natural selection and its influence on species development over time. But religious leaders objected to Darwin and his book on the grounds that they challenged religious beliefs that God was responsible for the creation of the world and all the creatures—humans and animals—that dwelled therein.

For his part, Darwin let the storm swirl around him without responding. His unwillingness to debate his views in public was due at least in part to his poor health. Throughout his adult life, in fact, he suffered from a bewildering array of illnesses, from the skin disease eczema to extreme bouts of nausea. Most of his biographers, however, agree that at least some of Darwin's health problems were anxiety-related. Darwin also felt less pressure to respond to critics because he had a champion in his friend Thomas Henry Huxley, a vibrant speaker and noted scientist in his own right. While Darwin remained at his farm in Downe, Huxley promoted the theory of evolution at universities and scientific meetings in England and elsewhere.

Darwin and God

By the time *The Origin of Species* was published, Darwin had suffered the loss of a favorite daughter and the death of his youngest son. He also had become an agnostic—someone who believes that there is no way to be certain whether God exists or not. Darwin believed that his agnosticism made it easier for him to develop his theories impartially, without religious prejudice either toward or against the existence of God.

The Origin of Species does not address human evolution directly. As scientists began to embrace his theory, however, Darwin turned to a direct examination of human origins, publishing *The Descent of Man, and Selection in Relation to Sex* in 1871. In this work Darwin hypothesized that humans and African apes had evolved from common ancestors. In addition, he suggested that humans chose mates according to the biological and cultural traits they possessed, just as birds chose the mates with the most brilliant plumage.

Together, *The Origin of Species* and *The Descent of Man* made Darwin's position plain: humans had evolved from an ancestral ape species that had responded to climatic changes by adapting for intelligence, evolving a bipedal gait (walking on two feet), and developing long nurturing periods for children. His follow-up volume, *The Expression of the Emotions in Man and Animals*, published in 1872, demonstrated the remarkable similarity between facial expressions in humans and animals, particularly apes.

Darwin also published a number of other books and papers, from a work dedicated to the interplay between insects and orchids to a study of vegetable mold. But he remained most famous for the theory of evolution he set forth in *The Origins of Species* and *The Descent of Man*.

In Darwin's final years, health problems confined him to home, but he was surrounded by a large family that cared for him. As he neared death, Darwin contemplated a simple burial in a country cemetery near his home. He suffered a seizure in March 1882 and died of a heart attack one month later, on April 19, 1882. Despite his wishes, the English scientific community clamored for a burial more suited to Darwin's stature as one of the most influential thinkers of the nineteenth century. He was given an elaborate state funeral and interred in Westminster Abbey in London.

Sources

Browne, Janet. *Charles Darwin: The Power of Place.* New York: Knopf, 2002.

Browne, Janet. *Charles Darwin: Voyaging.* New York: Knopf, 1995.

Chapman, Matthew. *Trials of the Monkey: An Accidental Memoir.* London: Duckworth, 2000.

Darwin, Charles. *The Autobiography of Charles Darwin.* 1876. Reprint. Kila, MT: Kessinger, 2004.

Thomas, Herbert. *Human Origins: The Search for Our Beginnings.* New York: Abrams, 1995.

Arthur Garfield Hays (1881-1954)
ACLU Attorney for the Defense in the Scopes "Monkey Trial"

Arthur Garfield Hays was born December 12, 1881, in Rochester, New York. He was the son of Isaac Hays and Laura Garson Hays. Both of Hays's parents had family ties to the lucrative garment manufacturing business, so the young Hays—named after two Republican Presidents—grew up in luxury.

Hays spent the first twelve years of his life in Rochester, New York, before moving with his family to New York City. He graduated from Columbia University in 1902 and received a law degree from the same institution in 1905. The following year he founded the first of two law firms, Hays, Kaufmann & Lindheim, and began a profitable career serving the interests of big businesses, actors and actresses, and international shipping tycoons. He later formed the partnership of Hays, St. John & Abramson. His wealthy clients paid him handsomely, but as the years passed by, Hays felt a growing desire to use his legal talents to promote social justice in America.

To that end, Hays joined the leadership of the American Civil Liberties Union (ACLU) in 1920, the same year that the ACLU was founded. Then as now, the ACLU's mission was to ensure that the protections enshrined in the U.S. Constitution's Bill of Rights are made available to all Americans. This mandate led the organization to defend people whose interests conflicted with the views of most Americans. These individuals included American Communists who were persecuted by the government and labor leaders seeking to unionize coal mining and other industries.

Leading Role in Scopes Trial

The ACLU's core beliefs eventually led it to take a leading role in the defense of John T. Scopes when he was prosecuted for teaching evolution in Tennessee in 1925. The Scopes trial was the first high-profile case for the ACLU, and the organization chose Hays to lead its efforts in Dayton.

Hays's duties during the trial included managing the expert testimony from scientists and religious scholars (ruled inadmissible as evidence by Judge John T. Raulston) and attempting, unsuccessfully, to keep the entire proceedings from becoming a debate between religion and science. In the view of Hays and the ACLU, the Scopes case was important because it was a clear instance in which the sentiments of the majority—the Tennessee law-makers and citizens who supported the anti-evolution Butler Act—threatened the civil rights of the minority.

When the jury in Dayton found Scopes guilty of violating the Butler Act, Hays participated in the appeal of the Scopes verdict to the Tennessee Supreme Court. He was deeply disappointed when the Court threw out the ruling against Scopes on a technicality. The Tennessee Supreme Court voided Scopes's sentence and would not hear an appeal. To his dismay, Hays no longer had a case. Since he could not mount an appeal in state court, he had no avenue to take the case to the U.S. Supreme Court. That had been his goal from the beginning of the proceedings, for he knew that the U.S. Supreme Court had the power to determine the unconstitutionality of the Butler Act once and for all.

Nevertheless, the ACLU's participation in the Scopes case greatly increased the organization's profile, and Hays went on to work on many high-profile cases. In many instances he represented unpopular defendants, including the Italian anarchists Nikola Sacco and Bartolomeo Vanzetti, who were put to death for a murder they claimed they did not commit. Hays also defended the Scottsboro Eight, a group of African American males accused of raping two white women in Alabama. He even helped his friend H. L. Mencken win a case for freedom of the press after an issue of Mencken's *American Mercury* magazine was banned because it contained a story about a prostitute.

A Steadfast Voice for Civil Liberties

In true ACLU fashion, Hays sometimes took positions that were extremely unpopular. For example, he defended Henry Ford's right to distribute anti-union leaflets at his Ford Motor Company factories. He also defended the freedom of speech rights of the Bund, a group of Americans who supported Adolf Hitler in the 1930s. In every case in which he engaged in work on behalf of the ACLU, Hays offered his services free of charge. Meanwhile, he continued to maintain a thriving law practice that represented an array of powerful corporations. He never felt that his work on behalf of large corporations conflicted with his ACLU cases. In every instance he felt he was promoting basic American rights, whether for industry or for individuals.

Despite his hectic schedule, Hays managed to write several books. *Let Freedom Ring*, first published in 1928, contains his reflections on the Scopes trial. He also penned a 1942 memoir, *City Lawyers: The Autobiography of a Law Practice*. Hays lost a fortune in the stock market crash of 1929 but regained his financial footing during the 1930s, when he was a vigorous supporter of President Franklin D. Roosevelt's New Deal programs.

Hays was married twice. His first wife was Blanche Marks, who he married in 1908 and divorced in 1924. That same year he wed Aline Davis Fleisher. He had two daughters, one by each marriage. He died of heart failure on December 14, 1954.

Sources

"Arthur Garfield Hays Dies at 73: Counsel to Civil Liberties Union." *New York Times,* December 15, 1954.

Hays, Arthur Garfield. *City Lawyers: The Autobiography of a Law Practice.* New York: Simon & Schuster, 1942.

Hays, Arthur Garfield. *Let Freedom Ring.* New York: Liveright Publishers, 1928. Reprint. New York: Da Capo Press, 1972.

Larson, Edward J. *Summer for the Gods: The Scopes Trial and America's Continuing Debate over Science and Religion.* Cambridge, MA: Harvard University Press, 1997.

Dudley Field Malone (1882-1950)
Assistant Defense Attorney for John T. Scopes

Dudley Field Malone was born June 3, 1882, in New York City. The son of a successful attorney, Malone grew up on the West Side of Manhattan and graduated from Francis Xavier College in 1903 with a major in French. He then attended Fordham University, earning a law degree in 1905. Within months of his departure from Fordham, he became involved in reform-based politics, particularly in opposition to the powerful and corrupt New York political machine known as Tammany Hall. He married Mary P. O'Gorman, a fellow Roman Catholic, in 1908.

Malone's skills as a lawyer and an orator made him a rising star in Democratic political circles. In 1912 he took a prominent role in the presidential campaign of Woodrow Wilson. When Wilson won, Malone was named assistant secretary of state. One of the great ironies of the Scopes trial is that Malone worked directly for William Jennings Bryan, who served as secretary of state in the Wilson administration from 1913 to 1915. The two men did not get along particularly well, and Malone continued to spend much of his time engaged in New York City politics.

From 1914 until 1917, Malone served as collector of the Port of New York, a federal position that supervised all the ships and cargo passing through Manhattan's terminals. It was during these years that Malone became increasingly active in social causes, among them the women's suffrage movement. Enraged by the treatment of female activists in Washington, D.C., Malone resigned from the Wilson administration in 1917.

In 1921 Malone divorced his first wife—a scandalous move for a politically-connected Roman Catholic. In order to pursue the divorce, he and his wife traveled to France. French divorce laws were more lenient, and the process took much less time. The experience of his own divorce convinced him to become a Paris-based divorce attorney.

From 1921 until the outbreak of World War II, Malone divided his time between his Paris law practice and numerous high-profile "underdog" trials in America. During these years he co-founded the Association against the Prohibition Amendment, labored to increase public acceptance of the young Soviet Union, and worked for the American Civil Liberties Union (ACLU) on several cases. By far the most prominent of these ACLU cases was the 1925 trial of John T. Scopes in Dayton, Tennessee.

At first the ACLU suggested that Malone might best serve Scopes's defense by carrying out legal research in New York. Malone thought otherwise. He wanted to be in the fray, and he proved during the course of the trial that his presence on the defense team was indispensable. He did cause a stir in Dayton upon his arrival, though. When he arrived in town with his second wife, women's suffrage activist Doris Stevens (who insisted on using her maiden name, to the shock of her contemporaries), the sophisticated couple seemed like foreigners from another country altogether.

While fellow defense attorney Clarence Darrow projected a relaxed, "everyman" demeanor during the trial, Malone set a different standard. Defying the sweltering heat that enveloped the courtroom, he did not remove his suit coat or tie until the trial's fifth day. On that afternoon, he dramatically folded his suit coat and draped it over a chair before launching into an impassioned speech on behalf of academic freedom, separation of church and state, and the use of the Bible for moral, rather than scientific, purposes.

Malone's speech was in response to a long oration by Bryan, the star of the team of prosecutors in the case. Bryan had ridiculed the theory of evolution and warned that teaching evolution would bring an avalanche of moral corruption and atheism onto young schoolchildren. At the conclusion of Bryan's remarks, the partisan spectators in the courtroom had cheered and applauded their champion.

Malone's Shining Moment

Malone's task—to respond to Bryan's comments before a hostile audience—was a daunting one. But historians and eyewitnesses alike agreed that Malone's dramatic reply to Bryan was the oratorical high point of the Scopes trial. Speaking so loudly that he could be heard clearly outside without the aid of the loudspeakers, Malone respectfully but thoroughly assailed Bryan's arguments with a passion and precision that brought grudging applause from the audience. "We feel we stand with progress," Malone said. "We feel we stand with science. We feel we stand with intelligence. We feel we stand with fundamental freedom in America. We are not afraid… Where is the fear? We defy it!"

A roar of approval erupted from the crowd inside the courtroom and outside on the lawn as Malone concluded his speech. Years later, Scopes wrote in his memoir that "Bryan was never the same afterward and if there were any turning points in the trial that day was one. Dudley Field Malone had shattered his former chief's unbounded optimism, which Darrow is commonly credited with having done later in the trial. Bryan had reached his peak before Darrow ever got him on the stand. If anything, Malone's debilitating coup probably made Bryan want to go on the stand, in the vain hope of regaining some of his tarnished glory."

At the end of the Scopes trial, Malone returned to his private practice in France. A *New York Times* obituary noted that while Malone was known as "the greatest international divorce lawyer" of the 1920s, "he had arranged more reconciliations than divorces for those who sought his help in their domestic problems." He was less successful with his own domestic arrangements. Malone divorced his second wife in 1929 and married actress Edna Louise Johnson in 1930. Together they had one son, Malone's only child.

Malone returned to the United States at the beginning of World War II, working as a general counsel for 20th Century-Fox Films. During this time, his resemblance to English prime minister Winston Churchill was so pronounced that Malone actually played Churchill in a 1943 film, *Mission to Moscow*. He died of a heart attack on October 5, 1950, in Culver City, California.

Sources

"Dudley F. Malone Dies in California," *New York Times,* October 6, 1950.

Larson, Edward J. *Summer for the Gods: The Scopes Trial and America's Continuing Debate over Science and Religion.* Cambridge, MA: Harvard University Press, 1997.

Moran, Jeffrey P. *The Scopes Trial: A Brief History with Documents.* New York: St. Martin's Press, 2002.

Scopes, John T. and James Presley. *Center of the Storm: Memoirs of John T. Scopes.* New York: Holt, Rinehart & Winston, 1967.

H. L. Mencken (1880-1956)
Journalist Who Provided Controversial Commentary on the Scopes "Monkey Trial"

Henry Louis Mencken was born in Baltimore, Maryland, on September 12, 1880. The son of August and Anna Abhau Mencken, he was the oldest of four siblings. Mencken's father and uncle owned a prosperous cigar factory, and when Mencken was three years old the family moved to a genteel three-story brick row house that was within easy walking distance of Baltimore's downtown business district. Except for one brief period, Mencken lived in this house for the rest of his life.

Mencken's childhood was pleasant. His parents stressed the importance of a well-rounded education, and young Henry excelled in school. As a child he attended Knapp's Institute, a private school for German Americans. He finished his scholastic career at Baltimore's Polytechnic Institute, a public high school that emphasized engineering and technical training. He graduated at the top of his class when he was only 16.

Mencken had a burning desire to be a writer. In his teens he began penning poetry and short stories, but he longed to be a newspaper reporter. Family expectations, however, led him to dutifully follow his father into the cigar-making business. In his spare time Mencken took correspondence courses and did his own independent reading, sometimes devouring a whole book in a single night.

Career Beginnings in Baltimore

When Mencken was 18, his father died unexpectedly. Released from his sense of obligation to the family business, Mencken quit the cigar factory and relentlessly pursued a newspaper job. Still a teenager, with no journalistic experience or college credits, Mencken strode into the *Baltimore Herald*. He asked to see the editor and requested a position with the paper. The editor told him that no jobs were available, but that he could check back from time to time. Mencken returned every single day until the editor relented and signed him on as a cub reporter.

From the very beginning of his career as a journalist, Mencken displayed two major assets. The first was his impressive writing ability. The second was his work ethic. He thought nothing of spending up to 18 hours a day on his newspaper duties, just from pure enjoyment of the job. During the Great Baltimore Fire of 1904, he worked feverishly on dispatches even as the offices of the *Baltimore Herald* burned to the ground. By the time the *Herald* closed in 1906, the 25-year-old Mencken had risen to the position of editor-in-chief. In his memoir *Newspaper Days, 1899-1906*, Mencken recalled that his early years of newspaper work were "the maddest, gladdest, damndest existence ever enjoyed by mortal youth."

After the *Baltimore Herald* closed its doors, a rival newspaper, the *Baltimore Sun*, promptly hired Mencken to write theater reviews and Sunday editorials. He also published two books during this time, one on playwright George Bernard Shaw and another on the German philosopher Friedrich Nietzsche. In 1908 he was hired to provide monthly book reviews for a popular New York-based magazine called *The Smart Set*.

Mencken used his column in *The Smart Set* (and later in his own magazine, *The American Mercury*) to promote serious authors, many of whom labored in obscurity until he discovered them. He was influential in promoting the careers of such major writers as F. Scott Fitzgerald, Theodore Dreiser, Sinclair Lewis, the African American writers of the "Harlem Renaissance," and Nobel Prize-winning playwright Eugene O'Neill.

A Rising Star

Although his duties at *The Smart Set* often took him to New York, and eventually led to a co-editorship of the magazine, Mencken never quit working for the *Baltimore Sun*. His allegiance to the *Sun* stemmed partly from the journalistic freedom he enjoyed at the paper. In 1910, for example, the editors of the newspaper asked him to write a regular column on whatever topic he wished. Calling his column "The Free Lance," Mencken began writing the kind of journalism that eventually made him famous around the world. The first targets of his sharp, mocking wit were local Baltimore society figures, but he soon began commenting on national figures and events. Throughout the 1910s and 1920s, Mencken penned numerous columns challenging middle-class American notions of democracy, religion, civic pride, popular entertainment, and morality.

Not surprisingly, Mencken's barbs were not well-received in some quarters. For example, his views were harshly condemned from many pulpits, even though his friends included many prominent theologians and liberal Christian pastors. In his biography of Mencken, *Disturber of the Peace,* William Manchester quoted one such irate preacher: "If a buzzard had laid an egg in a dunghill and the sun had hatched a thing like Mencken, the buzzard would have been justly ashamed of its offspring." Not surprisingly, Mencken was widely accused of being an atheist. But the writer described himself instead as a religious "skeptic" and agnostic—someone who believes that it is impossible to know whether God exists or not.

The *Sun* editors sometimes cringed at the uproar that flared up around some of Mencken's remarks. But his darkly witty and insightful columns attracted a wide following in Baltimore and around the country. When America entered World War I in 1917, his opposition to American involvement and his disrespectful attitude toward President Woodrow Wilson led *Sun* editors to dramatically lower his profile. But Mencken re-emerged at war's end with a whole new audience: educated young Americans who had been appalled by the war and who were united in their belief that most Americans were simple-minded and easily controlled by political and religious leaders. To these readers Mencken was a hero, a sharp-tongued, cynical observer of social hypocrisy and political manipulation.

In 1923 Mencken and George Jean Nathan co-founded *The American Mercury,* a national magazine that widened Mencken's readership considerably. By the time he arrived in Dayton, Tennessee, to cover the Scopes "Monkey Trial," H. L. Mencken was the best-known journalist in the United States.

Mencken in Dayton

Mencken's dispatches from the Scopes trial showcased both his talented pen and his hostility toward religion and rural social traditions. He reveled in hurling insults at the citizens of Dayton, the farmers in the surrounding mountains, the trial jury, the judge, and especially William Jennings Bryan. Mencken called the citizens of Dayton the "local primates," described their religious beliefs as "degraded nonsense hammered into yokel skulls," and claimed that most Dayton residents saw John T. Scopes as a "Satan" who, due to his youth, might yet be saved.

Detractors claimed that Mencken's reports from Dayton showed him to be a malicious and arrogant man. But Mencken and his defenders claimed that his harsh words stemmed from his firm belief in individual rights, education, and scientific progress. Mencken argued that Fundamentalist Christianity posed a genuine threat to school children who would have to compete as scientists and inventors in an increasingly global economy. Mencken asserted that his commentary was designed to make his readers think about important issues of the day and about how mass movements of all sorts could cloud individual judgment and choke individual freedoms.

In the aftermath of the Scopes trial, legends arose about the dangers Mencken faced while in Dayton. According to some accounts, his safety and even his life were threatened by angry members of the community. In reality, though, most of the anger directed at him remained civil in tone—and a lot of it came from ministers who offered to debate him or save his soul. "It is a fact that my dispatches from the courtroom were somewhat displeasing to local susceptibilities," Mencken admitted in his memoir *Heathen Days,* "and that my attempts to describe the town and its people were even more so, and it is also a fact that there was talk among certain bolder spirits of asking me to retire from the scene, but beyond that it did not go."

A Legend of American Journalism

Mencken's sharp-tongued commentaries on American society played well throughout the remainder of the 1920s, when most Americans were employed and secure. At the outset of the Great Depression, however, he fell out of favor. His comments began to seem less amusing and insightful to out-of-work Americans, especially when he criticized Franklin D. Roosevelt and the New Deal. To make matters worse, Mencken wrote favorably about Adolf Hitler and some of his social policies in the early 1930s. This attitude has been attributed to a variety of factors, including Mencken's own German heritage, his admiration for Germany's swift recovery from defeat in World War I, and his own anti-Semitic leanings (though Mencken never publicly defended Hitler's anti-Semitic policies).

Mencken severed ties with the *American Mercury* in 1933 and limited himself to his editorial work for the *Sun.* He also published several books and revised what is considered his most important work, *The American Language,* a multi-volume study of the evolution of American English. At age 50, he married for the first time. He met his wife, writer Sara Haardt, at an all-female college after delivering a tongue-in-cheek speech he called "How to Catch a Husband." Although her health was always poor, she and Mencken enjoyed a five-year marriage before her death in 1935. Those years were the only ones Mencken spent away from his childhood home. He and his wife lived in an apartment in another part of Baltimore.

After his wife's death, Mencken settled back into his family home for the final 20 years of his life. Late in the 1930s he began to publish autobiographical sketches about his childhood in Baltimore and his early years in journalism, mainly in the *New Yorker.* These sketches became the basis for a trilogy of memoirs, *Happy Days, Newspaper Days,* and *Heathen Days.* The memoirs were bestsellers and revived Mencken's reputation as a gifted, entertaining writer.

In 1948 Mencken suffered a stroke and became unable to read or write. He hired people to read for him—among them his biographer, William Manchester—but became frustrated when none of his readers could maintain the pace to which he was accustomed. His physical health improved to the point that he could make his way around the house and communicate with family and visitors, but he curtailed public appearances. He died in his sleep on January 29, 1956, at the family home on Hollins Street.

Mencken left numerous unpublished writings upon his death. One book, *Minority Report,* was released by Alfred A. Knopf the year Mencken died. Others, including his diaries, were sealed for thirty years at his request. These have since been published, as well as volumes of his collected correspondence.

Sources
Bode, Carl. *Mencken.* Baltimore, MD: Johns Hopkins University Press, 1986.

"H. L. Mencken, 75, Dies in Baltimore." *New York Times,* January 30, 1956.

Manchester, William. *Disturber of the Peace: The Life of H. L. Mencken,* New York: Harper & Row, 1950. Revised ed. Cambridge, MA: University of Massachusetts Press, 1986.

Mencken, H. L. *Happy Days, 1880-1892.* New York: Alfred A. Knopf, 1940. Reprint. Baltimore, MD: Johns Hopkins University Press, 1996.

Mencken, H. L. *Heathen Days, 1890-1936.* New York: Alfred A. Knopf, 1943. Reprint. Baltimore, MD: Johns Hopkins University Press, 1996.

Mencken, H. L. *Newspaper Days, 1899-1906.* New York: Alfred A. Knopf, 1941. Reprint. Baltimore, MD: Johns Hopkins University Press, 1996.

Stenerson, Douglas C. *H. L. Mencken: Iconoclast from Baltimore.* Chicago, IL: University of Chicago Press, 1971.

John T. Raulston (1868-1956)
Presiding Judge in the Scopes "Monkey Trial"

John Tate Raulston was born September 22, 1868, in rural Marion County, Tennessee. His father, William Doran Raulston, and mother, Comfort Matilda Tate Raulston, supported their family through farming. He was one of seven siblings, all schooled in the Bible by their mother and local Methodist ministers.

Raulston earned a degree from U. S. Grant University (now Tennessee Wesleyan College) and completed his law studies at the University of Chattanooga while working in the law offices of William D. Spear. Raulston was admitted to the bar in 1896. He spent the next several years teaching school before finally opening his own law practice in Whitwell, Tennessee, in 1902.

Raulston served one term in the Tennessee state legislature, from 1902 to 1904. Thereafter he worked in a firm in South Pittsburgh, Tennessee, until 1918, when he was elected judge of Tennessee's eighteenth district. He spent the next several years as a circuit-riding judge, traveling through seven counties on a regular rotating schedule. When he arrived in each county seat, he would hear all the cases that had accumulated since his last visit.

Raulston's quiet judicial career came to an end in 1925, when John T. Scopes was arrested for teaching evolution in a public school in Dayton, Tennessee, in clear violation of the state's Butler Act. As famous lawyers such as William Jennings Bryan and Clarence Darrow lined up for the prosecution and the defense, respectively, Raulston adjusted his circuit-riding schedule so that the Scopes trial could proceed quickly. Raulston saw the case as a way to increase his own local popularity and possibly even capture nationwide attention. As Edward J. Larson noted in *Summer for the Gods*, Raulston "apparently felt called by God to preside over this trial and would not let the opportunity slip through his hands."

Sympathetic to the Prosecution

On a personal level, Raulston approved of the state's anti-evolution law and saw the Scopes case as a clear violation of that law. His views were evident from the outset of the legal proceedings. At the preliminary hearing against Scopes on May 25, 1925, Raulston convened a grand jury, read the anti-evolution statute, and then read the first chapter of Genesis from the Bible. The grand jury indicted Scopes in a matter of hours.

During the actual trial in Dayton, Raulston ruled against the defense on several important issues. For example, he refused to allow the defense to call expert witnesses to the stand to testify on the science of evolution or ways in which the theory could be reconciled with Christian religious beliefs. Instead, he only allowed the defense to submit written testimony from these experts that could be used in appeals to the state Supreme Court. Raulston also denied defense requests that he halt the state-sanctioned prayers that began each session of court, even though some of them were clearly biased against evolutionary science.

By the sixth day of the Scopes trial, Clarence Darrow had become so frustrated by the judicial rulings that he leveled an insulting reference to Raulston's lack of impartiality. This insult earned Darrow a contempt of court citation. When court next convened, Darrow apologized for his remark, and Raulston accepted the apology and withdrew the contempt citation. This exchange paved the way for Darrow's famous showdown with Bryan on July 20, 1925, the final day of testimony in the trial.

Raulston ordered the trial proceedings to be held outside on that day because of concerns about the heat and the courthouse floor's ability to support the weight of the assembled legal teams, jurors, and spectators. He allowed Darrow to call Bryan to the stand as an "expert witness" on the Bible and then looked on quietly as Darrow grilled Bryan mercilessly on Biblical miracles and ancient history. Finally, as the argument grew heated, Raulston halted Darrow's questions and adjourned court for the day.

A Fateful Legal Misstep

The following morning, Raulston ordered Bryan's testimony from the previous day stricken from the court record. Darrow then asked that the jury retire and come back with a guilty verdict against Scopes. This legal maneuver prevented Bryan from calling Darrow to the stand (as they had previously agreed), and it also paved the way for an appeal of the verdict to a higher court. Raulston instructed the jury, and in nine minutes the jurors returned with a guilty verdict. Raulston set Scopes's fine at the minimum amount of $100.

The fact that Raulston imposed the fine later gave Tennessee's Supreme Court a technicality upon which it could throw out the case. It was the *jury,* and not *Raulston,* who should have set the level of fine, according to the high court. The high court reversed Scopes's conviction. This "victory" was actually a bitter disappointment to Scopes, Darrow, and the rest of the defense team, for it meant that the state Supreme Court had avoided addressing the constitutionality of the Butler Act—and the legality of teaching evolution in public schools. One legal error on Raulston's part thus allowed the anti-evolution Butler Act to remain in the Tennessee statute books, uncontested, for the next 40 years.

If Raulston thought the Scopes trial would increase his popularity with his constituents in Tennessee, he was proven wrong. In 1926 he failed in his bid for re-election to his circuit judge post. He never served in a public office again, although he once tried to run for governor of Tennessee.

Raulston worked for the remainder of his life as a partner in the firm of Raulston, Raulston & Swafford. He accumulated a sizable fortune representing corporate clients from the coal and railroad industries. Occasionally he lectured on the topic of law as it related to the teaching of evolution. His *New York Times* obituary suggests that in the wake of the Scopes trial Raulston "moderated his views of fundamentalism and education," taking the position that science classes might not corrupt the morals of young students.

Raulston married twice. His first wife, Estelle Otto Faller, died in 1916, and he later married Eva Davis. He suffered a nervous breakdown in 1950 and then fractured his hip in a fall. He was seldom seen in public after that, and he died in South Pittsburgh, Tennessee, on July 11, 1956. He was survived by Davis and two daughters.

Sources

Dictionary of American Biography, Supplement 6: 1956-1960. New York: American Council of Learned Societies, 1980.

"John T. Raulston, Jurist, 87, Dead." *New York Times,* July 12, 1956.

Larson, Edward J. *Summer for the Gods: The Scopes Trial and America's Continuing Debate over Science and Religion.* Cambridge, MA: Harvard University Press, 1997.

Moran, Jeffrey P. *The Scopes Trial: A Brief History with Documents.* New York: St. Martin's Press, 2002.

John T. Scopes (1900-1970)
Public School Teacher and Defendant in the Scopes "Monkey Trial"

John Thomas Scopes was born on August 3, 1900, in Paducah, Kentucky. He was the youngest of five children, and the only boy. Scopes's father, Thomas, was a native of England who found work in the United States as a railroad machinist. Thomas Scopes became an American citizen shortly before John Scopes was born. Scopes's mother, Mary Alva Brown, was a native Kentuckian and the granddaughter of a prominent Presbyterian clergyman.

John Scopes was profoundly influenced by his free-thinking parents, particularly his self-educated father. In his memoir, *Center of the Storm,* Scopes recalled the fact that his father read to the family from the works of Mark Twain, Jack London, Charles Dickens—and Charles Darwin, the British naturalist who developed evolutionary theory. When Thomas Scopes was fired for refusing to work as a strikebreaker during a railroad walkout, he became an ardent union organizer and a Socialist. Later in life he severed ties with a church because he felt the church leaders were acting in opposition to Bible teachings.

Scopes attended church and Sunday school as a child, but he remembered leaving one Sunday school class after challenging the teacher's views. When he was thirteen, the family moved to Danville, Illinois, where he and his sister were treated harshly in school because of their Southern accents and Kentucky origins. He found acceptance when the family moved on to Salem, Illinois (which was also the birthplace of William Jennings Bryan). By that time Scopes was in high school. Tall and athletic, he played basketball and occasionally got into trouble for driving with his friends to neighboring counties to buy alcohol.

William Jennings Bryan served as commencement speaker at Scopes's high school the year he graduated. Scopes later recalled in his memoir that he and a few friends, sitting within earshot of Bryan, snickered during Bryan's speech. This earned Scopes a withering look from Bryan at the time. Six years later, when Bryan and Scopes met again at the famous trial in Dayton, Bryan recalled the incident.

Scopes began his college education at the University of Illinois, but a strange illness forced him out of classes. He later speculated that it might have been a mild case of polio. After working as a railroad worker in order to save for tuition, he entered the University of Kentucky. There he made an interesting decision. He chose classes based not on their content, but on the quality and personality of the professor. Thus he spent three years taking a wide variety of courses, from education and child psychology to law, zoology, math, and chemistry. By his senior year he realized that he had never chosen a major. This meant that he had to work very hard as a college senior to fulfill the requirements of the major he finally did choose—law.

Drifting into a Teaching Career

During Scopes's enrollment at the University of Kentucky, the Kentucky legislature considered a bill to ban the teaching of evolution in public school classrooms. Scopes was very proud that some of the professors he had studied under publicly spoke out against this proposal. The Kentucky legislature voted down the bill.

Scopes earned a bachelor's degree in law from the University of Kentucky in 1924. Feeling that he would eventually become an attorney, he decided to teach for a few years and save money to attend law school. Late in the summer of 1924 he accepted a position at Central High School in Dayton, Tennessee, at a salary of $150 per month. He was expected to teach mathematics and serve as the school's football coach, even though he admitted he knew very little about football. Scopes moved to Dayton, rented a room in the spacious home of a local store owner, and soon knew almost everyone in town. He attended church and socialized with some of his older students. As a young bachelor, he had few other social options in the small town.

During the spring term of 1925, the principal of Central High became ill. He asked Scopes to fill in and lead a science class that he normally taught for the remainder of the year. Later Scopes could not recall whether he actually taught evolution during his stint as a substitute science teacher. He was aware, however, that the textbook he used—*A Civic Biology* by George W. Hunter—did cover the topic.

Scopes had planned to leave Dayton as soon as the school year ended and spend the summer with his parents. Instead, intrigued by a pretty girl, he lingered for an extra week. In those few extra days, his life changed dramatically.

Taking on the Butler Act

In March 1925, the Tennessee state legislature passed a law called the Butler Act. This law made it a crime to teach "any theory that denies the story of the Divine Creation of man as taught in the Bible, and to teach instead that man has descended from a lower order of animals." The fine for breaking this law ranged from $100 to $500, a significant sum for a Tennessee school teacher at the time.

The American Civil Liberties Union (ACLU) in New York City believed that this new law was unconstitutional, and that it could have a chilling effect on all kinds of scientific research. Determined to challenge the Butler Act in the American court system, the ACLU announced that it would provide free legal help to any teacher in Tennessee who would admit to teaching evolution in a science class between March and June of 1925. The ACLU further guaranteed to pay any fines handed down by the courts against any such teacher.

The ACLU stand intrigued a group of Dayton's citizens, led by a pro-evolution businessman named George W. Rappleyea. They summoned Scopes to a popular drugstore, bought him a soft drink, and persuaded him to serve as the test case for the constitutionality of the law. Scopes pulled a copy of *A Civic Biology* off the shelf in the drugstore and flipped to the pages on evolution. According to Scopes's memoir, he then turned to the assembled men and declared, "There's our text, provided by the state. I don't see how a teacher can teach biology without teaching evolution."

Scopes was a perfect candidate to challenge the law. He was young, scholarly-looking, and a bachelor with no ties to Dayton. He was promptly arrested for teaching evolution, and Rappleyea and his allies, eager for national recognition and tourist dollars, contacted the American Civil Liberties Union.

Over the next few weeks Scopes was overwhelmed by the level of national interest in the case. When he traveled to New York City to meet with the ACLU, it seemed that everyone wanted to meet him. Newspaper reporters mobbed him and prominent scientists invited him to lectures. The quiet country teacher from Kentucky was suddenly a celebrity.

The only significant impact Scopes had on the trial itself occurred during these preliminary meetings with the ACLU in New York. The leaders of the ACLU did not want controversial attorney Clarence Darrow to take part in the "Monkey Trial" proceedings. But when Scopes heard that William Jennings Bryan had volunteered to help the prosecution, he insisted that Darrow be named to his defense team. Anticipating a "gouging, roughhouse battle," Scopes thought Darrow and Dudley Field Malone were better suited to match wits against Bryan than the attorneys hand-picked by the ACLU.

Scopes's predictions about the "roughhouse" nature of the trial proved accurate. Even though he did not testify at the trial, his name was at the center of a heated debate that was covered by live radio broadcast feeds and newspapers from all over America. Outside the courtroom, Dayton took on a carnival atmosphere as both anti-evolutionists and supporters of evolution gathered to listen to the proceedings and argue among themselves. At times the furor was more than Scopes could bear. One afternoon he escaped to go swimming with prosecuting attorney William Jennings Bryan, Jr., and wound up being scolded for returning late to court.

A Guilty Verdict

As the trial progressed, Scopes's defense team realized that it had no chance of winning over the jury, composed of local residents who had a generally anti-evolution outlook. Scopes's defense team finally decided to ask the jury for a guilty verdict. This was quickly supplied, and Scopes was given his only chance to speak at the trial. The young teacher stood before the judge and the large crowd and spoke briefly. He said: "Your honor, I feel that I have been convicted of violating an unjust statute. I will continue in the future, as I have in the past, to oppose this law in any way I can. Any other action would be in violation of my ideals of academic freedom, that is to teach the truth as guaranteed in our Constitution, of personal and religious freedom."

In the immediate aftermath of the "Monkey Trial," Scopes was deluged with mail. Fundamentalist pastors wanted to convert him to Christianity. Young women proposed marriage. He was even offered a lecture tour. Scopes never opened most of the mail, though. Instead he and some friends piled it all in a field and set it on fire. He wanted nothing more to do with the controversy, and he expressed relief when the state supreme court overturned his conviction on a technicality.

Immediately after the trial, Scopes received a generous academic scholarship, collected from university professors throughout the country. The gift allowed him to pursue a master's degree in geology at the University of Chicago. After earning that degree, he was made a candidate for a fellowship that would have brought him a Ph.D. But the president of the university denied him the fellowship, writing: "Your name has been removed from consideration… As far as I am concerned, you can take your atheistic marbles and play elsewhere."

Armed with his master's degree, Scopes went to work for the Gulf Oil Company as a surveyor in Venezuela. There he met Mildred Walker, a Roman Catholic. He married her in 1930, after himself converting to Roman Catholicism "to please my bride." That same year he was fired by Gulf Oil for refusing to cross a national border to conduct an illegal survey.

Scopes returned to graduate school, but he never completed his degree. Instead, in 1933, he took a job with the United Gas Corporation and spent the next three decades working in Texas and Louisiana. A self-confessed workaholic who regularly spent 50 to 60 hours at his duties each week, he nevertheless found time for his wife and two sons, John Jr. and William. He retired in 1964.

Throughout his life Scopes regularly received mail from students and adults interested in the "Monkey Trial." He never answered any of it. He felt that if he took time to reply to one letter, he ought to reply to them all, and his workload did not provide that amount of leisure. The only time he participated in any activity related to the trial was in 1960, when his wife persuaded him to attend premiere activities for the film *Inherit the Wind*. This tour brought him back to Dayton for the first time since 1930. After wandering Dayton's streets for the first time in more than three decades, he expressed surprise at how little the town had changed.

Scopes published his memoir in 1967, and the book brought him notoriety yet again. The book received glowing reviews in the Tennessee press and prompted a flurry of newspaper editorials praising the teaching of evolution in public schools. A short time later, the Tennessee legislature repealed the Butler Act. More than 40 years after the end of his trial, Scopes was finally vindicated. He died in Shreveport, Louisiana, three years later, on October 21, 1970.

Sources

American National Biography. New York: Oxford University Press, 1999.

Larson, Edward J. *Summer for the Gods: The Scopes Trial and America's Continuing Debate over Science and Religion.* Cambridge, MA: Harvard University Press, 1997.

Scopes, John T., and James Presley. *Center of the Storm: Memoirs of John T. Scopes.* New York: Holt, Rinehart & Winston, 1967.

Tom Stewart (1892-1972)
Local Prosecutor in the Scopes "Monkey Trial"

Arthur Thomas "Tom" Stewart was born on January 11, 1892, in Dunlap, Tennessee. He studied at the Pryor Institute in Jasper, Tennessee, and earned a bachelor's degree from Emory College (now Emory University) in Atlanta, Georgia. He returned to his home state to study law at Cumberland University and was admitted to the bar in 1913. Six years later he moved to Winchester, Tennessee, and lived there the rest of his life. From 1923 until 1939 he divided his time between the private practice of law and his duties as district attorney for Tennessee's eighteenth district.

It was in the latter capacity that Stewart was called upon to prosecute John T. Scopes in the evolution trial of 1925. Stewart headed a large team of prosecutors that included William Jennings Bryan, William Jennings Bryan, Jr., Ben and J. Gordon McKenzie, Sue and Herbert Hicks, and Wallace C. Haggard.

In Stewart's opinion, the case against Scopes was quite simple and based on narrow legal limits. The state legislature of Tennessee had passed a law that was approved by the majority of its citizens, and John Scopes had broken that law. To Stewart, this fact precluded all debate on whether religion or evolution should be taught in the classrooms of Tennessee.

Even before the trial began, Stewart realized that it would be difficult to keep the proceedings from degenerating into a debate on the merits of evolution. He vigorously objected to the inclusion of any expert witnesses on behalf of the defense, and he also tried in vain to keep William Jennings Bryan from taking the stand for interrogation by Clarence Darrow. During the famous exchange between Darrow and Bryan, Stewart raised objections more than ten times. He reminded the judge that Bryan's testimony as an expert on the Bible had no pertinence to the trial. "We are attaining no evidence here," he complained to the judge as Darrow grilled Bryan in the summer heat. But Bryan silenced the earnest prosecutor by demanding the right to answer Darrow's challenges.

Stewart ultimately won his case when the jury returned a guilty verdict against Scopes. But the victory was a strange one, for it came only after Darrow asked the jury to find his client guilty in order to assure that the defense could file an appeal with a higher court. Stewart did not participate in the appeal process, which ended abruptly when the Tennessee Supreme Court overturned Scopes's conviction on a technicality.

After the Scopes trial ended, Stewart returned to his normal routine. By the late 1930s he had become a prominent political figure in the state. In 1938 Tennessee's Senator Nathan L. Bachman died in office, and Stewart became a candidate in a race for the balance of Bachman's term. Stewart won and became a Democratic U.S. senator for Tennessee in 1939. He served in that capacity for ten years until he was defeated in the 1948 primary election by fellow Democrat Estes Kefauver.

After his defeat, Stewart returned to Winchester and his private law practice. He died there on October 10, 1972. He was married to Helen Turner and had five children. Interestingly, Stewart is remembered more for the week he spent in Dayton, Tennessee, prosecuting John Scopes than for his many years of service in the United States Senate.

Sources

Dictionary of American Biography, Supplement 9. New York: Charles Scribner's Sons, 1994.

Larson, Edward J. *Summer for the Gods: The Scopes Trial and America's Continuing Debate over Science and Religion.* Cambridge, MA: Harvard University Press, 1997.

Moran, Jeffrey P. *The Scopes Trial: A Brief History with Documents.* New York, NY: St. Martin's Press, 2002.

PRIMARY SOURCES

Bishop Ussher Calculates the Day that God Created the World

Certain editions of the St. James Bible—*especially those used by fundamentalist Christians in the 1920s—featured the calculations of Bishop James Ussher (1581-1656), a prominent theologian in the Church of Ireland. In his work* Annals of the World, *first published in Latin in 1650, Ussher used the combined ages of Adam's descendants as well as known dates of events in Israelite history to arrive at an exact day, month, and year in which God created the earth. During the Scopes "Monkey Trial," prosecuting attorney William Jennings Bryan referred to his Bible—and specifically the portion of the Bible that featured Ussher's calculations—in citing the date of Noah's flood at 2349 BC.*

This excerpt from Annals of the World *shows that Bishop Ussher assumed each day of creation mentioned in the Book of Genesis consisted of exactly twenty-four hours. During his famous courtroom duel with defense attorney Clarence Darrow, however, Bryan himself contradicted this notion in his testimony.*

Note: In the text below, JP refers to the Julian (Roman) year, beginning January 1, 4713 BC. Unlike the "backwards" numbering of the Christian calendar, the Julian calendar runs forwards from 1-10, etc. The abbreviation "Ge" refers to the Book of Genesis, and the numbers that follow this abbreviation refer to specific chapters and verses within that book.

1a AM, 710 JP, 4004 BC

1. In the beginning God created the heaven and the earth. [Ge 1:1] The beginning of time; according to our chronology, happened at the start of the evening preceding the 23rd day of October (on the Julian calendar), 4004 BC or 710 JP....

2. On the first day [Ge. 1: 1-5] of the world (Sunday, October 23), God created the highest heaven and the angels. When he finished, as it were, the roof of this building, he started with the foundation of this wonderful fabric of the world. He fashioned this lower-most globe, consisting of the deep and of the earth....

3. On the second day [Ge. 1:6-8] (Monday, October 24) after the firmament or heaven was finished, the waters above were separated from the waters here below, enclosing the earth.

4. On the third day [Ge. 1:9-13] (Tuesday, October 25), when these waters below ran together into one place, the dry land appeared. From

---

this collection of the waters God made a sea, sending out from here the rivers, which were to return there again....

5. On the fourth day (Wednesday, October 26), the sun, the moon and the rest of the stars were created. [Ge. 1:14-19].

6. On the fifth day (Thursday, October 27), fish and flying birds were created and commanded to multiply and fill the sea and the earth.

7. On the sixth day (Friday, October 28), the living creatures of the earth were created, as well as the creeping creatures [Ge. 1:24-27]. Last of all, man was created in the image of God, which consisted in the capacity of the mind to have a knowledge of the divine... Lest [Adam] should be destitute of a suitable companion, God took a rib out of his side while he slept and fashioned it into a woman....

8. Now on the seventh day (Saturday, October 29), when God had finished his work which he intended, he then rested from all labour.

[Using the ages given to Adam and his descendants in the Book of Genesis, Bishop Ussher also affixed a precise date to Noah's flood, including the day, month, and year.]

1656a AM, 2365 JP, 2349 BC

33. Methuselah, the eighth from Adam, died when he was nine hundred and sixty-nine years old. He was the oldest man that ever lived. [Ge. 5:24-27]

34. On the tenth day of the second month of this year (Sunday, November 30), God commanded Noah that in that week he should prepare to enter the ark. Meanwhile the world, totally devoid of all fear, sat eating and drinking and marrying and giving in marriage. [Ge. 7:1-4]

35. In the 600th year of the life of Noah, on the seventeenth day of the second month (Sunday, December 7), he, together with his children and living creatures of all kinds, had entered into the ark. God sent a rain on the earth for forty days and forty nights. The waters flooded the earth for a hundred and fifty days. [Ge. 7:4, 6, 11-13, 17, 24]

Source: *Annals of the World,* by James Ussher, "The Annals of the Old Testament from the Beginning of the World," 1650, revised edition updated by Larry and Marion Pierce. Green Forest, AR: Master Books, 2003.

Charles Darwin Explains His Theory of Human Evolution

In his classic 1855 work The Origin of Species by Means of Natural Selection; Or, The Preservation of Favored Races in the Struggle for Life, *Charles Darwin touched lightly on human evolution. His subsequent work,* The Descent of Man, and Selection in Relation to Sex (1871), *concentrated more heavily on human ancestry and the physical similarities between humans and apes. In the following passage from* The Descent of Man, *Darwin outlines the scientific evidence of his time indicating a close evolutionary relationship between humans, monkeys, and apes. At the end of this excerpt, Darwin explicitly states his belief that man and all other vertebrate animals share a common ancestry.*

The Bodily Structure of Man.—It is notorious that man is constructed on the same general type or model with other mammals. All the bones in his skeleton can be compared with corresponding bones in a monkey, bat, or seal. So it is with his muscles, nerves, blood-vessels and internal viscera. The brain, the most important of all organs, follows the same law, as shewn by Huxley and other anatomists....

Man is liable to receive from the lower animals, and to communicate to them, certain diseases as hydrophobia [rabies], variola [smallpox], the glanders [a bacterial infection], &c.; and this fact proves the close similarity of their tissues and blood, both in minute structure and composition, far more plainly than does their comparison under the best microscope, or by the aid of the best chemical analysis. Monkeys are liable to many of the same non-contagious diseases as we are; thus [Johann R.] Rengger, who carefully observed for a long time the *Cebus Azarae* in its native land, found it liable to catarrh [bronchial infection], with the usual symptoms, and which when often recurrent led to consumption [tuberculosis]. These monkeys suffered also from apoplexy, inflammation of the bowels, and cataract in the eye. The younger ones when shedding their teeth often died from fever. Medicines produced the same effect on them as on us. Many kinds of monkeys have a strong taste for tea, coffee, and spirituous liquors: they will also, as I myself have seen, smoke tobacco with pleasure. [Alfred] Brehm asserts that the natives of north-eastern Africa catch the wild baboons by exposing vessels with strong beer, by which they are made drunk. He has seen some of these animals, which he kept in confinement, in this state; and he gives a laughable account of their behaviour and strange grimaces. On the following morning they were very cross and dismal; they held their aching heads with both

153

hands and wore a most pitiable expression: when beer or wine was offered them, they turned away with disgust, but relished the juice of lemons. An American monkey, an Ateles, after getting drunk on brandy, would never touch it again, and thus was wiser than many men. These trifling facts prove how similar the nerves of taste must be in monkeys and man, and how similarly their whole nervous system is affected.

Man is infested with internal parasites, sometimes causing fatal effects, and is plagued by external parasites, all of which belong to the same genera or families with those infesting other mammals. Man is subject like other mammals, birds, and even insects, to that mysterious law, which causes certain normal processes, such as gestation, as well as the maturation and duration of various diseases, to follow lunar periods. His wounds are repaired by the same process of healing; and the stumps left after the amputation of his limbs occasionally possess, especially during an early embryonic period, some power of regeneration, as in the lowest animals.

The whole process of that most important function, the reproduction of the species, is strikingly the same in all mammals, from the first act of courtship by the male to the birth and nurturing of the young. Monkeys are born in almost as helpless a condition as our own infants; and in certain genera the young differ fully as much in appearance from the adults, as do our children from their full-grown parents. It has been urged by some writers as an important distinction, that with man the young arrive at maturity at a much later age than with any other animal; but if we look to the races of mankind which inhabit tropical countries the difference is not great, for the orang is believed not to be adult till the age of from ten to fifteen years. Man differs from woman in size, bodily strength, hairyness, &c., as well as in mind, in the same manner as do the two sexes of many mammals. It is, in short, scarcely possible to exaggerate the close correspondence in general structure, in the minute structure of the tissues, in chemical composition and in constitution, between man and the higher animals, especially the anthropomorphous apes....

Thus we can understand how it has come to pass that man and all other vertebrate animals have been constructed on the same general model, why they pass through the same early stages of development, and why they retain certain rudiments in common. Consequently we ought frankly to admit their community of descent: to take any other view, is to admit that our own structure and that of all the animals around us, is a mere snare laid to entrap our judgment. This conclusion is greatly strengthened, if we look to the members of the whole animal series, and consider the evidence derived from their affinities or classification, their geographical distribution and geological succession. It is only our natural prejudice, and that arrogance which made our forefathers declare that they were descended from demi-gods, which leads us to demur to this conclusion. But the time will before long come when it will be thought wonderful, that naturalists, who were well acquainted with the comparative structure and development of man and other mammals, should have believed that each was the work of a separate act of creation.

Source: Darwin, Charles. *The Descent of Man, and Selection in Relation to Sex.* London, J. Murray, 1871. Reprint. Princeton, NJ: Princeton University Press, 1981.

Tennessee's 1925 Statute Prohibiting the Teaching of Evolution in Public Schools

On March 13, 1925, state lawmakers in Tennessee passed a statute introduced by Representative John Butler that explicitly prohibited public school teachers in the state from teaching evolution. Eight days later, Tennessee Governor Austin Peay signed the legislation, also known as the Butler Act, into law. "The people must have the right to regulate what is taught in their schools," stated Peay. Following is the text of the statute.

AN ACT prohibiting the teaching of the Evolution Theory in all the Universities, Normals and all other public schools of Tennessee, which are supported in whole or in part by the public school funds of the State, and to provide penalties for the violations thereof.

Section 1. *Be it enacted by the General Assembly of the State of Tennessee,* That it shall be unlawful for any teacher in any of the Universities, Normals and all other public schools of the State which are supported in whole or in part by the public school funds of the State, to teach any theory that denies the story of the Divine Creation of man as taught in the Bible, and to teach instead that man has descended from a lower order of animals.

Section 2. *Be it further enacted,* That any teacher found guilty of the violation of this Act, Shall be guilty of a misdemeanor and upon conviction, shall be fined not less than One Hundred ($100.00) Dollars nor more than Five Hundred ($500.00) Dollars for each offense.

Section 3. *Be it further enacted,* That this Act take effect from and after its passage, the public welfare requiring it.

Passed March 13, 1925

W. F. Barry, *Speaker of the House of Representatives*
L. D. Hill, *Speaker of the Senate*
Approved March 21, 1925.
Austin Peay, *Governor.*

Source: Public Acts of the State of Tennessee, 64th General Assembly, 1925, Chapter 237.

H. L. Mencken Describes Jury Selection in Dayton

This editorial by Baltimore journalist H. L. Mencken deeply angered Dayton's citizens when it was reprinted in Chattanooga newspapers. The nominal subject of Mencken's column was the jury selection process for the Scopes "Monkey Trial," but the journalist devoted most of his column to insulting remarks about the religious beliefs and local culture of the people of Dayton. Mencken's comments were driven by a profound and lifelong disgust toward what he perceived as ignorance and superstition, but this disdain revealed his own bigotry toward rural people in general. The individuals he mentions in the first paragraph of his column are prominent community leaders in the Baltimore area.

Chattanooga, Tenn., July 11. — Life down here in the Cumberland mountains realizes almost perfectly the ideal of those righteous and devoted men, Dr. Howard A. Kelly, the Rev. Dr. W. W. Davis, the Hon. Richard H. Edmonds and the Hon. Henry S. Dulaney. That is to say, evangelical Christianity is one hundred per cent triumphant. There is, of course, a certain subterranean heresy, but it is so cowed that it is almost inarticulate, and at its worst it would pass for the strictest orthodoxy in such Sodoms of infidelity as Baltimore. It may seem fabulous, but it is a sober fact that a sound Episcopalian or even a Northern Methodist would be regarded as virtually an atheist in Dayton. Here the only genuine conflict is between true believers. Of a given text in Holy Writ one faction may say this thing and another that, but both agree unreservedly that the text itself is impeccable, and neither in the midst of the most violent disputation would venture to accuse the other of doubt.

To call a man a doubter in these parts is equal to accusing him of cannibalism. Even the infidel Scopes himself is not charged with any such infamy. What they say of him, at worst, is that he permitted himself to be used as a cat's paw by scoundrels eager to destroy the anti-evolution law for their own dark and hellish ends. There is, it appears, a conspiracy of scientists afoot. Their purpose is to break down religion, propagate immorality, and so reduce mankind to the level of the brutes. They are the sworn and sinister agents of Beelzebub, who yearns to conquer the world, and has his eye especially upon Tennessee. Scopes is thus an agent of Beelzebub once removed, but that is as far as any fair man goes in condemning him. He is young and yet full of folly. When the secular arm has done execution upon him, the pastors will tackle him and he will be saved.

The selection of a jury to try him, which went on all yesterday afternoon in the atmosphere of a blast furnace, showed to what extreme lengths the salvation of the local primates has been pushed. It was obvious after a few rounds that the jury would be unanimously hot for Genesis. The most that Mr. Darrow could hope for was to sneak in a few men bold enough to declare publicly that they would have to hear the evidence against Scopes before condemning him. The slightest sign of anything further brought forth a peremptory challenge from the State. Once a man was challenged without examination for simply admitting that he did not belong formally to any church. Another time a panel man who confessed that he was prejudiced against evolution got a hearty round of applause from the crowd.

The whole process quickly took on an air of strange unreality, at least to a stranger from heathen parts. The desire of the judge to be fair to the defense, and even polite and helpful, was obvious enough—in fact, he more than once stretched the local rules of procedure in order to give Darrow a hand. But it was equally obvious that the whole thing was resolving itself into the trial of a man by his sworn enemies. A local pastor led off with a prayer calling on God to put down heresy; the judge himself charged the grand jury to protect the schools against subversive ideas. And when the candidates for the petit jury came up Darrow had to pass fundamentalist after fundamentalist into the box—some of them glaring at him as if they expected him to go off with a sulphurous bang every time he mopped his bald head.

In brief this is a strictly Christian community, and such is its notion of fairness, justice and due process of law. Try to picture a town made up wholly of Dr. Crabbes and Dr. Kellys, and you will have a reasonably accurate image of it. Its people are simply unable to imagine a man who rejects the literal authority of the Bible. The most they can conjure up, straining until they are red in the face, is a man who is in error about the meaning of this or that text. Thus one accused of heresy among them is like one accused of boiling his grandmother to make soap in Maryland. He must resign himself to being tried by a jury wholly innocent of any suspicion of the crime he is charged with and unanimously convinced that it is infamous. Such a jury, in the legal sense, may be fair. That is, it may be willing to hear the evidence against him before bumping him off. But it would certainly be spitting into the eye of reason to call it impartial.

The trial, indeed, takes on, for all its legal forms, something of the air of a religious orgy. The applause of the crowd I have already mentioned. Judge

Raulston rapped it down and threatened to clear the room if it was repeated, but he was quite unable to still its echoes under his very windows. The court-house is surrounded by a large lawn, and it is peppered day and night with evangelists. One and all they are fundamentalists and their yells and bawlings fill the air with orthodoxy. I have listened to twenty of them and had private discourse with a dozen, and I have yet to find one who doubted so much as the typographical errors in Holy Writ. They dispute raucously and far into the night, but they begin and end on the common ground of complete faith. One of these holy men wears a sign on his back announcing that he is the Bible cham-pion of the world. He told me today that he had studied the Bible four hours a day for thirty-three years, and that he had devised a plan of salvation that would save the worst sinner ever heard of, even a scientist, a theater actor or a pirate on the high seas, in forty days. This gentleman denounced the hard-shell Baptists as swindlers. He admitted freely that their sorcerers were powerful preachers and could save any ordinary man from sin, but he said that they were impotent against iniquity. The distinction is unknown to city theologians, but is as real down here as that between sanctification and salvation. The local experts, in fact, debate it daily. The Bible champion, just as I left him, was chal-lenged by one such professor, and the two were still hard at it an hour later.

Most of the participants in such recondite combats, of course, are yokels from the hills, where no sound is heard after sundown save the roar of the catamount and the wailing of departed spirits, and a man thus has time to ponder the divine mysteries. But it is an amazing thing that the more polished classes also participate actively. The professor who challenged the Bible cham-pion was indistinguishable, to the eye, from a bond salesman or city bootleg-ger. He had on a natty palm beach suit and a fashionable soft collar and he used excellent English. Obviously, he was one who had been through the local high school and perhaps a country college. Yet he was so far uncontaminated by infidelity that he stood in the hot sun for a whole hour debating a point that even bishops might be excused for dodging, winter as well as summer.

The Bible champion is matched and rivaled by whole herds of other metaphysicians, and all of them attract good houses and have to defend themselves against constant attack. The Seventh Day Adventists, the Camp-bellites, the Holy Rollers and a dozen other occult sects have field agents on the ground. They follow the traveling judges through all this country. Every-where they go, I am told, they find the natives ready to hear them and dispute with them. They find highly accomplished theologians in every village, but even in the county towns they never encounter a genuine skeptic. If a man has doubts in this immensely pious country, he keeps them to himself.

Dr. Kelly should come down here and see his dreams made real. He will find a people who not only accept the Bible as an infallible handbook of history, geology, biology and celestial physics, but who also practice its moral precepts—at all events, up to the limit of human capacity. It would be hard to imagine a more moral town than Dayton. If it has any bootleggers, no visitor has heard of them. Ten minutes after I arrived a leading citizen offered me a drink made up half of white mule and half of coca cola, but he seems to have been simply indulging himself in a naughty gesture. No fancy woman has been seen in the town since the end of the McKinley administration. There is no gambling. There is no place to dance. The relatively wicked, when they would indulge themselves, go to Robinson's drug store and debate theology.

In a word, the new Jerusalem, the ideal of all soul savers and sin exterminators. Nine churches are scarcely enough for the 1,800 inhabitants: many of them go into the hills to shout and roll. A clergyman has the rank and authority of a major-general of artillery. A Sunday-school superintendent is believed to have the gift of prophecy. But what of life here? Is it more agreeable than in Babylon? I regret that I must have to report that it is not. The incessant clashing of theologians grows monotonous in a day and intolerable the day following. One longs for a merry laugh, a burst of happy music, the gurgle of a decent jug. Try a meal in the hotel; it is tasteless and swims in grease. Go to the drug store and call for refreshment: the boy will hand you almost automatically a beaker of coca cola. Look at the magazine counter: a pile of *Saturday Evening Posts* two feet high. Examine the books: melodrama and cheap amour. Talk to a town magnifico; he knows nothing that is not in Genesis.

I propose that Dr. Kelly be sent here for sixty days, preferably in the heat of summer. He will return to Baltimore yelling for a carboy of pilsner and eager to master the saxophone. His soul perhaps will be lost, but he will be a merry and a happy man.

Source: Mencken, H. L. "Mencken Likens Trial to Religious Orgy, with Defendant a Beelzebub." *Baltimore Evening Sun,* July 11, 1925.

Mencken Sizes Up the Lawyers

Baltimore journalist H. L. Mencken attended the Scopes "Monkey Trial" not in the capacity of a reporter, but in that of an editorialist for the Baltimore Sun *(and syndicated newspapers around the country). In this dispatch, Mencken offers praise for defense attorney Arthur Hays and prosecuting attorney Tom Stewart. He also refers in admiring terms to a Clarence Darrow speech that warned that if the Butler Act was not struck down as unconstitutional, the nation would be set on a path of intolerance and ignorance. "If today you can take a thing like evolution and make it a crime to teach in the public schools," Darrow said, "tomorrow you can make it a crime to teach it in the private schools, and the next year you can make it a crime to teach it in the hustings or in the churches." But Mencken, a self-described religious "skeptic," characterizes defense lawyer William Jennings Bryan in extremely negative terms, painting him as an agent of ignorance and superstition who represents a threat to future generations of Americans. At the end of the piece, for example, he compares him unfavorably to Wat Tylor, a commoner who incited riots among the working class in the Middle Ages.*

Dayton, Tenn., July 14.— The net effect of Clarence Darrow's great speech yesterday seems to be precisely the same as if he had bawled it up a rainspout in the interior of Afghanistan. That is, locally, upon the process against the infidel Scopes, upon the so-called minds of these fundamentalists of upland Tennessee. You have but a dim notion of it who have only read it. It was not designed for reading, but for hearing. The clanging of it was as important as the logic. It rose like a wind and ended like a flourish of bugles. The very judge on the bench, toward the end of it, began to look uneasy. But the morons in the audience, when it was over, simply hissed it.

During the whole time of its delivery the old mountebank, Bryan, sat tight-lipped and unmoved. There is, of course, no reason why it should have shaken him. He has those hill billies locked up in his pen and he knows it. His brand is on them. He is at home among them. Since his earliest days, indeed, his chief strength has been among the folk of remote hills and forlorn and lonely farms. Now with his political aspirations all gone to pot, he turns to them for religious consolations. They understand his peculiar imbecilities. His nonsense is their ideal of sense. When he deluges them with his theological bilge they rejoice like pilgrims disporting in the river Jordan.

The town whisper is that the local attorney-general, Stewart, is not a fundamentalist, and hence has no stomach for his job. It seems not improbable. He is a man of evident education, and his argument yesterday was confined very strictly to the constitutional points—the argument of a competent and conscientious lawyer, and to me, at least very persuasive.

But Stewart, after all, is a foreigner here, almost as much so as Darrow or Hays or Malone. He is doing his job and that is all. The real animus of the prosecution centers in Bryan. He is the plaintiff and prosecutor. The local lawyers are simply bottle-holders for him. He will win the case, not by academic appeals to law and precedent, but by direct and powerful appeals to the immemorial fears and superstitions of man. It is no wonder that he is hot against Scopes. Five years of Scopes and even these mountaineers would begin to laugh at Bryan. Ten years and they would ride him out of town on a rail, with one Baptist parson in front of him and another behind.

But there will be no ten years of Scopes, nor five years, nor even one year.

Such brash young fellows, debauched by the enlightenment, must be disposed of before they become dangerous, and Bryan is here, with his tight lips and hard eyes, to see that this one is disposed of. The talk of the lawyers, even the magnificent talk of Darrow, is so much idle wind music. The case will not be decided by logic, nor even by eloquence. It will be decided by counting noses—and for every nose in these hills that has ever thrust itself into any book save the Bible there are a hundred adorned with the brass ring of Bryan. These are his people. They understand him when he speaks in tongues. The same dark face that is in his own eyes is in theirs, too. They feel with him, and they relish him.

I sincerely hope that the nobility and gentry of the lowlands will not make the colossal mistake of viewing this trial of Scopes as a trivial farce. Full of rustic japes and in bad taste, it is, to be sure, somewhat comic on the surface. One laughs to see lawyers sweat. The jury, marched down Broadway, would set New York by the ears. But all of that is only skin deep.

Deeper down there are the beginnings of a struggle that may go on to melodrama of the first caliber, and when the curtain falls at least all the laughter may be coming from the yokels. You probably laughed at the prohibitionists, say, back in 1914. Well, don't make the same error twice.

As I have said, Bryan understands these peasants, and they understand him. He is a bit mangy and flea-bitten, but by no means ready for his harp.

He may last five years, ten years or even longer. What he may accomplish in that time, seen here at close range, looms up immensely larger than it appears to a city man five hundred miles away. The fellow is full of such bitter, implacable hatreds that they radiate from him like heat from a stove. He hates the learning that he cannot grasp. He hates those who sneer at him. He hates, in general, all who stand apart from his own pathetic commonness. And the yokels hate with him, some of them almost as bitterly as he does himself. They are willing and eager to follow him—and he has already given them a taste of blood.

Darrow's peroration yesterday was interrupted by Judge Raulston, but the force of it got into the air nevertheless. This year it is a misdemeanor for a country school teacher to flout the archaic nonsense of Genesis. Next year it will be a felony. The year after the net will be spread wider. Pedagogues, after all, are small game; there are larger birds to snare—larger and juicier. Bryan has his fishy eye on them. He will fetch them if his mind lasts, and the lamp holds out to burn. No man with a mouth like that ever lets go. Nor ever lacks followers.

Tennessee is bearing the brunt of the first attack simply because the civilized minority, down here, is extraordinarily pusillanimous.

I have met no educated man who is not ashamed of the ridicule that has fallen upon the State, and I have met none, save only judge Neal [Scopes's only attorney from Tennessee], who had the courage to speak out while it was yet time. No Tennessee counsel of any importance came into the case until yesterday and then they came in stepping very softly as if taking a brief for sense were a dangerous matter. When Bryan did his first rampaging here all these men were silent.

They had known for years what was going on in the hills. They knew what the country preachers were preaching—what degraded nonsense was being rammed and hammered into yokel skulls. But they were afraid to go out against the imposture while it was in the making, and when any outsider denounced it they fell upon him violently as an enemy of Tennessee.

Now Tennessee is paying for that poltroonery. The State is smiling and beautiful, and of late it has begun to be rich. I know of no American city that is set in more lovely scenery than Chattanooga, or that has more charming homes. The civilized minority is as large here, I believe, as anywhere else.

It has made a city of splendid material comforts and kept it in order. But it has neglected in the past the unpleasant business of following what was going on in the cross roads Little Bethels.

The Baptist preachers ranted unchallenged.

Their buffooneries were mistaken for humor. Now the clowns turn out to be armed, and have begun to shoot.

In his argument yesterday judge Neal had to admit pathetically that it was hopeless to fight for a repeal of the anti-evolution law. The Legislature of Tennessee, like the Legislature of every other American state, is made up of cheap job-seekers and ignoramuses.

The Governor of the State is a politician ten times cheaper and trashier. It is vain to look for relief from such men. If the State is to be saved at all, it must be saved by the courts. For one, I have little hope of relief in that direction, despite Hays' logic and Darrow's eloquence. Constitutions, in America, no longer mean what they say. To mention the Bill of Rights is to be damned as a Red.

The rabble is in the saddle, and down here it makes its first campaign under a general beside whom Wat Tylor seems like a wart beside the Matterhorn.

Source: Mencken, H. L. "The Scopes Trial: Darrow's Eloquent Appeal Wasted on Ears That Heed Only Bryan, Says Mencken." *Baltimore Evening Sun,* July 14, 1925.

Bryan Argues Against Testimony from Defense "Experts"

On the fifth day of the Scopes "Monkey Trial," Judge John T. Raulston heard arguments about the admissibility of expert evidence from scientists and religious leaders brought to Dayton by the defense team. Bryan objected to the prospect of exposing the jury to long testimony from these biologists and theologians. He describes his objections in the following excerpt from the trial transcript.

Bryan's objections were upheld by Raulston. As a result, testimony from scientists and religious leaders for the defense was limited to written briefs. These briefs were submitted by Clarence Darrow and the rest of the Scopes defense team in anticipation of a guilty verdict, so that they could be used during the appeals process.

Tell me that the parents of this day have not any right to declare that children are not to be taught this doctrine [of evolution]? Shall not be taken down from the high plane upon which God put man? Shall be detached from the throne of God and be compelled to link their ancestors with the jungle, tell that to these children? Why, my friend, if they believe it, they go back to scoff at the religion of their parents! And the parents have a right to say that no teacher paid by their money shall rob their children of faith in God and send them back to their homes, skeptical, infidels, or agnostics, or atheists.

This doctrine that they want taught, this doctrine that they would force upon the schools, where they will not let the Bible be read! ...

[Scientists] take all life as a mystery that nobody can explain, and they want you to let them commence there and ask no questions. They want to come in with their little padded up evolution that commences with nothing and ends nowhere. They do not dare to tell you that it ended with God. They come here with this bunch of stuff that they call evolution, that they tell you that everybody believes in, but do not know that everybody knows as a fact, and nobody can tell how it came, and they do not explain the great riddle of the universe—they do not deal with the problems of life—they do not teach the great science of how to live—and yet they would undermine the faith of these little children in that God who stands back of everything and whose promise we have that we shall live with him forever by and by. They shut God out of the world. They do not talk about God. Darwin says the beginning of all things is a mystery unsolvable by us. He does not pretend to say how these things started....

Our contention is, even if they put God back [into the process of evolution], it does not make it harmonious with the Bible. The court is right that unless they put God back there, it must dispute the Bible.... They did not tell us where in this long period of time, between the cell at the bottom of the sea and man, where man became endowed with the hope of immortality. They did not, if you please, and most of them do not go to the place to hunt for it, because more than half of the scientists in this country ... do not believe there is a God or personal immortality, and they want to teach that to these children, and take that from them, to take from them their belief in a God who stands ready to welcome his children.

And your Honor asked me whether it has anything to do with the principle of the virgin birth. Yes, because this principle of evolution disputes the miracle; there is no place for the miracle in this train of evolution, and the Old Testament and the New are filled with miracles, and if this doctrine is true, this logic eliminates every mystery in the Old Testament and the New, and eliminates everything supernatural, and that means they eliminate the virgin birth—that means that they eliminate the resurrection of the body—that means that they eliminate the doctrine of atonement and they believe man has been rising all the time, that man never fell, that when the Savior came there was not any reason for His coming, there was no reason why He should not go as soon as He could, that He was born of Joseph or some other co-respondent, and that He lies in his grave, and when the Christians of this state have tied their hands and said we will not take advantage of our power to teach religion to our children, by teachers paid by us, these people come in from the outside of the state and force upon the people of this state and upon the children of the taxpayers of this state a doctrine that refutes not only their belief in God, but their belief in a Savior and belief in heaven, and takes from them every moral standard that the Bible gives us....

Your Honor, we first pointed out that we do not need any experts in science.... And when it comes to Bible experts, every member of the jury is as good an expert on the Bible as any man that they could bring, or that we could bring. The one beauty about the word of God is, it does not take an expert to understand it. They have translated that Bible into five hundred languages, they have carried it into nations where but a few can read a word, or write, to people who never saw a book, who never read, and yet can understand the Bible, and they can accept the salvation that that Bible offers, and they can know more about that book by accepting Jesus and feeling in their hearts the sense of their sins forgiven than all of the skeptical outside Bible experts that could come in here to talk to the people of Tennessee about the construction that they place upon the Bible, that is foreign to the construction that the people here place on it. Therefore, your Honor, we believe that this evidence is not competent.... Why should we prolong this case?

We can bring our experts here for the Christians; for every one they can bring who does not believe in Christianity, we can bring more than one who believes in the Bible and rejects evolution, and our witnesses will be just as good experts as theirs on a question of that kind. We could have a thousand or a million witnesses, but this case as to whether evolution is true or not, is not going to be tried here, within this city; if it is carried to the state's courts, it will not be tried there, and if it is taken to the great court at Washington, it will not be tried there. No, my friends, no court of the law, and no jury, great or small, is going to destroy the issue between the believer and the unbeliever. The Bible is the word of God; the Bible is the only expression of man's hope of salvation. The Bible, the record of the Song of God, the Savior of the world, born of the virgin Mary, crucified and risen again. That Bible is not going to be driven out of this court by experts who come hundreds of miles to testify that they can reconcile evolution, with its ancestor in the jungle, with man made by God in his image, and put here for purposes as a part of the divine plan. No, we are not going to settle that question here, and I think we ought to confine ourselves to the law and to the evidence that can be admitted in accordance with the law. Your court is an office of this state, and we who represent the state as counsel are officers of the state, and we cannot humiliate the great state of Tennessee by admitting for a moment that people can come from anywhere and protest against the enforcement of this state's laws on the grounds that it does not conform with their ideas, or because it banishes from our schools a thing they believe in and think ought to be taught in spite of the protest of those who employ the teacher and pay him his salary.

The facts are simple, the case is plain, and if those gentlemen want to enter upon a larger field of educational work on the subject of evolution, let us get through with this case and then convene a mock court for it will deserve the title of mock court if its purpose is to banish from the hearts of the people the word of God as revealed!

Source: Allen, Leslie H. *Bryan and Darrow at Dayton.* New York: Russell and Russell, 1925.

Dudley Malone Speaks on Science, Religion, and the Quest for Truth

William Jennings Bryan made his first major oration of the Scopes trial on Thursday, July 16, 1925, on the trial's fifth day. His remarks were part of a prosecution effort to convince Judge John T. Raulston not to allow several defense "experts" to take the witness stand. After Bryan completed his remarks, defense attorney Dudley Field Malone rose and delivered a dramatic reply. Years later, John Scopes himself described Malone's speech as the highlight of the trial. Even Tennessee lawmaker John Butler—author of the state's anti-evolution act that was at the center of the trial—reportedly declared that Malone's address ranked as "the finest speech of the century."

In this excerpt from his impassioned oration, Malone discusses the different aims of science and religion and challenges Bryan to debate the assembled scientists and theologians who support evolution. In addition, he expresses confidence that American teachers and young people can study science without becoming morally corrupt. Malone's efforts came to naught, however, as Raulston sided with Bryan and his allies on the issue of hearing the defense's expert witnesses.

If the court please, it does seem to me that we have gone far afield in this discussion. However, probably this is the time to discuss everything that bears on the issues that have been raised in this case, because after all, whether Mr. Bryan knows it or not, he is a mammal, he is an animal and he is a man. But, your Honor, I would like to advert to the law, and to remind the court that the heart of the matter is the question of whether there is liability under this law.

I have been puzzled and interested at one and the same time at the psychology of the prosecution and I find it difficult to distinguish between Mr. Bryan the lawyer in this case; Mr. Bryan, the propagandist outside of this case; and the Mr. Bryan who made a speech against science and for religion just now—Mr. Bryan my old chief and friend. I know Mr. Bryan. I don't know Mr. Bryan as well as Mr. Bryan knows Mr. Bryan, but I know this, that he does believe—and Mr. Bryan, your Honor, is not the only one who believes in the Bible. As a matter of fact there has been much criticism, by indirection and implication, of this text, or synopsis, if you please, that does not agree with their ideas. If we depended on the agreement of theologians, we would all be infidels....

Are we to hold mankind to a literal understanding of the claim that the world is 6,000 years old, because of the limited vision of men who believed the world was flat, and that the earth was the center of the universe, and that man is the center of the earth? …Are we to have our children know nothing about science except what the church says they shall know? I have never seen harm in learning and understanding, in humility and open-mindedness, and I have never seen clearer the need of that learning than when I see the attitude of the prosecution, who attack and refuse to accept the information and intelligence, which expert witnesses will give them.

Mr. Bryan may be satisfactory to thousands of people. It is in so many ways that he is satisfactory to me; his enthusiasm, his vigor, his courage, his fighting ability these long years for the things he thought were right. And many a time I have fought with him, and for him; and when I did not think he was right, I fought just as hard against him. This is not a conflict of personages; it is a conflict of ideas, and I think this case has been developed by men of two frames of mind.

Your Honor, there is a difference between theological and scientific men. Theology deals with something that is established and revealed; it seeks to gather material, which they claim should not be changed; it is literal, it is not to be interpreted. That is the theological mind. It deals with theology. The scientific is a modern thing, your Honor…. The difference between the theological mind and the scientific mind is that the theological mind is closed, because that is what is revealed and is settled. But the scientist says no, the Bible is the book of revealed religion, with rules of conduct, and with aspirations—that is the Bible. The scientist says, take the Bible as guide, as an inspiration, as a set of philosophies and preachments in the world of theology.

And what does this law do? We have been told here that this was not a religious question. I defy anybody, after Mr. Bryan's speech, to believe that this was not a religious question. Mr. Bryan brought all of the foreigners into this case. Mr. Bryan had offered his services from Miami, Florida; he does not belong in Tennessee. If it be wrong for American citizens from other parts of this country to come to Tennessee to discuss issues which we believe, then Mr. Bryan has no right here, either.…

These gentlemen say the Bible contains the truth—if the world of science can produce any truth or facts not in the Bible as we understand it, then destroy science, but keep the Bible. And we say, "Keep your Bible." Keep it as your consolation, keep it as your guide, but keep it where it belongs, in the world of your own conscience, in the world of your individual judgment, in the world of the Protestant conscience that I heard so much about when I was a boy, keep your Bible in the world of theology where it belongs and do not try to tell an intelligent world and the intelligence of this country that these books written by men who knew none of the accepted fundamental facts of science can be put into a course of science, because what are they doing here? This law says what? It says that no theory of creation can be taught in a course of science, except one which conforms with the theory of divine creation as set forth in the Bible. In other words, it says that only the Bible shall be taken as an authority on the subject of evolution in a course on biology....

I believe and we believe that men who are God-fearing, who are giving their lives to study and observation, to the teaching of the young—are the teachers and scientists of this country in a combination to destroy the morals of the children to whom they have dedicated their lives? Are preachers the only ones in America who care about our youth? Is the church the only source of morality in this country? And I would like to say something for the children of the country. We have no fears about the young people of America. They are a pretty smart generation. Any teacher who teaches the boys and girls today an incredible theory—we need not worry about those children of this generation paying much attention to it. The children of this generation are pretty wise. People, as a matter of fact I feel that the children of this generation are probably much wiser than many of their elders. The least that this generation can do, your Honor, is to give the next generation all the facts, all the available data, all the theories, all the information that learning, that study, that observation has produced—give it to the children in the hope of heaven that they will make a better world of this than we have been able to make it. We have just had a war with twenty million dead. Civilization is not so proud of the work of the adults. Civilization need not be so proud of what the grown-ups have done. For God's sake let the children have their minds kept open—close no doors to their knowledge; shut no door from them. Make the distinction between theology and science. Let them have both. Let them both be taught. Let them both live....

There is never a duel with the truth. The truth always wins and we are not afraid of it. The truth is no coward. The truth does not need the law. The truth does not need the forces of government. The truth does not need Mr. Bryan. The truth is imperishable, eternal, and immortal and needs no human agency to support it. We are ready to tell the truth as we understand it and we do not fear all the truth that they can present as facts. We are ready. We are ready. We feel we stand with progress. We feel we stand with science. We feel we stand with intelligence. We feel we stand with fundamental freedom in America. We are not afraid. Where is the fear? We meet it! Where is the fear? We defy it!

Source: Allen, Leslie H. *Bryan and Darrow at Dayton.* New York: Russell and Russell, 1925.

Darrow's Cross-Examination of Bryan

A large crowd had gathered on what was expected to be the final day of the Scopes "Monkey Trial." In a surprise move, however, defense attorney Clarence Darrow called prosecuting attorney William Jennings Bryan to the witness stand as an expert on the Bible. Two hours of riveting debate followed as Bryan, who had the audience squarely in his corner, entered into a tense verbal duel with Darrow. Their sharp exchanges were highlighted by Darrow's repeated challenges to Bryan's stated belief in Biblical literalism (that every event and story in the Bible is literally true), and by Bryan's stated determination to defend the Bible against "atheists and agnostics" such as Darrow.

Following are excerpts from Darrow's interrogation of Bryan, which took place on Monday, July 20, 1925.

Darrow: You have given considerable study to the Bible, haven't you, Mr. Bryan?

Bryan: Yes sir, I have tried to.

Darrow: Well, we all know you have. We are not going to dispute that at all. But you have written and published articles almost weekly, and sometimes have made interpretations of various things?

Bryan: I would not say interpretations, Mr. Darrow, but comments on the lesson.

Darrow: If you comment to any extent these comments have been interpretations?

Bryan: I presume that my discussion might be to some extent interpretations, but they have not been primarily intended as interpretations.

Darrow: But you have studied that question, of course?

Bryan: Of what?

Darrow: Interpretation of the Bible.

Bryan: On this particular question?

Darrow: Yes, sir.

Bryan: Yes, sir.

Darrow: Then you have made a general study of it?

Bryan: Yes, I have; I have studied the Bible for about fifty years, or sometime more than that, but, of course, I have studied it more as I have become older than when I was but a boy.

Darrow: Do you claim that everything in the Bible should be literally interpreted?

Bryan: I believe everything in the Bible should be accepted as it is given there; some of the Bible is given illustratively. For instance: "Ye are the salt of the earth." I would not insist that man was actually salt, or that he had flesh of salt, but it is used in the sense of salt as saving God's people….

[After questioning Bryan on the matters of the story of Jonah and the whale and the account of the sun standing still as described in the Book of Joshua, Darrow moved on to probe Bryan's views of the great flood described in the Book of Genesis.]

Darrow: You believe the story of the flood to be a literal interpretation?

Bryan: Yes, sir.

Darrow: When was that Flood?

Bryan: I would not attempt to fix the date. The date is fixed….

Darrow: About 4004 B.C.?

Bryan: That has been the estimate of a man that is accepted today. I would not say it is accurate.

Darrow: That estimate is printed in the Bible?

Bryan: Everybody knows, at least, I think most of the people know, that was the estimate given.

Darrow: But what do you think that the Bible, itself says? Don't you know how it was arrived at?

Bryan: I never made a calculation.

Darrow: A calculation from what?

Bryan: I could not say.

Darrow: From the generations of man?

Bryan: I would not want to say that.

Darrow: What do you think?

Bryan: I do not think about things I don't think about.

Darrow: Do you think about things you do think about?

Bryan: Well, sometimes.

(Laughter from audience)

Policeman: Let us have order....

Stewart [District Attorney]: Your honor, he is perfectly able to take care of this, but we are attaining no evidence. This is not competent evidence.

Bryan: These gentlemen have not had much chance—they did not come here to try this case. They came here to try revealed religion. I am here to defend it and they can ask me any question they please.

The Court [Judge Raulston]: All right.

(Applause from the audience.)

Darrow: Great applause from the bleachers.

Bryan: From those whom you call "yokels."

Darrow: I have never called them yokels.

Bryan: That is the ignorance of Tennessee, the bigotry.

Darrow: You mean who are applauding you?

(Applause from the audience.)

Bryan: Those are the people whom you insult.

Darrow: You insult every man of science and learning in the world because he does not believe in your fool religion.

The Court: I will not stand for that.

Darrow: For what he is doing?

The Court: I am talking to both of you....

[Order was restored and further questioning commenced.]

Darrow: How long ago was the Flood, Mr. Bryan?

Bryan: Let me see Ussher's calculation about it....It is given here, as 2348 years B.C.

Darrow: Well, 2348 years B.C. You believe that all the living things that were not contained in the ark were destroyed?

Bryan: I think the fish may have lived.

Darrow: Outside of the fish?

Bryan: I cannot say.

Darrow: You cannot say?

Bryan: No, except that just as it is, I have no proof to the contrary.

Darrow: I am asking you whether you believe?

Bryan: I do.

Darrow: That all living things outside of fish were destroyed?

Bryan: What I say about the fish is merely a matter of humor.

Darrow: You are not satisfied there is any civilization that can be traced back 5,000 years?

Bryan: I would not want to say there is because I have no evidence of it that is satisfactory.

Darrow: Would you say there is not?

Bryan: Well, so far as I know, but when the scientists differ, from 24,000,000 to 306,000,000 in their opinion, as to how long ago life came here. I want them nearer, to come nearer together before they demand of me to give up my belief in the Bible.

Darrow: Do you say that you do not believe that there were any civilizations on this earth that reach back beyond 5,000 years?

Bryan: I am not satisfied by any evidence that I have seen.

Darrow: Let me make this definite. You believe that every civilization on the earth and every living thing, except possibly the fishes, that came out of the ark were wiped out by the Flood?

Bryan: At that time.

Darrow: At that time. And then, whatever human beings, including all the tribes, that inhabited the world, and have inhabited the world, and who run their pedigree straight back, and all the animals, have come onto the earth since the Flood?

Bryan: Yes.

Darrow: Within 4200 years. Do you know a scientific man on the face of the earth that believes any such thing?

Bryan: I cannot say, but I know some scientific men who dispute entirely the antiquity of man as testified to by other scientific men.

Darrow: Oh, that does not answer the question. Do you know of a single scientific man on the face of the earth that believes any such thing as you stated, about the antiquity of man?

Bryan: I don't think I have ever asked one the direct question.

Darrow: Quite important, isn't it?

Bryan: Well, I don't know as it is.

Darrow: It might not be?

Bryan: If I had nothing else to do except speculate on what our remote ancestors were and what our remote descendants have been, but I have been more interested in Christians going on right now, to make it much more important than speculation on either the past or the future.

Darrow: You have never had any interest in the age of the various races and people and civilization and animals that exist upon the earth today? Is that right?

Bryan: I have never felt a great deal of interest in the effort that has been made to dispute the Bible by the speculations of men, or the investigations of men.

Darrow: Are you the only human being on earth who knows what the Bible means?

Stewart: I object.

The Court: Sustained.

Darrow: You do know that there are thousands of people who profess to be Christians who believe the earth is much more ancient and that the human race is much more ancient?

Bryan: I think there may be.

Darrow: And you have never investigated to find out how long man has been on the earth?

Bryan: I have never found it necessary.

Darrow: For any reason, whatever it is?

Bryan: To examine every speculation; but if I had done it I never would have done anything else.

Darrow: I ask for a direct answer.

Bryan: I do not expect to find out all those things, and I do not expect to find out about races.

Darrow: I didn't ask you that. Now, I ask you if you know if it was interesting enough, or important enough for you to try to find out about how old these ancient civilizations were?

Bryan: No; I have not made a study of it.

Darrow: Don't you know that the ancient civilizations of China are 6,000 or 7,000 years old, at the very least?

Bryan: No, but they would not run back beyond the creation, according to the Bible, 6,000 years.

Darrow: You have never in all your life made any attempt to find out about the other peoples of the earth—how old their civilizations are—how long they had existed on the earth, have you?

Bryan: No, sir. I am not afraid now that you will show me any.... I have all the information I need to live and die by.

Darrow: And that's all you're interested in?

Bryan: I am not looking for any more on religion.

Darrow: You don't care how old the earth is, how old man is, and how long the animals have been here?

Bryan: I am not so much interested in that.

Darrow: You have never made any investigation to find out?

Bryan: No, sir, I have never.

Darrow: All right....

[Darrow continued to question Bryan about various Biblical miracles, finally arriving at the creation account in the Book of Genesis.]

Darrow: Have you any idea how old the earth is?

Bryan: No.

Darrow: The book you have introduced in evidence tells you, doesn't it?

Bryan: I don't think it does, Mr. Darrow.

Darrow: Let's see whether it does; is this the one?

Bryan: That is the one, I think.

Darrow: It says B.C. 4004?

Bryan: That is Bishop Ussher's calculation.

Darrow: That is printed in the Bible you introduced?

Bryan: Yes, sir.

Darrow: And numerous other Bibles?

Bryan: Yes, sir....

Darrow: Would you say that the earth was only 4,000 years old?

Bryan: Oh no; I think it is much older than that.

Darrow: How much?

Bryan: I couldn't say.

Darrow: Do you say whether the Bible itself says it is older than that?

Bryan: I don't think the Bible says itself whether it is older or not.

Darrow: Do you think the earth was made in six days?

Bryan: Not six days of twenty-four hours.

Darrow: Doesn't it say so?

Bryan: No, sir.

Stewart: I want to interpose another objection. What is the purpose of this examination?

Bryan: The purpose is to cast ridicule on everybody who believes in the Bible, and I am perfectly willing that the world shall know that these gentlemen have no other purpose than ridiculing every Christian who believes in the Bible.

Darrow: We have the purpose of preventing bigots and ignoramuses from controlling the education of the United States and you know it, and that is all.

Bryan: I am glad to bring out that statement. I want the world to know that this evidence is not for the view Mr. Darrow and his associates have filed affidavits here stating, the purposes of which I understand it, is to show that the Bible story is not true.

Malone: Mr. Bryan seems anxious to get some evidence in the record that would tend to show that those affidavits are not true.

Bryan: I am not trying to get anything into the record. I am simply trying to protect the word of God against the greatest atheist or agnostic in the United States!

(Applause from the audience.)

Bryan: I want the papers to know I am not afraid to get on the stand in front of him and let him do his worst! I want the world to know!

(Prolonged applause from the audience.)

Darrow: I wish I could get a picture of these clappers.

[*The attorneys for the prosecution and defense argued about the admissibility of Bryan's testimony, even as an affidavit for an appeal. Bryan again defended his answers, claiming that he welcomed an opportunity to assert his beliefs.*]

The Court: Are you about through, Mr. Darrow?

Darrow: I want to ask a few more questions about the creation.

The Court: I know. We are going to adjourn when Mr. Bryan comes off the stand for the day. Be very brief, Mr. Darrow. Of course, I believe I will make myself clearer. Of course, it is incompetent testimony before the jury. The only reason I am allowing this to go in at all is that they may have it in the appellate court as showing what the affidavit would be.

Bryan: The reason I am answering is not for the benefit of the superior court. It is to keep these gentlemen from saying I was afraid to meet them and let them question me, and I want the Christian world to know that any atheist, agnostic, unbeliever, can question me anytime as to my belief in God, and I will answer him.

Darrow: I want to take an exception to this conduct of this witness. He may be very popular down here in the hills. I do not need to have his explanation for his answer....

Bryan: Your honor, they have not asked a question legally and the only reason they have asked any question is for the purpose, as the question about Jonah was asked, for a chance to give this agnostic an opportunity to criticize a believer in the world of God; and I answered the question in order to shut his mouth so that he cannot go out and tell his atheistic friends that I would not answer his questions. That is the only reason, no more reason in the world.

Malone: Your honor on this very subject, I would like to say that I would have asked Mr. Bryan—and I consider myself as good a Christian as he is—

every question that Mr. Darrow has asked him for the purpose of bringing out whether or not there is to be taken in this court a literal interpretation of the Bible, or whether, obviously, as these questions indicate, if a general and literal construction cannot be put upon the parts of the Bible which have been covered by Mr. Darrow's questions. I hope for the last time no further attempt will be made by counsel on the other side of the case, or Mr. Bryan, to say the defense is concerned at all with Mr. Darrow's particular religious views or lack of religious views. We are here as lawyers with the same right to our views. I have the same right to mine as a Christian as Mr. Bryan has to his, and we do not intend to have this case charged by Mr. Darrow's agnosticism or Mr. Bryan's brand of Christianity.

(Applause from the audience.)

[Darrow then began his last string of questions.]

Darrow: Mr. Bryan, do you believe that the first woman was Eve?

Bryan: Yes.

Darrow: Do you believe she was literally made out of Adams's rib?

Bryan: I do.

Darrow: Did you ever discover where Cain got his wife?

Bryan: No, sir; I leave the agnostics to hunt for her.

Darrow: You have never found out?

Bryan: I have never tried to find.

Darrow: You have never tried to find?

Bryan: No.

Darrow: The Bible says he got one, doesn't it? Were there other people on the earth at that time?

Bryan: I cannot say.

Darrow: You cannot say. Did that ever enter your consideration?

Bryan: Never bothered me.

Darrow: There were no others recorded, but Cain got a wife.

Bryan: That is what the Bible says.

Darrow: Where she came from you do not know. All right. Does the statement, "The morning and the evening were the first day," and "The morning and the evening were the second day," mean anything to you?

Bryan: I do not think it necessarily means a twenty-four-hour day.

Darrow: You do not?

Bryan: No.

Darrow: What do you consider it to be?

Bryan: I have not attempted to explain it. If you will take the second chapter—let me have the book. (Examining Bible.) The fourth verse of the second chapter says: "These are the generations of the heavens and of the earth, when they were created in the day that the Lord God made the earth and the heavens," the word "day" there in the very next chapter is used to describe a period. I do not see that there is any necessity for construing the words, "the evening and the morning," as meaning necessarily a twenty-four-hour day, "in the day when the Lord made the heaven and the earth."

Darrow: Then, when the Bible said, for instance, "and God called the firmament heaven. And the evening and the morning were the second day," that does not necessarily mean twenty-four hours?

Bryan: I do not think it necessarily does.

Darrow: Do you think it does or does not?

Bryan: I know a great many think so.

Darrow: What do you think?

Bryan: I do not think it does.

Darrow: You think those were not literal days?

Bryan: I do not think they were twenty-four-hour days.

Darrow: What do you think about it?

Bryan: That is my opinion—I do not know that my opinion is better on that subject than those who think it does.

Darrow: You do not think that?

Bryan: No. But I think it would be just as easy for the kind of God we believe in to make the earth in six days as in six years or in 6,000,000 years or in 600,000,000 years. I do not think it important whether we believe one or the other.

Darrow: Do you think those were literal days?

Bryan: My impression is they were periods, but I would not attempt to argue as against anybody who wanted to believe in literal days.

Darrow: Do you have any idea of the length of the periods?

Bryan: No; I don't....

Darrow: I will read ... to you from the Bible: "And the Lord God said unto the serpent, because thou hast done this, thou art cursed above all cattle, and above every beast of the field; upon thy belly shalt thou go and dust shalt thou eat all the days of thy life." Do you think that is why the serpent is compelled to crawl upon its belly?

Bryan: I believe that.

Darrow: Have you any idea how the snake went before that time?

Bryan: No, sir.

Darrow: Do you know whether he walked on his tail or not?

Bryan: No, sir. I have no way to know.

(Laughter from the audience.)

Darrow: Now, you refer to the cloud that was put in heaven after the flood, the rainbow. Do you believe in that?

Bryan: Read it.

Darrow: All right, Mr. Bryan, I will read it for you.

Bryan: Your Honor, I think I can shorten this testimony. The only purpose Mr. Darrow has is to slur at the Bible, but I will answer his question. I will answer it all at once, and I have no objection in the world, I want the world to know that this man, who does not believe in a God, is trying to use a court in Tennessee—

Darrow: I object to that.

Bryan: —to slur at it, and while it will require time, I am willing to take it.

Darrow: I object to your statement. I am examining you on your fool ideas that no intelligent Christian on earth believes.

[At that point Judge Raulston adjourned the court for the day.]

Source: Allen, Leslie H. *Bryan and Darrow at Dayton.* New York: Russell and Russell, 1925.

Clarence Darrow Asks the Jury to Return a "Guilty" Verdict

On July 21, 1925, the eighth day of the Scopes Trial, defense attorney Clarence Darrow announced that since Judge Raulston refused to admit the testimony of defense experts, there was little left to do but find Scopes guilty. At that point, he added, the legal battle over the case could move along to the court of appeals.

Darrow's explicit request for a guilty verdict brought the "Monkey Trial" to an oddly subdued and anticlimactic close. The jury filed out, and nine minutes later it returned with a verdict in hand. The foreman announced that they found John T. Scopes guilty as charged. Following is the complete text of Darrow's final remarks to the jury.

May I say a few words to the jury? Gentlemen of the jury, we are sorry to have not had a chance to say anything to you. We will do it some other time. Now, we came down to offer evidence in this case and the court has held under the law that the evidence we had is not admissible, so all we can do is to take an exception and carry it to a higher court to see whether the evidence is admissible or not. As far as this case stands before the jury, the court has told you very plainly that if you think my client taught that man descended from a lower order of animals, you will find him guilty, and you heard the testimony of the boys on those questions and heard read the books, and there is no dispute about the facts.

Scopes did not go on the stand, because he could not deny the statements made by the boys. I do not know how you may feel, I am not especially interested in it, but this case and this law will never be decided until it gets to a higher court, and it cannot get to a higher court probably, very well, unless you bring in a verdict. So, I do not want any of you to think we are going to find any fault with you as to your verdict. I am frank to say, while we think it is wrong, and we ought to have been permitted to put in our evidence, the court felt otherwise, as he had a right to hold. We cannot argue to you gentlemen under the instructions given by the court—we cannot even explain to you that we think you should return a verdict of not guilty. We do not see how you could. We do not ask it. We think we will save our point and take it to the higher court and settle whether the law is good, and also whether he should have permitted the evidence. I guess that is plain enough.

Source: Allen, Leslie H. *Bryan and Darrow at Dayton.* New York: Russell and Russell, 1925.

Bryan's Closing Summation

The sudden conclusion of the Scopes trial robbed William Jennings Bryan of the opportunity to deliver a summation speech that he had prepared for the jury. But instead of tucking the speech in a drawer to gather dust, Bryan spent the next few days after the trial delivering it to appreciative crowds all around Tennessee. He then returned to Dayton, where he was scheduled to make a public address to supporters. But he died in his sleep upon his return to Dayton, a mere six days after the trial had ended. Following is an excerpt from the summation that Bryan delivered to Tennessee audiences in the last few days of his life.

Religion is not hostile to learning; Christianity has been the greatest patron learning has ever had. But Christians know that "the fear of the Lord is the beginning of wisdom" now just as it has been in the past, and they therefore oppose the teaching of guesses that encourage godlessness among the students.

Neither does Tennessee undervalue the service rendered by science. The Christian men and women of Tennessee know how deeply mankind is indebted to science for benefits conferred by the discovery of the laws of nature and by the designing of machinery for the utilization of these laws. Give science a fact and it is not only invincible, but it is of incalculable service to man. If one is entitled to draw from society in proportion to the service that he renders to society, who is able to estimate the reward earned by those who have given to us the use of steam, the use of electricity and enabled us to utilize the weight of water that flows down the mountainside? Who will estimate the value of the service rendered by those who invented the phonograph, the telephone and the radio? Or, to come more closely to our home life, how shall we recompense those who gave us the sewing machine, the harvester, the threshing machine, the tractor, the automobile and the method now employed in making artificial ice? The department of medicine also opens an unlimited field for invaluable service. Typhoid and yellow fever are not feared as they once were. Diphtheria and pneumonia have been robbed of some of their terrors, and a high place on the scroll of fame still awaits the discovery of remedies for arthritis, cancer, tuberculosis and other dread diseases to which mankind is heir.

Christianity welcomes truth from whatever source it comes and is not afraid that any real truth from any source can interfere with the divine truth that comes by inspiration from God Himself. It is not scientific truth to which

Christians object, for true science is classified knowledge, and nothing therefore can be scientific unless it is true...

Evolution is not truth; it is merely a hypothesis—it is millions of guesses strung together. It had not been proven in the days of Darwin—he expressed astonishment that with two or three million species it had been impossible to trace any species to any other species—it had not been proven in the days of Huxley, and it has not been proven up to today. It is less than four years ago that Professor Bateson came all the way from London to Canada to tell the American scientists that every effort to trace one species to another had failed—every one. He said he still had faith in evolution but had doubts about the origin of species. But of what value is evolution if it cannot explain the origin of species? While many scientists accept evolution as if it were a fact, they all admit, when questioned, that no explanation has been found as to how one species developed into another.

Darwin suggested two laws, sexual attraction and natural selection. Sexual selection has been laughed out of the classroom and natural selection is being abandoned, and no new explanation is satisfactory even to scientists. Some of the more rash advocates of evolution are want to say that evolution is as firmly established as the law of gravitation or the Copernican theory. The absurdity of such a claim is apparent when we remember that any one can prove the law of gravitation by throwing a weight into the air and that any one can prove the roundness of the earth by going around it, while no one can prove evolution to be true in any way whatever...

Let us, then, hear the conclusion of the whole matter. Science is a magnificent material force, but it is not a teacher of morals. It can perfect machinery, but it adds no moral restraints to protect society from the misuse of the machine. It can also build gigantic intellectual ships, but it constructs no moral rudders for the control of storm-tossed human vessels. It not only fails to supply the spiritual element needed, but some of its unproven hypotheses rob the ship of its compass and ... endanger its cargo.

In war, science has proven itself an evil genius; it has made war more terrible than it ever was before. Man used to be content to slaughter his fellow man on a single plane—the earth's surface. Science has taught him to go down into the water and shoot up from below, and to go up into the clouds and shoot down from above, thus making the battlefield three times as bloody as it was before; but science does not teach brotherly love. Science has made war so hellish that civilization was about to commit suicide; and now we are told that newly discovered instruments of destruction will make the cruelties of the late war seem trivial in comparison with the cruelties of wars that may come in the future. If civilization is to be saved from the wreckage threatened by intelligence not consecrated by love, it must be saved by the moral code of the meek and lowly Nazarene. His teachings, and His teachings alone, can solve the problems that vex hearts and perplex the world.

The world needs a savior more than it ever did before, and there is only one name under heaven given among men whereby we must be saved. It is this name that evolution degrades, for, carried to its logical conclusion, it robs Christ of the glory of a Virgin birth, of the majesty of His deity and mission, and of the triumph of His resurrection. It also disputes the doctrine of the atonement.

This case is no longer local; the defendant ceases to play an important part. The case has assumed the proportions of a battle royal between unbelief that attempts to speak through so-called science and the defenders of the Christian faith, speaking through the legislators of Tennessee.

It is again a choice between God and Baal; it is also a renewal of the issue in Pilate's court. In that historic trial—the greatest in history—force, impersonated by Pilate, occupied the throne. Behind it was the Roman Government, mistress of the world, and behind the Roman Government were the legions of Rome. Before Pilate stood Christ, the Apostle of love. Force triumphed; they nailed him to the tree and those who stood around mocked and jeered and said, "He is dead." But from that day the power of Caesar waned and the power of Christ increased. In a few centuries the Roman Government was gone and its legions forgotten; while the crucified and risen Lord has become the greatest fact in history and the growing figure of all time.

Again force and love meet face to face, and the question, "What shall I do with Jesus?" must be answered. A bloody, brutal doctrine—evolution—demands, as the rabble did 1900 years ago, that He be crucified. That cannot be the answer of this jury, representing a Christian State and sworn to uphold the laws of Tennessee. Your answer will be heard throughout the world; it is eagerly awaited by a praying multitude. If the law is nullified, there will be rejoicing wherever God is repudiated, the Savior scoffed at, and the Bible ridiculed. Every unbeliever of every kind and degree will be happy.

If, on the other hand, the law is upheld and the religion of the school children protected, millions of Christians will call you blessed and, with hearts full of gratitude to God, will sing again that grand old song of triumph:

Faith of our Fathers, living still,
In spite of dungeon, fire and sword;
O, how our hearts beat high with joy,
Whene'er we heard that glorious word
Faith of our Fathers—holy faith;
We will be true to thee till death!

Source: Bryan, William Jennings. *Bryan's Last Speech: Undelivered Speech to the Jury in the Scopes Trial.* Oklahoma City: Sunlight Publishing Society, 1925.

Scopes Remembers the Monkey Trial—Forty Years Later

John T. Scopes penned a memoir in 1967, more than forty years after the celebrated "Monkey Trial" came to a close. The autobiography covers Scopes's memories of the trial in Dayton, as well as his later education and career as a petroleum geologist. In this excerpt, Scopes describes a return visit to Dayton, Tennessee, on the thirty-fifth anniversary of the "Monkey Trial" in 1960. During his visit he was a special guest at the world premiere of the Stanley Kramer-produced feature film, Inherit the Wind, *a fictionalized account of the trial. Scopes found the town much as he left it in 1925, with local opinion still fiercely divided on the famous trial and the issues it raised.*

Through the years I have had my share of interviews, crank letters, and telephone calls. Notoriety never completely releases its victims. July has usually been the worst time, as people remember it was the month of the Dayton trial. Again, in April and May when term papers are being written, the mail gets heavier with questions and requests. I made it a policy not to answer students' letters about the trial. I didn't have time to answer them all and I did not think it would be fair to answer them selectively. Many of my letters have come from preachers and from persons who have "got religion" and think I should get it too. Occasionally someone comes up with a new twist on religion and informs me of it. Others provide quotes from some part of the Bible for my particular benefit. Many write for autographs. I've never been able to understand how so many persons manage to find out how to get in touch with me.

In 1960 my role in the Dayton trial came to public attention anew because of the movie, *Inherit the Wind,* based upon the three-act play by Jerome Lawrence and Robert E. Lee, which in turn was inspired by the Dayton trial. Bertram Cates was the Scopeslike character in the movie, and I was to have a role in the build-up surrounding it. I had turned down a chance to see myself portrayed in the Broadway play years before. I'd been too busy and not interested enough to fly to New York to see it. In 1960 I changed my mind when Stanley Kramer, the producer, urged me to help promote the movie. I was to follow a carefully scheduled itinerary and to attend the premiere. As I pointed out to several newsmen, nothing in the trial or since had interrupted my normal routine as much as traveling to publicize *Inherit the*

Wind, and I probably wouldn't have gone if [wife] Mildred hadn't persuaded me to go. One reporter called me a "reluctant ballyhooist" and he was accurate enough. Of course, there were solid reasons for going. If nothing else, it was time to remind the people again of the importance of preserving their basic freedoms, as the defense had tried to do in the Dayton trial.

In July, I returned to Dayton for the thirty-fifth anniversary of the trial and the world premiere of *Inherit the Wind.* It was the first time I had been back since Mildred and I had driven through in late 1931. The town hadn't changed much. Many of the older people were dead. Others, such as Mack Jones, Whitney Morgan, and Fred Robinson, Jr., who were my age, were still around. I was the only surviving principal of the trial who attended; Bryan, Darrow, Hays, Raulston, Malone, and Neal all were dead. Others who had played lesser roles in the drama were there: F. R. Rogers, at whose home Bryan had died; Sue Hicks, now a judge; and J. B. Goodrich, W. G. Taylor, and J. H. Bowman, who had been jurors. (They have since died.) Rappelyea was not there; someone said he was in California. He had left Dayton many years before. I did not see Tom Stewart. A former U.S. Senator who had been defeated by Estes Kefauver in 1948, he was practicing law in Nashville. Nellie Kenyon, Warner Ogden (who was often mistaken for me, as he had been in 1925), Adolph Shelby Ochs, and others who had covered the trial attended the premiere, as did Watson Davis of Science Service, who had administered my scholarship fund; Rudd Brown, Bryan's granddaughter; and Miss Vera Raulston, a daughter of the judge. The mayor called it the second largest crowd in Dayton's history.

Doc Robinson was gone with the years. His drugstore, still there, had a new sign:

Shadows of the Dayton Trial
Scopes Soda
15 cents
Priced Now as Then
in Honor of Scopes' Return
to Dayton

Thirty-five years before, Dick Beamish, fresh from Philadelphia, had introduced the Beamish Specials to Dayton's drugstores. Ironically, because I had survived and had returned, my name supplanted Dick's on the most famous soda of the day, proof enough that true fame is fleeting while notoriety is enduring.

Major J. J. Rogers proclaimed a Scopes Trial Day and formally gave me the key to the city. Yet, not everyone was satisfied. That morning, a radio series called "Open Bible" began, featuring the Reverend Paul Levengood, director of the Tennessee Mountain Mission. "The devil is here in Dayton and is having a heyday," he said, in tones that sounded like an echo of 1925, and he probably was right. It made me suspect that if the trial had been held again, in 1960, the verdict would have been the same.

I couldn't see that the trial had altered the basic beliefs of most Daytonites. Teachers still had to sign a pledge that they wouldn't teach evolution. I was not surprised. A way of belief that has existed for decades cannot be radically modified overnight. A single event, such as the trial, accomplishes little in the changing of a culture. Prejudice is not unique to Tennessee; it is ubiquitous and not easily eradicated. On its simplest level, prejudice means people are afraid of what they don't know and don't understand. By these criteria, who of us is not afflicted by prejudice?

A plaque in Dayton recalled the sweating summer that the movie evoked. It read:

> Here, from July 10 to 21, 1925, John Thomas Scopes, a County High School teacher, was tried for expounding the theory of simian descent of man, in violation of a lately passed state law. William Jennings Bryan assisted the prosecution: Clarence Darrow, Arthur Garfield Hayes [sic] and Dudley Field Malone the defense. Scopes was convicted.

Myths die hard and Dayton is not the only place in America where evolution is still thought to mean that *homo sapiens* descended from monkeys rather than from common ancestors.

I enjoyed the movie. Of course, it altered the facts of the real trial. I was never jailed and I hadn't met my future wife until years later in Venezuela. I didn't mind such small liberties. They had to invent romance for the balcony set. Also, Matthew Harrison Brady, the Bryanlike character, died nearer the close of the trial than Bryan had. What was important, though, the film captured the emotions in the battle of words between Bryan and Darrow, who was represented by a character called Henry Drummond.

After the premiere at Dayton I rode the ballyhoo trail to Boston, New York, Washington, and Los Angeles. Inevitably I was interviewed over and over. Would I do it again? "If I were a young man with no outside obligations," I invariably replied, "my decision would be the same as it was in 1925. I would go home and think about it. I would sleep on it. And the next day I would do it again."

Source: Scopes, John T. "Shadows of the Dayton Trial," from *Center of the Storm: Memoirs of John T. Scopes*. New York: Holt, Rinehart, and Winston, 1967.

Tennessee Repeals the Butler Act

Tennessee's Butler Act remained a state law until 1967, when a Tennessee school teacher named Gary L. Scott threatened to challenge the statute in court. This caught the attention of leaders of the state legislature who feared the possible negative publicity of a "Scopes II" trial. After heated debate, the Tennessee state government overturned the Butler Act on May 13 (with an effective date of September 1, 1967).

PUBLIC ACTS
OF THE
STATE OF TENNESSEE
PASSED BY THE
EIGHTY - FIFTH GENERAL ASSEMBLY
1967

CHAPTER NO. 237
House Bill No. 48
(By Smith, Galbreath, Bradley)
SUBSTITUTED FOR : SENATE BILL NO. 46
(By Elam)
AN ACT to repeal Section 498 - 1922, Tennessee Code Annotated, prohibiting the teaching of evolution.

Be it enacted by the General Assembly of the State of Tennessee :

Section 1. Section 49 - 1922, Tennessee Code Annotated, is repealed.

Section 2. This Act shall take effect September 1, 1967.

Passed : May 13, 1967

Source: Public Acts of the State of Tennessee, 85th General Assembly, 1967, Chapter 27.

Introducing "Intelligent Design" in Dover, Pennsylvania

In 2004, the Dover Area School District Board of Education released a statement on intelligent design that the board would require science teachers to read to their classes prior to any teaching about evolutionary theory. This excerpt, taken from the judicial opinion that Judge John E. Jones III offered in the case of Kitzmiller et. al. v. Dover Area School District et. al., *provides the text of the statement that brought protests from parents, citizens, and teachers in the district, ultimately leading to the court case.*

IN THE UNITED STATES DISTRICT COURT
FOR THE MIDDLE DISTRICT OF PENNSYLVANIA

TAMMY KITZMILLER, <u>et.al.</u>
Plaintiffs

v.

DOVER AREA SCHOOL DISTRICT, <u>et.al.</u>
Defendants

MEMORANDUM OPINION
December 20, 2005

<u>INTRODUCTION</u>

On October 18, 2004, the Defendant Dover Area School Board of Directors passed by a 6-3 vote the following resolution:

> Students will be made aware of gaps/problems
> in Darwin's theory and of other theories of
> evolution including, but not limited to,
> intelligent design.
> Note: Origins of Life is not taught.

On November 19, 2004, the Defendant Dover Area School District announced by press release that, commencing in January 2005, teachers would be required to read the following statement to students in the ninth grade biology class at Dover High School:

> The Pennsylvania Academic Standards require
> Students to learn about Darwin's Theory of Evolution
> and eventually to take a standardized test of which
> evolution is a part.

Because Darwin's Theory is a theory, it continues to be tested as new evidence is discovered. The Theory is not a fact. Gaps in the Theory exist for which there is no evidence. A theory is defined as a well-tested explanation that unifies a broad range of observations.

Intelligent Design is an explanation of the origin of life that differs from Darwin's view. The reference book, *Of Pandas and People,* is available for students who might be interested in gaining an understanding of what Intelligent Design actually involves.

With respect to any theory, students are encouraged to keep an open mind. The school leaves the discussion of the Origins of Life to individual students and their families. As a Standards-driven district, class instruction focuses upon preparing students to achieve proficiency on Standards-based assessments.

Source: Kitzmiller v. Dover Area Scool District, 400 F. Supp. 2d 707 (M.D. Pa. 2005).

Judge Jones's Ruling Against Intelligent Design in Public Schools

In this excerpt from the 2005 trial, Kitzmiller et. al. v. Dover Area School District et. al., federal judge John E. Jones III gives his reasons for finding in favor of the plaintiffs that intelligent design is religion and not science, and therefore should not be debated in a biology classroom. Jones's 82-page decision includes his suggestion that this decision should end all debate about introduction of intelligent design principles in public schools, no matter how strongly certain members of the community might support intelligent design.

Excerpts from the ruling by The Honorable John E. Jones III, United States District Court for the Middle District of Pennsylvania, case of *Kitzmiller et. al. v. Dover Area School District et. al.,* 2005.

4. Whether ID [Intelligent Design] Is Science

After a searching review of the record and applicable caselaw, we find that while ID arguments may be true, a proposition on which the Court takes no position, ID is not science. We find that ID fails on three different levels, any one of which is sufficient to preclude a determination that ID is science. They are: (1) ID violates the centuries-old ground rules of science by invoking and permitting supernatural causation; (2) the argument of irreducible complexity, central to ID, employs the same flawed and illogical contrived dualism that doomed creation science in the 1980s; and (3) ID's negative attacks on evolution have been refuted by the scientific community…. It is additionally important to note that ID has failed to gain acceptance in the scientific community, it has not generated peer-reviewed publications, nor has it been the subject of testing and research….

ID is predicated on supernatural causation, … as various expert testimony revealed. ID takes a natural phenomenon and, instead of accepting or seeking a natural explanation, argues that the explanation is supernatural. Further support for the conclusion that ID is predicated on supernatural causation is found in the ID reference book to which ninth grade biology students [in Dover, Pennsylvania] are directed, [*Of Pandas and People*]. *Pandas* states, in pertinent part, as follows:

> Darwinists object to the view of intelligent design *because it does not give a natural cause explanation* of how the various

forms of life started in the first place. Intelligent design means that various forms of life began abruptly, through an intelligent agency, with their distinctive features already intact — fish with fins and scales, birds with feathers, beaks, and wings, etc.

Stated another way, ID posits that animals did not evolve naturally through evolutionary means but were created abruptly by a non-natural, or supernatural, designer. Defendants' own expert witnesses acknowledged this point.

It is notable that defense experts' own mission, which mirrors that of the IDM [Intelligent Design Movement] itself, is to change the ground rules of science to allow supernatural causation of the natural world.... Not a single expert witness over the course of the six week trial identified one major scientific association, society or organization that endorsed ID as science. What is more, defense experts concede that ID is not a theory as that term is defined by the [National Association of Science] and admit that ID is at best "fringe science" which has achieved no acceptance in the scientific community.... In addition to failing to produce papers in peer-reviewed journals, ID also features no scientific research or testing.

After this searching and careful review of ID as espoused by its proponents, as elaborated upon in submissions to the Court, and as scrutinized over a six week trial, we find that ID is not science and cannot be adjudged a valid, accepted scientific theory as it has failed to publish in peer-reviewed journals, engage in research and testing, and gain acceptance in the scientific community. ID, as noted, is grounded in theology, not science. Accepting for the sake of argument its proponents', as well as Defendants' argument that to introduce ID to students will encourage critical thinking, it still has utterly no place in a science curriculum. Moreover, ID's backers have sought to avoid the scientific scrutiny which we have now determined that it cannot withstand by advocating that the *controversy,* but not ID itself, should be taught in science class. This tactic is at best ingenuous, and at worst a canard. The goal of the IDM is not to encourage critical thought, but to foment a revolution which would supplant evolutionary theory with ID.

To conclude and reiterate, we express no opinion on the ultimate veracity of ID as a supernatural explanation. However, we commend to the attention of those who are inclined to superficially consider ID to be a true "scientific" alternative to evolution without a true understanding of the concept the foregoing detailed analysis. It is our view that a reasonable, objective observer would, after reviewing both the voluminous record in this case, and our narrative, reach the inescapable conclusion that ID is an interesting theological argument, but that it is not science.

Source: Kitzmiller v. Dover Area School District, 400 F. Supp. 2d 707 (M.D. Pa. 2005).

A Christian Explains His Belief in Darwinian Evolution

Ted Peters teaches systematic theology at Pacific Lutheran Theological Seminary and the Graduate Theological Union in Berkeley, California. He is co-author, with Martinez Hewlett, of the book Evolution from Creation to New Creation (2003). *In the following article, he explains how he reconciles his strong Christian faith with his belief in Darwin's evolutionary theory.*

In the dust storm kicked up by proponents of "Intelligent Design" over what should be taught in the public schools, the science of evolutionary biology—the Darwinian model of evolution—is dubbed as materialistic, reductionistic, and atheistic. The Intelligent Design advocates suggest that to be a Christian one must take a stand against Darwinism. According to them, to pursue scientific research under the principles of random variation and natural selection is un-Christian. So-called "theistic evolutionists" (a phrase actually coined by the creationists as a term of derision) are accused of selling out to the enemy.

In turn the scientific establishment tries to assert that to be religious is like having a disease that quarantines a person against participation in science. To accuse someone of holding a religious view about evolution helps to defend the hegemony of the Darwinian model in the public schools. Why? Because science is not subject to First Amendment proscriptions, while religion is. So, if you label your opponents "religious," you get the courts on your side.

The implication is that those who continue to believe in religious things are simply not smart enough to advance. When they become smart, they'll drop their religion and join the scientific community.

Intelligent Design proponents and creationists insist that the Darwinists are blinded by their atheism so they cannot see the limitations and gaps in their theory. These advocates argue that the very existence of complexity contradicts the standard theory of evolution, which assumes that change occurred gradually, slowly, step by step. They say that a qualitative leap to a higher order of complexity must be acknowledged, and that only an appeal to a transcendent intelligent designer provides an adequate explanation. Without quite using the word "stupid," intelligent design advocates suggest that insistence by Darwinists that natural selection suffices as an explanation shows at least a lack of open-mindedness.

What all of this leaves out is my group of friends and colleagues. I hang out with those so-called theistic evolutionists. We tend to think scientists are pretty smart. In fact, many of my colleagues are research scientists, even evolutionary biologists. We are convinced that the neo-Darwinian model of random genetic variation combined with natural selection provides the most adequate explanation for the development of life forms.

But my friends and colleagues are also religious, mostly Christian but with some other faiths mixed in. We think religious people can be pretty smart too. What is so important and what gets missed too often when the media covers the evolution wars is this: To be a Christian does not require that one be anti-Darwinian.

It's very possible that one could embrace the science of the Darwinian tradition and also embrace a Christian understanding of God at work in the natural world. I believe that God has used the evolution of life over deep time to serve a divine purpose for creation. This requires distinguishing between the strictly scientific Darwinian model and the atheism and related ideologies that have frequently been associated with evolution. The science is solid.

Christian faith seeks understanding, as St. Anselm put it. Historically, Christians have fallen in love with science. Faith loves science. Today, the Christian faith demands that our schools teach the best science, and only the best science. To teach inferior science would be stupid and, yes, irreligious.

Source: Peters, Ted. "Intelligent Religion: Are Science and Faith Really Incompatible?" *Sojourners*, December 2005.

An ID Proponent Explains Intelligent Design

Stephen C. Meyer is director and Senior Fellow of the Center for Science and Culture at the Discovery Institute, a conservative Seattle-based institution that describes itself as a champion of free market economic ideas, representative democracy, libertarian ideals of citizenship, and "Intelligent Design" theory. In the following article, Meyer explains his belief in intelligent design.

In December 2004 New Mexico Public Television scheduled, advertised and then, under pressure, canceled a documentary explaining the scientific case for a theory of biological origins known as intelligent design.

In the same month, a renowned British philosopher, Antony Flew, made worldwide news when he repudiated a lifelong commitment to atheism, citing among other factors, evidence of intelligent design in the DNA molecule.

Also in December, the ACLU filed suit to prevent a Dover, Penn. school district from informing its students about the theory of intelligent design.

In February, *The Wall Street Journal* reported that an evolutionary biologist with two doctorates had been punished for publishing a peer-reviewed scientific article making a case for this same theory.

More recently, the Pope, the President of the United States and the Dalai Lama have each weighed in on the subject.

But what is this theory of intelligent design? And why does it arouse such passion and inspire such apparently determined efforts to suppress it?

According to a spate of recent media reports, intelligent design is a new "faith-based" alternative to evolution—an alternative based entirely on religion rather than scientific evidence.

As the story goes, intelligent design is just creationism repackaged by religious fundamentalists in order to circumvent a 1987 Supreme Court prohibition against teaching creationism in the public schools.

Over the last year, many major U.S. newspapers, magazines and broadcast outlets have run stories repeating this same trope.

But is it accurate?

As one of the architects of the theory of intelligent design, and the director of a research center that supports the work of scientists developing the theory, I know that it isn't.

The modern theory of intelligent design was not developed in response to a legal setback for creationists in 1987. Instead, it was first formulated in the late 1970s and early 1980s by a group of scientists—Charles Thaxton, Walter Bradley, Roger Olson, and Dean Kenyon—who were trying to account for an enduring mystery of modern biology: the origin of the digital information encoded along the spine of the DNA molecule.

In the book *The Mystery of Life's Origin*, Thaxton and his colleagues first developed the idea that the information-bearing properties of DNA provided strong evidence of a prior but unspecified designing intelligence. *Mystery* was published in 1984 by a prestigious New York publisher—three years before the Edwards v. Aguillard decision.

Even as early the 1960s and 70s, physicists had begun to reconsider the design hypothesis. Many were impressed by the discovery that the laws and constants of physics are improbably "finely-tuned" to make life possible. As British astrophysicist Fred Hoyle put it, the fine-tuning of numerous physical parameters in the universe suggested that "a superintellect had monkeyed with physics" for our benefit.

Nevertheless, only the most committed conspiracy theorist could see in these intellectual developments a concealed legal strategy or an attempt to smuggle religion into the classroom.

But what exactly is the theory of intelligent design?

Contrary to media reports, intelligent design is not a religious-based idea, but instead an evidence-based scientific theory about life's origins—one that challenges strictly materialistic views of evolution. According to Darwinian biologists such as Oxford's Richard Dawkins, livings systems "give the appearance of having been designed for a purpose." But, for modern Darwinists, that appearance of design is entirely illusory.

Why? According to neo-Darwinism, wholly undirected processes such as natural selection and random mutations are fully capable of producing the intricate designed-like structures in living systems. In their view, natural selection can mimic the powers of a designing intelligence without itself being directed by an intelligence.

In contrast, the theory of intelligent design holds that there are tell-tale features of living systems and the universe that are best explained by an intelligent cause. The theory does not challenge the idea of evolution defined as change over time, or even common ancestry, but it does dispute Darwin's idea that the cause of biological change is wholly blind and undirected.

Either life arose as the result of purely undirected material processes or a guiding intelligence played a role. Design theorists favor the latter option and argue that living organisms look designed because they really were designed.

But why do we say this? What tell-tale signs of intelligence do we see in living organisms?

Over the last 25 years, scientists have discovered an exquisite world of nanotechnology within living cells. Inside these tiny labyrinthine enclosures, scientists have found functioning turbines, miniature pumps, sliding clamps, complex circuits, rotary engines, and machines for copying, reading and editing digital information—hardly the simple "globules of plasm" envisioned by Darwin's contemporaries.

Moreover, most of these circuits and machines depend on the coordinated function of many separate parts. For example, scientists have discovered that bacterial cells are propelled by miniature rotary engines called flagellar motors that rotate at speeds up to 100,000 rpm. These engines look for all the world as if they were designed by the Mazda corporation, with many distinct mechanical parts (made of proteins) including rotors, stators, O-rings, bushings, U-joints, and drive shafts.

Is this appearance of design merely illusory? Could natural selection have produced this appearance in a neo-Darwinian fashion one tiny incremental mutation at a time? Biochemist Michael Behe argues 'no.' He points out that the flagellar motor depends upon the coordinated function of 30 protein parts. Yet the absence of any one of these parts results in the complete loss of motor function. Remove one of the necessary proteins (as scientists can do experimentally) and the rotary motor simply doesn't work. The motor is, in Behe's terminology, "irreducibly complex."

This creates a problem for the Darwinian mechanism. Natural selection preserves or "selects" functional advantages. If a random mutation helps an organism survive, it can be preserved and passed on to the next generation. Yet, the flagellar motor has no function until after all of its 30 parts have been assembled. The 29 and 28-part versions of this motor do not work. Thus, natural selection can "select" or preserve the motor once it has arisen as a functioning whole, but it can do nothing to help build the motor in the first place.

This leaves the origin of molecular machines like the flagellar motor unexplained by the mechanism—natural selection—that Darwin specifically proposed to replace the design hypothesis.

Is there a better alternative? Based upon our uniform and repeated experience, we know of only one type of cause that produces irreducibly complex systems, namely, intelligence. Indeed, whenever we encounter irreducibly complex systems—such as an integrated circuit or an internal combustion engine—and we know how they arose, invariably a designing engineer played a role.

Thus, Behe concludes—based on our knowledge of what it takes to build functionally-integrated complex systems—that intelligent design best explains the origin of molecular machines within cells. Molecular machines appear designed because they were designed.

The strength of Behe's design argument can be judged in part by the response of his critics. After nearly ten years, they have mustered only a vague just-so story about the flagellar motor arising from a simpler subsystem of the motor—a tiny syringe—that is sometimes found in bacteria without the other parts of the flagellar motor present. Unfortunately, for advocates of this theory recent genetic studies show that the syringe arose after the flagellar motor—that if anything the syringe evolved from the motor, not the motor from the syringe.

But consider an even more fundamental argument for design. In 1953 when Watson and Crick elucidated the structure of the DNA molecule, they made a startling discovery. The structure of DNA allows it to store information in the form of a four-character digital code. Strings of precisely sequenced chemicals called nucleotide bases store and transmit the assembly instructions—the information—for building the crucial protein molecules and machines the cell needs to survive.

Francis Crick later developed this idea with his famous "sequence hypothesis" according to which the chemical constituents in DNA function like letters in a written language or symbols in a computer code. Just as English letters may convey a particular message depending on their arrangement, so too do certain sequences of chemical bases along the spine of a DNA molecule convey precise instructions for building proteins. The arrangement of the chemical characters determines the function of the sequence as a whole. Thus, the DNA molecule has the same property of "sequence specificity" that characterizes codes and language. As Richard Dawkins has acknowledged, "the machine code of the genes is uncannily computer-like." As Bill Gates has noted, "DNA is like a computer program, but far, far more advanced than any software we've ever created."

After the early 1960s, further discoveries made clear that the digital information in DNA and RNA is only part of a complex information processing system—an advanced form of nanotechnology that both mirrors and exceeds our own in its complexity, design logic and information storage density.

Where did the digital information in the cell come from? And how did the cell's complex information processing system arise? Today these questions lie at the heart of origin-of-life research. Clearly, the informational features of the cell at least appear designed. And to date no theory of undirected chemical evolution has explained the origin of the digital information needed to build the first living cell. Why? There is simply too much information in the cell to be explained by chance alone. And the information in DNA has also been shown to defy explanation by reference to the laws of chemistry. Saying otherwise would be like saying that a newspaper headline might arise as the result of the chemical attraction between ink and paper. Clearly "something else" is at work.

Yet, the scientists arguing for intelligent design do not do so merely because natural processes—chance, laws or the combination of the two—have failed to explain the origin of the information and information processing systems in cells. Instead, they also argue for design because we know from experience that systems possessing these features invariably arise from intelligent causes. The information on computer screen can be traced back to a user or programmer. The information in a newspaper ultimately came from a writer—from a mental, rather than a strictly material, cause. As the pioneering information theorist Henry Quastler observed, "information habitually arises from conscious activity."

This connection between information and prior intelligence enables us to detect or infer intelligent activity even from unobservable sources in the distant past. Archeologists infer ancient scribes from hieroglyphic inscriptions. SETI's search for extraterrestrial intelligence presupposes that information imbedded in electromagnetic signals from space would indicate an intelligent source. As yet, radio astronomers have not found information-bearing signals from distant star systems. But closer to home, molecular biologists have discovered information in the cell, suggesting—by the same logic that underwrites the SETI program and ordinary scientific reasoning about other informational artifacts—an intelligent source for the information in DNA.

DNA functions like a software program. We know from experience that software comes from programmers. We know generally that information—whether inscribed in hieroglyphics, written in a book or encoded in a radio signal—always arises from an intelligent source. So the discovery of information in the DNA molecule, provides strong grounds for inferring that intelligence played a role in the origin of DNA, even if we weren't there to observe the system coming into existence.

Thus, contrary to media reports, the theory of intelligent design is not based upon ignorance or religion but instead upon recent scientific discoveries and upon standard methods of scientific reasoning in which our uniform experience of cause and effect guides our inferences about what happened in the past.

Of course, many will still dismiss intelligent design as nothing but warmed over creationism or as a "religious masquerading as science." But intelligent design, unlike creationism, is not based upon the Bible. Design is an inference from biological data, not a deduction from religious authority.

Even so, the theory of intelligent design may provide support for theistic belief. But that is not grounds for dismissing it. To say otherwise confuses the evidence for a theory and its possible implications. Many scientists initially rejected the Big Bang theory because it seemed to challenge the idea of an eternally self-existent universe and pointed to the need for a transcendent cause of matter, space and time. But scientists eventually accepted the theory despite such apparently unpleasant implications because the evidence strongly supported it. Today a similar metaphysical prejudice confronts the theory of intelligent design. Nevertheless, it too must be evaluated on the basis of the evidence not our philosophical preferences or concerns about its possible religious implications. Antony Flew, the long-time atheistic philosopher who has come to accept the case for design, insists correctly that we must "follow the evidence wherever it leads."

Source: Meyer, Stephen C. "Not by Chance: From Bacterial Propulsion Systems to Human DNA, Evidence of Intelligent Design is Everywhere." *National Post* (Canada), December 1, 2005.

A Defense of Intelligent Design as Science

Is intelligent design science? Will its suppression by science educators actually result in more interest in the topic, as is often the case with banned books? In this Washington Times *editorial, Tom Bethell defends intelligent design and suggests that students will be more curious about it if the government tries to ban teaching it in science classes. Bethell, who is a senior editor with the* American Spectator *and author of* The Politically Incorrect Guide to Science, *asserts that intelligent design is indeed science and that Darwinians cannot accept the gaps in their theory. Bethell also likens intelligent design to the construction and programming of computers.*

Evolutionists are ecstatic about U.S. District Judge John E. Jones's ruling in the Dover, Pa., school board case, claiming it is a major setback for the intelligent design movement. The judge declared intelligent design cannot be so much as discussed in biology classes in area public schools—a prohibition giving rise to free-speech concerns. Intelligent design is a "mere relabeling of creationism," he said.

But it is doubtful this ruling is even remotely a setback for intelligent design. For decades, the judiciary has dealt these "setbacks" to any and all critics of evolution. In that time, the intelligent design movement, which began perhaps 20 years ago, has gone from strength to strength.

If it had been advanced courtesy of the public schools, the judge's ruling would indeed have been a setback. But the schools had nothing to do with it. Intelligent design has gained adherents because a sizable number of Americans are capable of reading and thinking for themselves.

The best-known advocates of intelligent design have not attempted to advance their cause through state coercion in the schools. They understand how counterproductive such a strategy can be. Liberalism got a bad name to the extent that legislatures and courts tried to make it compulsory and its rivals illegal. The leading institutional supporter of intelligent design, the Discovery Institute in Seattle, issued a public statement after the judge's ruling, saying it "continues to oppose efforts to mandate teaching about the theory of intelligent design in public schools."

Discovery had opposed the original school board's mandating a brief statement in favor of intelligent design to be read to ninth-grade biology students. It is that school board action that was declared unconstitutional by the judge.

Attempts in the 1980s to legislate "balanced treatment" of life's origins were Bible-based and could legitimately be called "creationist." All were struck down, eventually by the Supreme Court. But contrary to Judge Jones's ruling, arguments that incline people to accept intelligent design are scientific, and to that extent, appropriate to the science class. They deal with such matters as the complexity of organisms at the cellular and microcellular level, the paucity of the fossil record, which has not revealed the transitional forms Darwinians anticipated, and the feebleness of the Darwinian mechanism of evolution ("the survival of the fittest").

Still, this doesn't explain why design-based theories have gained so much traction in recent years. Perhaps the most important reason has been overlooked. The rise of computer science and information technology has caused many intelligent people not just to think about issues of design and the difficulties involved.

Software designers understand how precisely such information must be specified. There is no room for error. Yet each cell of the body contains a DNA chain of 3 billion nucleotides, encoded in such a way it specifies construction of all the proteins.

No one knows the source of this code or how it arose. It cannot have been by accident, but accident is the only method available to the evolutionists, who believe as a matter of dogma that early life arose from the random collision of atoms and molecules and nothing else.

It used to be said that most DNA is "junk," because it didn't seem to do anything useful. But leading genome scientists such as Francis Collins of the National Human Genome Research Institute no longer believe that. And Microsoft's Bill Gates has said DNA "is like a computer program, but far, far more advanced than any software we have created."

The British philosopher Antony Flew said a year ago he was emboldened to turn away from atheism because he saw the implications of the structure of DNA. The cell itself, thought in Darwin's day to be a "simple little lump of protoplasm," is now understood to have the complexity of a high-tech factory.

There are 300 trillion cells in the human body, and each "knows" its function. Cell biologists do not know how these things happen, or how they arose.

In recent weeks, I have been on many talk-radio programs, discussing my book "The Politically Incorrect Guide to Science," which includes chapters on evolution and intelligent design. What I can attest from this experience is that intelligent design arouses passionate reactions—on both sides of the issue. The phone-banks light up, as talk show hosts tell me. People are intensely interested, and (to the dismay of some professionals in the field) they feel entitled to have an opinion and express it.

I dare say not one of these people developed their interest in public school. This interest will surely only increase in years ahead. If the Pennsylvania case acts as a precedent, students in public schools will not be allowed to learn about these things in biology. But when did such prohibitions ever work?

Some students are already sure to be thinking: "What is it in biology that we are not allowed to be taught?" Books banned in Boston notoriously became best-sellers, and design banned from biology will resurface in computer studies. Or is Bill Gates to be relabeled a closet creationist?

Source: Bethell, Tom. "Banned in Biology." *Washington Times*, December 26, 2005.

Why Intelligent Design Is Not Science

Robert George Sprackland is an evolutionary zoologist and systematist specializing in macroevolution. He is also director of the Virtual Museum of Natural History (www.curator.org). In the following article, he explains his opposition to teaching intelligent design in public science classrooms.

One of the most confrontational issues before American school boards and administrators is the effort by some Christian fundamentalists to have their views on life and its origins taught in science classes as a scientifically valid alternative to biological evolution.

This is no ordinary philosophical debate in which semantics is all that is at stake. Rather, the leaders of the creationism and intelligent design (ID) movements seek to undermine and overthrow the teachings of science and critical thought and replace them with their specific interpretation of Christianity.

Harsh words? Not when ID advocates misrepresent the evidence, methods and interpretations of science to push for equal treatment of their religious ideas in school science curricula. The fact that representatives of a single religious viewpoint—not Christianity writ large, but a branch of Evangelicals—have led the public to believe creationism is an actual scientific alternative to evolution is appalling and dangerous.

"It says we've failed as scientists and science educators to convey the nature of science and its values to the American public," says Bruce Alberts, the outgoing president of the National Academy of Sciences.

The issue continues to plague science education, suggesting that few school people have a deep understanding of the issue and its extremely broad ramifications. America will continue to fall behind in medicine, technology, and other fields of science as long as our children are denied a good science education—one based on an understanding of what is, and is not, science.

Science Majors Who Can't Define "Science"

In my three decades as a science teacher, I have met many university science majors who cannot properly define "science." Premedical and nursing students coming into my classes showed less and less understanding of basic biology each new year.

Think what that can mean to you when you or someone you love is hospitalized. Many of the 120,000 accidental deaths each year due to physician error might be eliminated if practitioners were given a better science education.

"Science," from the Latin word *sciere,* means "to know." Though science has been practiced for thousands of years, modern science came into being in the 1600s. Modern science has a few universally accepted ground rules.

To qualify as science, an activity must be based on two things: (1) *objective information.* This is called fact, although it may be interpreted subjectively. For example, flame is hot (fact), but is it the air, "ether," burned wood, something else, or a combination that bears the heat? (2) *explanation of nature and natural phenomena by means of natural processes.* Explanations that involve supernatural forces (including God) are by definition not scientific and are by definition beyond the realm of science.

Science proceeds as free of preconceptions as humanly possible. Scientists make only one universal assumption in their work: Reality is real. If you recall the Chinese sage wondering if he was a man who dreamt he was a butterfly or a butterfly who dreamt he was a man, you know that philosophers love to debate the nature and, well, reality of reality.

To scientists it is irrelevant if we are butterfly or man—we have to work with the reality that we can perceive and access. Science is not about the search for truth or proving the existence of anything; rather, it is a process of interpreting and understanding nature without recourse to the supernatural.

Based on this definition of science, scientists rightly claim that evolution is a fact. Evolution has been observed, analyzed, and subjected to innumerable tests and observations for more than 150 years and has not encountered any evidence to suggest that it is not a fact. The theory of evolution is not about *if* evolution happens but rather an explanation of *how* it happens. Let me restate that: **Evolution is a fact; the explanation of how it happens is a theory.**

The ID/creationists believe the Genesis story or a creation story that gives scientific credence to an "intelligent designer" should be taught in science classes. There are numerous reasons to argue against that position, but the only important reason is this: There is no scientific evidence that supports, in any way, the Genesis accounts or the existence of an "intelligent designer." There is, however, a staggering amount of evidence that supports evolutionary theory, and the evidence increases every day.

New Guises for Old Ideas

What is intelligent design? Courts have repeatedly ruled that teaching creationism in public schools is an unconstitutional promotion of a religious viewpoint. In response, new guises for old ideas have been invented. Creationism began as biblical literalism, evolved into creationism, and then creation science.

The newest resurrection calls itself intelligent design theory. Its proponents have devised a so-called wedge strategy specifically to find and exploit weaknesses in school boards to get creation-based lessons into science classrooms. Nature, they claim, is too complex and unlikely to have arisen by chance. Complexity is therefore "proof" of a creator.

ID/creationism is not science because its answers cannot be verified through experiment or scientific methods and are not subject to being discarded or modified if evidence shows where they are wrong. The ID/creationist's goal is to insert a narrow interpretation of the Bible into America's public schools and claim it is science. It is a move to impose religious beliefs on the curriculum, and as such it is vigorously anti-science and anti-intellectual (and unconstitutional).

The tradition of local control of school governance allows proponents of ID/creationism to tackle the issue with smaller governing bodies instead of a strong national department. To circumvent the First Amendment's prohibition of the establishment of a religion, they use arguments that are couched in scientific terms but have no credible science behind them. In response, out of a genuine concern to be fair—or due to lack of knowledge about science—some school boards have required science teachers to give equal time to intelligent design.

A major tactic in creation-evolution debates has been to keep scientists busy playing word games. Creationists lob old and already resolved questions at the scientific community. In turn, scientists repeat the fallacies of creation arguments and point out that these questions have been answered in great detail many times—some as long ago as the late 1800s.

An egregious example is the so-called problem that the laws of physics prohibit an increase in complexity because energy in a system runs down over time. Evolution, goes the ID argument, cannot be scientific, for if life becomes increasingly complex over time, thermodynamic law is violated. What they fail to point out is that entropy occurs in a closed system—one that has no energy input.

But Earth is not a closed system. It constantly receives far more energy from the sun per day than it uses in a millennium, making the earth a distinctly open system. This massive energy influx makes evolution possible.

The "problem" of evolution violating thermodynamics should be relegated to the rubbish heap of history. Until it is, scientists will have to continue reminding ID proponents and the public of what thermodynamics says and why biological evolution does not violate this foundation of physics.

Hitting Emotions Instead of Science

Other tactics are to appeal to emotions instead of science by calling for equal time and recognition of an "intelligent designer." The equal time tactics plays on the desire to be fair by giving equal time for an alternative explanation about the origins and diversity of life.

But the issue is not about presenting "the other side" of an argument, for the following reasons:

- Most religions, including the overwhelming majority of Christians, accept biological evolution as a fact.

- Other faiths, from the Australian aborigines to the Tibetan lamas, have very different creation stories from the one championed by the creationists.

- The Darwinian theory of evolution remains the only *scientific* explanation for the diversity of life that has withstood scientific testing. There is no scientific theory to compete with Darwinism—and no reason to present religion as science.

The "intelligent designer" tactic implicitly sidesteps naming "God." Evolutionists may be many things—and many of them are religious people—but they have the integrity to call their precepts by proper names. ID/creationists, in exploiting ignorance of science and scientific methods, hide their intellectual lights under bushels and their deity in a closet.

212

Who do ID proponents think the intelligent designer may be? Are they suggesting it could be Mr. Spock, Mork from Ork, or maybe E.T.? No, of course not (even if at times it seems as though our society was engineered by Mork). By whatever name we call this entity, it is by definition supernatural. The creator of nature would be beyond the constraints of our physics and the realm of science to seek or explain.

This does not mean there is no God, or that science can disprove God. Rather, God and deity are not subjects for scientific inquiry. Thus, whether we call an ultimate creator God, Goddess, or Intelligent Designer, the subject is not appropriate to a science curriculum.

Hoping to Dazzle with Degrees

A final tactic might be called the credential tactic. Many ID/Creationists hold doctorates in engineering, physics, and theology (and very rarely biology) but lack experience in the study of evolutionary biology. They assume the public will be dazzled by advanced degrees and believe that one Ph.D. is as good as another.

But if you wouldn't buy milk at the library or magazines from a shoe store, why would you "buy" information about biology from a lawyer, engineer, or physicist?

Why must we promote proper science in science class? Ensuring that only science is taught in science courses is not a trivial matter. Science is an essential component of modern experience, and students who fail to understand it will find fewer job possibilities. Science provides the entry to technology and underlies ecology, medicine, and many other critical disciplines.

In the twenty-first century, our nation depends more than ever on an educated populace that should be at the forefront of intellectual accomplishment. To achieve this, we must ensure that students learn about science in science classes.

When societies have perverted and redefined science, the result has been tragedy. "In Nazi Germany, relativity was considered 'Jewish science' and therefore unacceptable, while in the Soviet Union, modern genetics was rejected as un-Marxist in favor of the ravings of the chairman Lysenko," wrote anatomist Ejnar Fjerdingstad in July in *Science*.

The Nazis also misinterpreted the science of genetics in their eugenics movement, while China's Chairman Mao ran the nation's agricultural practices with his own "science." More Soviet and Chinese citizens were to die of starvation from this disregard for science than from combat during World War II. Those who mold science to political, religious, or philosophical aims do so at great peril to the rest of us.

Reasons Not to Teach It

If the ID/creation movement comes to your district, you may use these valid reasons why it should not be taught in a science class:

- ID/creationism is not science. It is not derived from scientific methods, cannot be tested, and does not allow for its source material (Genesis) to be corrected in the presence of facts.

- There is no "debate" about the validity of evolution. Scientists consider evolution as fact and the explanation of how it occurs as theory, which in science means a well-supported body of ideas and explanations. The only debates about evolution in the scientific community deal with specifics of how evolution occurs.

- ID criticizes biology but offers no new scientific model to replace Darwinism. Having no scientific alternative theory disqualifies ID from being a science.

- Science is an intellectual activity that requires questioning, testing, and revising ideas in the face of new evidence; ID is dogmatic, untestable, and a first step toward converting the entire science curriculum into religious instruction. (Remember that fundamentalists find unacceptable several other topics, including the Big Bang, the age of the earth, dinosaurs existing long before humans, germs as causes of disease, and quantum mechanics, among others, affecting the science of cosmology, geology, paleontology, medicine, and physics.)

Schools have neither the obligation nor the time to discuss creation stories in a science class. There are too many creation stories, and none is scientific. Discussion of these stories would be appropriate in a comparative religion or philosophy class, but not in a science class.

Science gives us great and important insights into the nature of our past and present and helps us forge into the future. It can do that only if science is allowed to be science, whether or not we like what reality may show us.

Educators and scientists may not be able to convince those whose agenda is as political as it is religious. But if we fail, there are many other nations ready and willing to assume our position as world leader in science innovation and application.

Source: Sprackland, Robert George. "A Scientist Tells Why 'Intelligent Design' is NOT Science." *The Education Digest,* January 2006. Originally published in longer form in *American School Board Journal,* November 2005.

IMPORTANT PEOPLE, PLACES, AND TERMS

18th Amendment
Ratified in 1919, this amendment outlawed the sale or production of alcoholic beverages throughout America. Better known as Prohibition, the amendment was repealed by the 21st Amendment in 1933.

19th Amendment
This constitutional amendment, ratified in 1920, gave women the right to vote in national elections.

Admissible evidence
Testimony and documents that can be entered into a trial after being deemed relevant to the case. A judge makes the determination of admissibility.

Affidavit
Oral statements put into writing, or written reports, submitted to a court.

Agnostic
A person who believes that it is not possible to know or prove whether God exists.

American Civil Liberties Union (ACLU)
An organization dedicated to defending freedom of speech and minority rights in the United States.

Appeal
An opportunity to have a higher court review a verdict rendered in a lower court. All cases must go through the appeals process before reaching the U.S. Supreme Court.

Atheist
A person who does not believe that God, heaven, or hell exists.

Bible Belt
  A term coined in reference to a group of Southern states particularly influenced by fundamentalist Christianity.

Bill of Rights
  The portion of U.S. and state Constitutions that lists basic rights of all citizens of the nation or its states.

Bryan University
  A Christian college in Dayton, Tennessee, founded in honor of William Jennings Bryan.

Bryan, William Jennings (1860-1925)
  Populist Democratic politician and reformer who served as a prosecuting attorney in the Scopes trial.

Bryan, William Jennings Jr. (1889-1978)
  California-based attorney who assisted his father, William Jennings Bryan, in the prosecution of John Scopes.

Butler Act
  Name given to the legislation criminalizing the teaching of evolution in public schools in Tennessee. The act went into law in 1925 and was repealed in 1967.

Butler, John Washington (1875-1952)
  Member of Tennessee House of Representatives who authored the Butler Act, making the teaching of evolution in Tennessee's public schools a criminal misdemeanor.

Civic Biology, A
  The title of the biology textbook Scopes used to teach evolution to Dayton high school science students.

Cold War
  The political, military, and economic rivalry that endured between the United States and the Soviet Union—and their respective allies—from the end of World War II to the dissolution of the USSR in 1991.

218

Contempt of Court

An action defying the authority of a U.S. court, either by ignoring the rules of the court, disobedience of a court order, or disrespectful behavior toward the judge. Criminal contempt charges can result in fines and jail time.

Creation Science

A movement in the 1970s and 1980s that unsuccessfully sought to incorporate a God-based theory of creation into public school science classes.

Darrow, Clarence (1857-1938)

Famous trial lawyer and admitted agnostic who served on the defense team in John Scopes's court case and its appeal.

Darwin, Charles (1809-1882)

Nineteenth century naturalist who developed the theory of how living organisms evolve into new species over time. Darwin proposed the theory of evolution by natural selection, or "survival of the fittest."

Dawson, Charles (1864-1916)

Amateur fossil collector partly responsible for the "Piltdown Man" fossil forgery in the early twentieth century.

Discovery Institute

A Seattle, Washington-based research and public relations center that champions the "intelligent design" theory of creation.

Edwards v. Aguillard

A 1987 case in which the U.S. Supreme Court struck down laws mandating the teaching of creation science in public schools. The High Court ruled that teaching creation science violated the Establishment Clause in the Bill of Rights.

Epperson v. Arkansas

A case that culminated with a 1968 U.S. Supreme Court decision striking down all anti-evolution legislation as a violation of the Establishment Clause in the Constitution's Bill of Rights.

Establishment Clause

A clause in the Constitution's Bill of Rights that specifically provides for the separation of church and state in American society; it also mandates that U.S. governmental institutions should not betray a preference for one particular religion or sect over any other.

Eugenics

A discredited movement to improve the human race genetically by sterilizing or otherwise "weeding out" allegedly undesirable or inferior members.

Evangelical

Protestant religious leaders and faiths that emphasize the authority of the gospel and the essential link between religious faith and salvation.

Evangelist

A Protestant pastor or missionary who delivers the evangelical message, often to large crowds, on topics pertaining to Christian salvation and social action.

Evolution

The development over geological time of species of animals, plants, and microorganisms.

Fortas, Abe (1910-1982)

U.S. Supreme Court justice who wrote the majority decision in *Epperson v. Arkansas,* a 1968 ruling that struck down all anti-evolution state statutes in the United States.

Free Thinker

Someone who rejects traditional authority and dogma, especially in the area of religious beliefs, in favor of independent or science-based thought and inquiry.

Fundamentalist

Someone who believes in the literal truth of the Bible and scriptures contained therein.

Hays, Arthur Garfield (1881-1954)

New York-based corporate lawyer and general counsel for the ACLU who served as defense attorney for John Scopes.

Homo erectus

An upright-walking pre-human, found in fossil form in Africa, Asia, and parts of southern Europe.

Hunter, George William (1873-1948)

College professor and author of the textbook *A Civic Biology,* which John Scopes said he used to teach evolution in defiance of Tennessee law.

Indictment

A formal issuing of a criminal charge, delivered by a grand jury.

Inherit the Wind

Broadway play and film of the same name based on the events of the Scopes trial. The play opened in 1955, the film premiered in 1960.

Intelligent Design

A modern movement that contends that a supernatural "intelligent designer" is responsible for the creation of the universe and the geological history of the earth.

Jones, John E. III (1955-   )

U.S. District Court Judge from Pennsylvania who ruled in 2005 against a state school board's efforts to introduce intelligent design themes into the public classroom.

Kitzmiller et. al. v. Dover Area School District et. al.

District court case in which federal judge John E. Jones III ruled that intelligent design did not meet the criteria of science and violated constitutional safeguards regarding the separation of church and state.

Lamarck, Chevalier de (1744-1829)

French zoologist of the early nineteenth century who theorized that changes in the environment could cause changes to animals and plants.

Malone, Dudley Field (1882-1950)

New York- and Paris-based attorney who served on John Scopes's defense team at the request of the ACLU.

Mencken, Henry Louis (H. L.) (1880-1956)

Baltimore-based journalist and social commentator who heaped scorn on Tennessee religious institutions, the Butler Act, and the behavior of William Jennings Bryan and his followers during the Scopes "Monkey Trial."

Misdemeanor

A minor crime usually resulting in payment of a fine, performance of community service, or a brief jail term.

Modernist
   Christian churches, denominations, and ministers that seek to reconcile church teachings and Biblical scripture with modern scientific and technological advances.

Natural Selection
   An element of Darwin's theory of evolution which holds that organisms with genetic characteristics that enable them to adapt to and thrive in their surrounding environment transmit these characteristics on to succeeding generations; over time, these descendents become a higher percentage of the overall species population, especially as members of the species with less beneficial genetic characteristics are eliminated.

Neal, John Randolph (1836-1889)
   Tennessee attorney who was the first attorney to volunteer his services to John Scopes.

Neanderthal Man
   A nineteenth-century fossil find from Germany that differed distinctly in appearance from modern human beings.

Pentecostal
   A Christian denomination marked by strict adherence to Biblical scripture, dramatic sermons, and rapturous behavior amongst its members.

Piltdown Man
   An elaborate hoax of the early twentieth century in which fossil remains of a human skull and an altered orangutan jaw were combined to create the long-sought "missing link" in human evolution; the fossil remains were finally discredited in the 1950s.

Rappleyea, George W.
   Dayton, Tennessee free-thinker who urged John Scopes to challenge the anti-evolution law.

Raulston, John Tate (1868-1956)
   The circuit court judge who presided over John Scopes's indictment and his trial.

Revealed Religion

In broad terms, any religion that is based on the revelations of a supreme being or deity; In Christianity, religious beliefs founded primarily on the revelations of God to humankind, especially as presented in Biblical scripture.

Robinson, Frank E. "Doc"

Dayton drug store owner and community leader who encouraged John Scopes to challenge Tennessee's anti-evolution law.

Scopes, John Thomas (1900-1970)

The defendant in the famous trial bearing his name. Scopes agreed to be charged with teaching evolution in defiance of an anti-evolution Tennessee state law.

Sequester

To remove a jury from a courtroom so the members cannot hear procedural arguments.

State of Tennessee v. John Thomas Scopes

The formal name for the 1925 court case better known as the Scopes "Monkey Trial."

Stewart, Arthur Thomas "Tom" (1892-1972)

District attorney for Rhea County and leader of the legal team that prosecuted John Scopes.

Ussher, Bishop James (1581-1656)

Renaissance cleric and scholar whose book, *Annals of the World,* used ancient texts from other cultures and the ages of patriarchs in the Bible to determine that God created the earth on October 23, 4004 BCE.

CHRONOLOGY

1658

Bishop James Ussher publishes *Annals of the World,* in which he dates the origin of creation to October 23, 4004 B.C.E. *See p. 7.*

1831-36

Charles Darwin sails on the *H.M.S. Beagle,* collecting animal and plant specimens from remote locations in South America and the Pacific Islands. *See p. 9.*

1857

Workers discover the first remains of Neanderthal Man in Germany. *See p. 10.*

1859

Darwin publishes *The Origin of Species by Natural Selection; Or, The Preservation of Favoured Races in the Struggle for Life.* See p. 9.

1871

Darwin publishes *The Descent of Man, and Selection in Relation to Sex,* a work that compares humans to other mammals and declares that the human species

evolved in Africa from ancestral apes. *See p. 9.*

1891

Eugène Dubois discovers a fossil pre-human in Java. He names it *Pithecanthropus erectus.* The name is later changed to *Homo erectus.* See p. 10.

1896

July 9 – William Jennings Bryan delivers his famous "Cross of Gold" speech, advocating a silver standard for America's monetary system. The speech earns him the first of three Democratic presidential nominations. See p. 13.

1907

July 29 – Clarence Darrow wins an acquittal for controversial labor leader William "Big Bill" Haywood in a murder trial in Boise, Idaho. *See p. 13.*

1912

November – Charles Dawson and Arthur Smith Woodward announce the discovery of "Piltdown Man," a human-like fossil featuring a skull with an apelike jaw. In 1953 the specimen is found to be a hoax. *See p. 11.*

1914

The first edition of *A Civic Biology,* by George William Hunter, is published. *See p. 23.*

1922

William Jennings Bryan travels to Kentucky, where he speaks against the teaching of evolution in public schools and unsuccessfully urges the state legislature to pass a law removing evolution from classrooms. *See p. 17.*

1923

Bryan continues his anti-evolution crusade, persuading state governments in Florida and Oklahoma to enact statutes severely restricting teaching of Darwin's theory. *See p. 17.*

1924

August 22 – Clarence Darrow undertakes a twelve-hour closing statement in a successful bid to save the lives of of convicted thrill-killers Nathan Leopold and Richard Loeb. *See p. 28.*

September – John T. Scopes begins teaching chemistry, physics, and mathematics at Central High School in Dayton, Tennessee. Scopes also serves as the football coach. *See p. 22.*

1925

January 21 – John Washington Butler of the Tennessee House of Representatives introduces legislation making it a criminal misdemeanor to teach any scientific theory in Tennessee public schools that is contrary to the story of creation described in Genesis. *See p. 17.*

February – Evangelist Billy Sunday carries out an 18-day religious revival in Memphis, Tennessee, urging state legislators to pass John W. Butler's anti-evolution statute. *See p. 18.*

March 13 – The Tennessee state legislature passes the Butler Act. *See p. 18.*

March 21 – Tennessee Governor Austin Peay signs the Butler Act into law. *See p. 18.*

May 4 – Tennessee's largest newspapers publish an announcement from the American Civil Liberties Union (ACLU) that the organization will provide free legal aid to any Tennessee public school teacher who challenges the Butler Act. *See p. 21.*

May 5 – Prominent citizens of Dayton, Tennessee, convince John T. Scopes to stand as defendant in a challenge to the Butler Act. *See p. 23.*

May 13 – William Jennings Bryan joins the prosecution team in the Scopes case. *See p. 27.*

May 14 – Learning of Bryan's interest in the Scopes case, Clarence Darrow offers to assist in Scopes's defense. *See p. 29.*

May 25 – A grand jury meeting in special session in Dayton indicts Scopes for teaching evolution in violation of the Butler Act.

June – Scopes and his first trial lawyer, John R. Neal, meet in New York City to choose the rest of Scopes's defense team. Scopes insists on including Clarence Darrow. *See p. 30.*

July 7 – William Jennings Bryan arrives in Dayton to prosecute Scopes. Bryan receives a hero's welcome. *See p. 36.*

July 9 – Scopes defense attorneys Dudley Malone and Clarence Darrow arrive in Dayton. *See p. 37.*

July 10 – The Scopes trial begins with a re-issue of the indictment and jury selection. *See p. 43.*

July 13 – Scopes's defense team argues that the indictment should be quashed on the basis that the Butler Act violates Tennessee's Bill of Rights. *See p. 48.*

July 14 – Judge Raulston ends court early after learning that a newspaper reporter "scooped" his decision to turn down the defense motion to quash the indictment. *See p. 56.*

July 15 – The prosecution begins and ends its case against Scopes; when the defense begins its case in the afternoon, the two legal camps argue over the admissibility of expert testimony from defense witnesses. *See p. 58.*

July 16 – Court proceedings are highlighted by orations by William Jennings Bryan, who condemns evolution as a false theory that corrupts youngsters, and Dudley Field Malone, who delivers an impassioned plea for academic freedom. *See p. 63.*

July 17 – Judge Raulston rules against the defense's introduction of expert witnesses to testify before the jury. Raulston allows the defense to use the weekend to prepare written statements to be introduced as affidavits for use on appeal. *See p. 75.*

July 19 – In statements to the press, Darrow accuses Bryan of avoiding a true debate by working to have the defense's expert witnesses excluded from the trial. *See p. 77.*

July 20 – Darrow calls Bryan to the stand as an "expert witness" on the Bible for the defense, sparking one of the most famous courtroom confrontations in American legal history. *See p. 80.*

July 21 – Darrow asks the jury to find his client guilty. The jury obliges, and Judge Raulston levies a minimal $100 fine against Scopes. *See p. 86.*

July 26 –William Jennings Bryan dies in his sleep in Dayton. *See p. 90.*

1927

January 17 – The Tennessee Supreme Court overturns John Scopes's conviction on a technicality, thus avoiding issuing a ruling about the constitutionality of the Butler Act. *See p. 94.*

1928

The state of Arkansas passes a law prohibiting the teaching of evolution in public school classrooms.

1955

January 10 – *Inherit the Wind*, a play based on the Scopes trial, opens on Broadway. *See p. 100.*

1960

October – The film version of *Inherit the Wind* makes its premiere in Dayton, Tennessee. *See p. 101.*

1965

Susan Epperson, a biology teacher, and H. H. Blanchard, a parent of two high school students, challenge the Arkansas anti-evolution law in court. *See p. 102.*

1967

May 17 – The Tennessee state legislature repeals the Butler Act. *See p. 102.*

John Scopes publishes his memoir, *Center of the Storm,* co-authored with James Presley.

1968

November 12 – Ruling in the case *Epperson v. Arkansas,* The United States Supreme Court strikes down all remaining state anti-evolution laws as being in violation of the Establishment Clause in the Bill of Rights. *See p. 103.*

1987

June 19 – In the case *Edwards v. Aguillard,* the United States Supreme Court bars the inclusion of creation science in public school curricula as a violation of the Establishment Clause in the Bill of Rights. *See p. 104.*

1990

The Discovery Institute, a leading force in the "Intelligent Design" movement, is founded in Seattle, Washington.

1996

October 22 – Pope John Paul II confirms a previous papal encyclical, *Humani generis* (1955), stating that the theory of evolution can be compatible with Roman Catholic doctrine, as evolution accounts for physical changes but does not account for the presence of an immortal soul in each human being.

2004

October – A school board in Dover, Pennsylvania, mandates that district science teachers read a statement about intelligent design before beginning any instruction on evolutionary theory. *See p. 104.*

2005

September 26 – Local parents challenge the legality of the Dover Board of Education's pro-intelligent design actions in the case *Kitzmiller et. al. vs. Dover Area School District et. al. See p. 105.*

November 7 – The Kansas state board of education issues a statement encouraging public school teachers to challenge the theory of evolution and offer students optional self-study on intelligent design.

November 8 – All eight members of the Dover, Pennsylvania, school board that supported the adoption of a policy mandating the reading of a statement about Intelligent Design in high school biology classes lose their seats in school board elections; they are replaced by a slate of candidates who ran on an anti-ID platform. *See p. 105.*

December 20 – In the *Kitzmiller* case, federal district court judge John E. Jones III rules that intelligent design does not meet established scientific criteria; mention of intelligent design in public schools therefore violates the Establishment Clause in the Bill of Rights. *See p. 105.*

SOURCES FOR FURTHER STUDY

Chapman, Matthew. *Trials of the Monkey: An Accidental Memoir.* London: Duckworth Literary Entertainments, 2000. Chapman, a direct descendant of Charles Darwin, travels to Dayton, Tennessee, where he revisits the Scopes trial and reflects on modern-day Dayton and Bryan University.

"Inherit the Wind." http://www.xroads.edu/~UG97/inherit/intro.html. A study of the play and film *Inherit the Wind,* with references to the Scopes trial and coverage of the changing perceptions of the often-performed work.

Larson, Edward J. *Summer for the Gods: The Scopes Trial and America's Continuing Debate over Science and Religion.* Cambridge, Massachusetts: Harvard University Press, 1997. Pulitzer Prize-winning study of the Scopes trial and subsequent debates on the issues raised at the trial.

Public Broadcasting System (PBS). "American Experience: Monkey Trial: An All-Out Duel between Science and Religion." http://www.pbs.org/amex/monkeytrial/index.html. A website with supporting documents for the "American Experience" television documentary on the Scopes trial. Includes timeline, photographs, and biographies.

Scopes, John T., and James Presley. *Center of the Storm: Memoirs of John T. Scopes.* New York: Holt, Rinehart & Winston, 1967. Scopes details how his childhood prepared him for the trial and reminisces at length about the trial.

University of Missouri, Kansas City. "Famous Trials in American History: Tennessee vs. John Scopes, the "Monkey Trial," 1925. http://www.law.umkc.edu/faculty/projects/ftrials/scopes.htm. The most comprehensive website on the Scopes trial. Includes an overview, biographies, timeline, excerpts from the trial transcript, editorial cartoons, and other newspaper coverage.

University of Utah Department of Math. "The Scopes Trial." http://www.math.utah.edu/~lars/scopes.pdf. Contains all of H. L. Mencken's columns on the Scopes trial, as well as other contemporary newspaper and magazine pieces on the trial.

BIBLIOGRAPHY

Books and Periodicals

"Active Political and Civic Career of W. J. Bryan, Thrice a Presidential Candidate." *New York Times,* July 27, 1925.

Alexander, T. H. *Austin Peay: A Collection of State Papers and Public Addresses.* Kingsport, TN: Southern Press, 1929.

"Anti-Evolution Act Invasion of Rights – Malone." *Knoxville Journal,* June 28, 1925.

"Argument by Clarence Darrow at Dayton Assailing Foes of Evolution." *New York Times,* July 14, 1925.

"Arthur Garfield Hays." *American National Biography.* New York: Oxford University Press, 1999.

"Arthur Garfield Hays Dies at 73: Counsel to Civil Liberties Union." *New York Times,* December 15, 1954.

Ashby, Leroy. *William Jennings Bryan: Champion of Democracy.* Boston, MA: Twayne Publishers, 1987.

Bethell, Tom. "Banned in Biology." *Washington Times,* December 26, 2005.

Bode, Carl. *Mencken.* Baltimore, MD: Johns Hopkins University Press, 1986.

"Bryan and Darrow Wage War of Words in Trial Interlude." *New York Times,* July 17, 1925.

"Bryan in Dayton, Calls Scopes Trial Duel to the Death." *New York Times,* June 8, 1925.

"Bryan Is Eulogized, Even by Opponents." *New York Times,* July 27, 1925.

Chapman, Matthew. *Trials of the Monkey: An Accidental Memoir.* London: Duckworth Literary Entertainment, 2000.

"Clarence Darrow Is Dead in Chicago." *New York Times,* March 14, 1938.

Darrow, Clarence. *Attorney for the Damned.* Edited by Arthur Weinberg. New York: Simon & Schuster, 1957. Reprint. Chicago: University of Chicago Press, 1987.

Darrow, Clarence. *The Story of My Life.* New York: Charles Scribner's Sons, 1932. Reprint. New York: Da Capo Press, 1996.

Darrow, Clarence. *Why I Am an Agnostic and Other Essays.* Amherst, NY: Prometheus Books, 1995.

Darwin, Charles. *The Autobiography of Charles Darwin.* New York: Barnes & Noble Books, 2005.

Darwin, Charles. *The Descent of Man, and Selection in Relation to Sex.* London: J. Murray, 1871. Reprint. New York: Barnes & Noble Books, 2004.

Darwin, Charles. *On the Origin of Species by Means of Natural Selection.* London: J. Murray, 1859. Reprint. New York: Penguin Books, 2005.

"Dudley F. Malone Dies in California." *New York Times,* October 6, 1950.

"Evolution Battle Rages out of Court." *New York Times,* July 22, 1925.

Gallup Polls. Available online at http://www.gallup.com

Graham, Fred P. "Court Ends Arkansas Darwinism Ban." *New York Times,* November 13, 1968.

"H. L. Mencken, 75, Dies in Baltimore." *New York Times,* January 30, 1956.

Hays, Arthur Garfield. *City Lawyers: The Autobiography of a Law Practice.* New York: Simon & Schuster, 1942.

Hays, Arthur Garfield. *Let Freedom Ring.* New York: Liveright Publishers, 1928. Reprint. New York: Da Capo Press, 1972.

Hunter, George William. *A Civic Biology.* New York: American Book Company, 1914.

Iannone, Carol. "The Truth about *Inherit the Wind.*" *First Things* 70, February 1997.

"John Tate Raulston." *Dictionary of American Biography,* Supplement 6: *1956-1960.* New York: American Council of Learned Societies, 1980.

"John T. Raulston, Jurist, 87, Dead." *New York Times,* July 12, 1956.

"Judge's Own Views." *Nashville Banner,* May 25, 1925.

Kazin, Michael. *A Godly Hero: The Life of William Jennings Bryan.* New York: Alfred A. Knopf, 2006.

Kazin, Michael. "What Would Bryan Do?" *Philadelphia Inquirer,* February 21, 2006.

Larson, Edward J. *Summer for the Gods: The Scopes Trial and America's Continuing Debate over Science and Religion.* Cambridge, MA: Harvard University Press, 1997.

Larson, Edward J. "The Scopes 'Monkey' Trial." Interview with Brian Lamb. *Booknotes: Stories from American History.* New York: Public Affairs, 2001.

"Malone Demands Freedom of the Mind." *New York Times,* July 17, 1925.

"Malone, Dudley Field." *American National Biography.* New York: Oxford University Press, 1999.

Manchester, William. *Disturber of the Peace: The Life of H. L. Mencken.* New York: Harper & Row, 1950. Revised edition. Cambridge, MA: University of Massachusetts Press, 1986.

Mencken, H. L. *Heathen Days: 1890-1936.* New York: Alfred A. Knopf, 1943. Reprint. Baltimore, MD: Johns Hopkins University Press, 1996.

Mencken, H. L. "Homo Neanderthalensis." *Baltimore Evening Sun,* June 29, 1925.

Mencken, H. L. "Mencken Likens Trial to Religious Orgy, with Defendant a Beelzebub." *Baltimore Evening Sun,* July 11, 1925.

Mencken, H. L. "The Scopes Trial: Darrow's Eloquent Appeal Wasted on Ears That Heed Only Bryan." *Baltimore Evening Sun,* July 14, 1925.

Moran, Jeffrey P. *The Scopes Trial: A Brief History with Documents.* New York: St. Martin's Press, 2002.

Nussbaum, Paul. "The Divide over Darwin." *Philadelphia Inquirer,* October 2, 2005.

Scopes, John T. and James Presley. *Center of the Storm: Memoirs of John T. Scopes.* New York: Holt, Rinehart & Winston, 1967.

Stenerson, Douglas C. *H. L. Mencken: Iconoclast from Baltimore.* Chicago: University of Chicago Press, 1971.

"Text of Bryan's Nine Questions on Religion and Darrow's Replies to the Commoner." *New York Times,* July 22, 1925.

Thomas, Herbert. *Human Origins: The Search for Our Beginnings.* New York: Harry N. Abrams, 1995.

Tierney, Kevin. *Darrow: A Biography.* New York: Crowell, 1979.

"Tom Stewart." *Dictionary of American Biography, Supplement 9.* New York: Charles Scribner's Sons, 1994.

Ussher, James. *The Annals of the World.* Revised and updated edition by Larry and Marion Pierce. Green Forest, AR: Master Books, 2003.

Worden, Amy. "It's a Revolution for Evolution: Voters Oust Backers of Intelligent Design." *Philadelphia Inquirer,* November 10, 2005.

Online

American Civil Liberties Union. "History of the ACLU." http://www.acluprocon.org/ACLU History/HistoryTable.html.

Bryan College. "About Bryan College." http://www.bryan.edu/about.html.

Discovery Institute. "The Origin of Intelligent Design." http://www.discovery.org/scripts.

Kitzmiller et. al. v. Dover Area School District et. al. http://www.pamd.uscourts.gov/kitzmiller/kitzmiller_342.pdf.

*Inherit the Wind.*http://www.xroads.edu/~UG97/inherit/intro.html.

Positive Atheism. "Positive Atheism's Big List of Quotations." http://www.positiveatheism.org/hist/quotes.

Public Broadcasting System (PBS). "American Experience: Monkey Trial: An All-Out Duel between Science and Religion." http://www.pbs.org/amex/monkeytrial/index.html.

University of Missouri, Kansas City. "Clarence Darrow Home Page." http://www.law.umkc.edu/faculty/projects/ftrials/Darrow.htm.

University of Missouri, Kansas City. "Famous Trials in American History: Leopold and Loeb." http://www.law.umkc.edu/faculty/projects/ftrials/leoploeb/leopold.htm.

University of Missouri, Kansas City. "Famous Trials in American History: Tennessee vs. John Scopes, the "Monkey Trial, 1925." http://www.law.umkc.edu/faculty/projects/ftrials/Scopes.htm.

University of Utah Department of Math. "The Scopes Trial." http://www.math.utah.edu/~lars/scopes.pdf.

DVD and VHS

American Experience: Monkey Trial: An All-Out Duel between Science and Religion. VHS. Public Broadcasting System (PBS) and Nebraska ETV, 2002.

PHOTO CREDITS

INDEX

(ill.) denotes illustration